Dedicated to

My Parents,

Veena Dhingra and Surjeet Kumar Dhingra
Whose blessing and guidance are the platform I stand on.

My Family,

Gunjan Dhingra and Soham Dhingra
Who supported me throughout this effort.

- Pragati Kumaar Dhingra

My parents,

Sheela Bhaskar and Vinod Bhaskar
Who gave me freedom to pave my own path in life.

My first mentor in industry,

Prashant Upadhyaya
Who taught me C beyond the textbooks.

- Priyanka Bhaskar

Preface

It is an observable fact that we are in the middle of a revolution – a technology revolution. As more and more devices get smarter and connected we have increasingly more automation and computer intelligence built into our daily lives. Self-driving cars and home automation are no longer things of future from a James Bond movie. Could a technical worker troubleshoot or program these complex software driven systems without fundamental knowledge of programming?

An implication of this revolution is that computer programming as a skill is no longer optional. Anyone pursuing education in any technical field has to be proficient in programming.

It is no coincidence that need for learning programming has been repeated many times over by eminent leaders from all walks of life including ex-US President Barak Obama and Facebook founder Mark Zuckerberg.

> *"Now we have to make sure all our kids are equipped for the jobs of the future – which means not just being able to work with computers, but developing the analytical and coding skills to power our innovation economy."*
>
> – **Barak Obama**.

You can view some of these messages on our site.
http://thebookofc.com/industry/importance-of-learning-programming/

Despite the widespread recognition of importance of learning programming in the modern world, our books and learning techniques for C programming are antiquated and have remained largely unchanged since long. Most textbooks are limited to theoretical explanation in a linear fashion that was created for a small geeky population five decades ago. This is not very effective for learning programming. It leaves the aspiring programmer with half knowledge that is inadequate for a job in today's world.

It should not be a two-step process to learn in college and then learn for the job. The whole purpose of education is prepare you for your career.

This is the gap we intend to fill with this book. Having combined industry experience of over three decades, we have significant exposure to practical programming in the form it is useful in the industry. It takes lesser effort to learn to program the right way than it takes to learn the wrong way and then relearn later on.

This book is intended for global audience that wants to learn real world C programming that can be applied to their career. This provides you the required approach, skills, knowledge, and practice to make learning programming a rewarding experience – a reward that shows up in your salary.

Like building a good physique requires a disciplined exercise regime; building a good practical programming muscle also requires you to be disciplined and do your exercises regularly. You would not see bulging biceps or a perfect figure in a day, but if you keep at it, we promise, you would be the one programmer everyone wants on their team.

How to use this book

If you master the contents of this book, you will acquire the right foundation and skills to help you program. Good news is that you can master the contents of this book with 3 simple rules.

1. For every example in this book, do not just read it. Type it in your code editor, run it and see its result. Just typing in the code gives you valuable practice. It is a great way to start building your programming muscle.
2. Attempt and solve every practice question. These practice questions have been very carefully designed to make sure that you understand and learn to apply the concepts covered

in that section and chapter. If you skip these exercises, your concept application will remain weak and you may face difficulties in further chapters.

3. If you get a solution wrong, do not give up. Solve it again until you get it right and understand what you did wrong. With programming, mistakes teach much more than all books and lectures combined.

We have provided all solutions with explanations for you on our website www.thebookofc.com. Use the website as your companion as you undertake this very rewarding journey of learning C.

Get In Touch With Us

Finally, we would love to hear back from you. You can get in touch with us on following email addresses.

1. feedback@thebookofc.com – If you found some concepts were hard to understand or if you found an error in the book then help us improve by letting us know. We will add clarifications on our website as well as improve future editions. If you found something useful or very well written, do let us know that too.
2. testimonial@thebookofc.com – If you would like to send us a testimonial and get featured on www.thebookofc.com then please write to us preferably with a photo.
3. contribute@thebookofc.com – If you solved a problem in a unique way or if you have an article that you would like to see published on www.thebookofc.com.

Contents

          feedback@thebookofc.com

feedback@thebookofc.com

Introduction to Programming

Welcome to the world of programming – your very own super powers to command and control computer systems present all around you.

What is a Program?

*A **program** is a set of instructions for a computer system to perform a well-defined task.*

What do these instructions look like?

Computers understand only binary language, composed of only 0s and 1s. However, we humans do not think or talk in 0s and 1s. So how do we issue instructions to a computer?

We create our instructions in a special human friendly language called "programming language". Then we use special software (compiler or interpreter software) to convert our instructions into binary language so that computer can understand and execute them. That is, we write our program in a programming language and then convert it into binary executable instructions.

*A **programming language** is a well-defined set of instruction building blocks along with rules for putting these building blocks together to create programs.*

There are two types of conversion software used to convert programs into binary executables – compiler and interpreter.

*A **compiler** reads the whole program at once and converts it into a set of binary instructions that are then executed by the computer.*

*An **interpreter** reads a program line by line. It converts and executes the program one line at a time.*

Languages that use a compiler are called compiled languages. Examples include C, C++, C#.NET etc.

Languages that use an interpreter are called interpreted languages. Examples include Python, PHP, etc.

What is Programming?

Programming is the art and science of creating computer programs.

The science aspect of programming is learning the language building blocks and syntax. This is similar to learning the fundamental notes of music that serve as building blocks for composing a song.

The programming language rules for writing programming building blocks are called **syntax** *of a language.*

The art aspect of programming begins after we have learned the science aspect. It involves putting our knowledge of programming building blocks to use for solving real world problems. This is similar to composing a new tune once we have mastered the fundamental notes of music.

Similar to music, learning programming requires rigor, focus, patience and a lot of practice. The more we practice, the better we get.

Prerequisites for Learning Programming

The most important prerequisite for learning programming is persistence. Like learning any new skill, programming too takes practice – lot of it.

Programming is not hard. It is methodical. It is one of those skills where everyday practice will make you better. Just don't give up. If you do not understand a particular concept first time around, take a short break and read it again and then practice it again. Don't let go until you get a hang of it. It is equally important to play around on your own. Try out different things and observe the results.

                    feedback@thebookofc.com

In this book, we assume basic familiarity with a computer usage and being able to launch various programs and run them independently.

We do not presume any prior knowledge of programming. This book takes a ground up approach explaining things from the most basic level. It is geared towards helping you write good quality code that industry expects. You would need a computer, preferably with internet connectivity, to practice and learn.

Solutions to all questions and exercises in this book are available online at our website www.thebookofc.com.

While you have source code available for all exercises, it would help you tremendously to attempt the exercises on your own. In case you need help, feel free to use the source code provided. However, type in the source code yourself instead of copy pasting it. Typing in the source code will help you see aspects of programming that you miss when you copy paste.

Setting Up Programming Environment

In order to learn programming you shall find a good programming environment to be extremely helpful. We strongly recommend using an Integrated Development Environment (IDE). It would make learning programming much more easier. Also, most professional settings use a modern IDE, so there would be a continuity in your effort as you graduate from a learner to a professional.

For the purpose of this book, you can use Eclipse IDE. http://thebookofc.com/environment/set-up/ outlines the setup instructions.

If you already have a different modern IDE setup then feel free to continue using it. Contents of this book are not dependent on a certain environment. Our only caution is to stay away from antiquated development environments and compilers.

This book conforms to C11 ISO standard. This is the international C standard that was defined in the year 2011. Any modern IDE that supports C11 can be used.

Hello World

Let's begin our C journey with the traditional "Hello World" program. This simple program instructs the computer to print Hello World message on your screen.

Here is the code.

```c
#include <stdio.h>

int main(int argc, char * argv[]) {
    /* Use printf to print a message */
    printf("Hello World\n");
    return 0;
}
```

Go ahead and type it in your IDE. Running hello world program will help you test your programming environment as well as help you get familiar with your IDE.

For now, we will use the following program structure (syntax) without worrying too much about the rest of the contents.

```c
#include <stdio.h>

int main(int argc, char * argv[]) {

    <We write code here>

    return 0;
}
```

The details of this program structure will become clearer as we learn and advance through this book. For now just remember that main is a function and when you execute a program, execution starts with the code inside main function.

feedback@thebookofc.com

The first line of main function in our example is

```
/* Use printf to print a message */
```

This is a comment. Comment is not code. It is placed purely for our convenience, for us to document important information about the code that we are writing. "/*" characters signify starting of comment and "*/" signify end of comment. System never processes a comment. It is skipped entirely.

A comment can span multiple lines. For example,

```
/* This
   is
   a
   valid
   comment
*/
```

C supports another format of comments as shown below

```
// This is also a valid comment
```

This alternative format starts with "//" and ends with the end of line. Everything from // till the end of line is considered to be part of comment. You can extend this comment format to multiple lines by placing \ (backslash character) as the last character on the comment line, where the comment is continued to next line. For example,

```
// This \
is \
multiline \
comment
```

Typical usage of // comment format is limited to a single line.

It is a good programming practice to write sensible comments that help the reader understand the code better. Comments also help you quickly recollect things when you are reading your own code after some time.

Now let us spend a moment understanding the meat of the program where all the action happened. It was this statement:

```
printf("Hello World\n");
```

`printf` statement is used for printing something to the output console. `printf` is short for print formatted.

After `printf`, we have a pair of parentheses that enclose the message to be printed in double quotes. The message inside the double quotes is printed as is.

The `\n` at the end of `Hello World` message is a newline character. This tells the system to add a new line and position the cursor on next line after printing `Hello World` on the console.

All statements in C terminate with a semicolon.

The `return` statement for now signifies end of program for us. We will get deeper into `return` statement later in this book. Until then, just remember this is how our programs end.

Practice questions : -
1. Now that you have learned how to print Hello World, modify this program to instruct your computer to print your name and greet you.

Let's play around a little with our new shiny working environment.

Syntax Errors and Fixing Them

Let's remove the closing double quote of `printf` statement in Hello World program. Your program should now look like this

```
#include <stdio.h>

int main (int argc, char * argv[]) {
    printf("Hello World\n);
}
```

                    feedback@thebookofc.com

Try compiling the above program. You should see a compilation error and compilation should fail. This is because we broke the syntax rules of the language by not closing the double quotes of the message that we wanted to print.

Errors that are a result of incorrect program syntax are called
syntactical errors *or simply* ***syntax errors***.

Compiler flags these errors for you along with some helpful error and warning messages that help you locate and fix syntactical errors quickly. Here is a sample compilation result for the above syntactical error.

```
../helloWorld.c:12:10: warning: missing terminating '"'
character [-Winvalid-pp-token]
        printf ("Hello World\n);
                ^
../helloWorld.c:12:10: error: expected expression
../helloWorld.c:14:2: error: expected '}'
```

Let's take a moment to learn how to read these messages.

The first component of the message `../helloWorld.c` is the path to the source code file from which error or warning was reported.

The next two numbers separated by a colon are the line number and character number in the source file specifying the exact location of the error or warning. In this sample `12:10` specify the location as 10th character of 12th line in source file `../helloWorld.c`

Next is type of message - typically error or warning. Warning means code looks fishy even though compilation can proceed with the reported issue. It is a flag for you to review your code and make sure it is correct. Error, on the other hand, means compilation cannot be completed successfully until the reported issue is fixed.

Next is the warning or error description of the issue encountered during compilation. If you ever find yourself with an issue that you don't know how to solve, searching the internet for the exact error description is always the best starting point.

Armed with this knowledge, let's revisit the warnings and errors above and figure out how we should interpret and handle them.

The first message we received was a warning from file `../helloWorld.c` line 12, character 10 that pointed out that closing double quote was not found.

```
../helloWorld.c:12:10: warning: missing terminating '"'
character [-Winvalid-pp-token]
        printf ("Hello World\n);
                ^
```

It also has two additional lines. First, it prints the offending line of source code. And in second line, it prints a karat (also called caret) symbol (^) pointing out the exact location of the reported issue. As you can see, it is the opening double quote for which compiler could not locate the corresponding closing quote.

However, this is still a warning - not an error yet. Let's look at the next message

```
../helloWorld.c:12:10: error: expected expression
```

This reports an error at exactly the same location, file `../helloWorld.c` line 12, character 10. What happened? Since compiler could not find a closing double quote, it interpreted everything that followed as part of the statement that was to be printed - including the closing parentheses and terminating semicolon. As a result, compiler could not make sense of the statement - it has an opening parentheses with no closing parentheses, an opening double quote with no closing double quote and no terminating semicolon. Hence, compiler complained about not finding a valid expression.

Let's move to the final error

```
../helloWorld.c:14:2: error: expected '}'
```

Why was this error reported? After all we had closing brace at the end of the program.

          feedback@thebookofc.com

This is typical of syntactical errors - first error leads to a cascade of subsequent errors as first error leads to misinterpretation of code that follows.

Thus it is a good strategy to start with the compilation errors and warnings from top - fix the first one and recompile before you proceed further. By following this approach, you will end up saving a lot of effort.

Variables and Data Types

Variables

Remember simple algebraic equations from math class:

$$\frac{x}{y} = 2$$

In this equation, x and y are variables that can take on any values as long as chosen values satisfy the equation.

For example, {x=10, y=5} or {x=2, y=1} are valid values that can be assigned to x and y in this equation.

Since values assigned to x and y can *vary*, they are called *variables*. The concept of variables is similar in programming world. It is a name, like x and y above, that denotes a computer memory address that can hold a value.

*A **variable** is a name that refers to an address in memory.*

The value stored at that location could change (vary) over time. However, at one point in time, a variable can hold only one value.

Data Type

C requires us to declare the type of data that a variable can store.

What do we mean by type of data?

Type indicates if a variable can store an integer value, or a fraction, or a character, etc. In C, each variable has an associated data type that specifies the type of data that it can store.

__Data type__ of a variable specifies the type of value that can be stored in that variable.

　　feedback@thebookofc.com

C allows you to declare variables of several native (or in-built) data types. C also allows you to define your own new data types called user defined data types. For now, we will learn about two native data types – `int` and `double`.

Variables of `int` data type can hold integer numbers such as -8, 0, 72 etc.

Variables of `double` data type can hold decimal numbers such as -2.995, 45.3009, 3.14 etc.

Keywords

If we wanted to tell C about data types of our variables, we would need special words that are understood by C.

*Set of special words that are understood by C compiler and have a special meaning are called **keywords**.*

Here are the keywords used to tell C about the data types that we just learned,

`int` – for integer data type
`double` – for double data type

C is a case sensitive language. Uppercase and Lowercase names are considered different names. That means `int` is a keyword, `Int` or `INT` is not.

We shall learn more keywords as we progress through this book.

Declaring Variables

Before we can use a variable in your program, we have to declare it, i.e. tell C what is the name of the variable and what type of value it can store. We can declare our variables with a declaration statement that takes following form.

```
data_type variable_name = initial_value;
```

For example:

```
int marks = 99;
```

This statement declares an integer variable named `marks` and assigns it an initial value of 99.

Assigning an initial value to a variable at the time of declaration is called **initializing** the variable.

Initializing is optional; you can declare a variable without initializing it. However, as a good programming practice, you should always initialize all variables that you declare.

Same declaration statement without initialization would appear as below.

```
int marks;
```

Note that in C all statements end with a semicolon.

An example of declaring and initializing a double variable is shown below.

```
double average_marks = 93.4;
```

A variable can have one and only one data type. It is not possible to have two different data types associated with one variable.

Each variable name can be declared once and only once in a code block. A code block is enclosed in braces {} like we had around body of `main` function in our Hello World example.

In C, all variables must be declared before they can be used. Also, all declarations should be made before we write any other code statement. In other words, we cannot have any declarations in the middle or end of a code block.

For us, at this stage, it means that all our declarations would be at the beginning of the `main` function – where we currently start writing our code.

Practice questions : -
1. Which of the following are valid variable declarations?
    1. `double celsius = 37.2;`
    2. `int rank = 1`
    3. `kelvin = 273;`
    4. `int count = 7;`
    5. `double int pi = 3.14;`
    6. `int double = 9;`

Now let's put our knowledge to practice. Let us write a program to declare a variable, initialize it, and print its value.

```c
#include <stdio.h>

int main (int argc, char * argv[]) {
    int test = 101;
    printf("Value of test = %d\n", test);
    return 0;
}
```

Let's examine the body of `main` function more closely.

```c
int test = 101;
```

This statement declares a variable named `test`, which can hold an integer value and assigns it an initial value of 101. If we were to now print the value of variable `test`, we should see 101 printed.

```c
printf("Value of test = %d\n", test);
```

This statement prints text `Value of test =` followed by integer value stored in variable `test` and a newline. Let's understand how this statement works.

The whole string enclosed in double quotes is called format string. `%d` in the format string is the format specifier for integer data type. `%d` format specifier tells our system that value stored in the variable name after comma should be printed as an integer value.

`printf` statement prints the entire format string as is with format specifier replaced with value of the variable.

Run the above program and you should see following output.

```
Value of test = 101
```

Practice questions : -
2. Write a program that declares an `int` variable named runs and initialises it to zero. Print its value. Next, assign value 50 to variable runs and print its value again.

C allows us to declare multiple variables in a single statement. E.g.

```
int maths_marks = 95, science_marks = 99;
```

Notice that in this statement data type is specified only once - at the beginning of the statement. All variables declared in the single statement will have the same data type, in this example - `int`.

Above statement declares two variables - `maths_marks` and `science_marks` and are initializes them to 95 and 99 respectively.

Here is the same statement without initialization.

```
int maths_marks, science_marks;
```

Practice questions : -
3. Which of the following are valid variable declarations?
    1. `double average, int maths, science;`
    2. `int maths, int science;`
    3. `int average, temperature = 32;`
    4. `int maths, science, english;`

It is also possible to print values of multiple variables in a single `printf` statement.

For example,

                    feedback@thebookofc.com

```c
#include <stdio.h>

int main (int argc, char * argv[]) {
    int height = 163, weight = 72;
    printf("Height is %d and weight is %d\n", height,
weight);
    return 0;
}
```

Let's begin with following statement,

```c
int height = 163, weight = 72;
```

This statement declares two integer variables; `height` and `weight`; and initializes them to 163 and 72 respectively. Note that a comma separates declarations of variables height and weight.

```c
printf("Height is %d and weight is %d\n", height, weight);
```

This statement prints the value of variables `height` and `weight`. How does it decide the order in which to print the values?

The answer is _positional matching_ – when we have more than one format specifier in the format string, C matches first format specifier with first variable in the list, second format specifier with second variable in the list and so on.

Hence, the first `%d` in the format string is matched to first variable in the list – `height`; and second `%d` in the format string is matched to second variable in the list – `weight`.

Run the above program and you should see following output

```
Height is 163 and weight is 72
```

Just as `%d` is format specifier for `int` data type, the corresponding print format specifier for `double` data type is `%f`.

<u>**Practice questions : -**</u>
4. What will be the output of following program?

```c
#include <stdio.h>

int main (int argc, char * argv[]) {
    int physics = 9, maths = 8;
    double average = 8.5;
    printf("physics is %d, maths is %d, and average is
%f\n", physics, maths, average);
    return 0;
}
```

5. What will be the output of following program?

```c
#include <stdio.h>

int main (int argc, char * argv[]) {
    int test = 9;
    printf("test = %d\n", test);
    test = 10;
    printf("test = %d\n", test);
    return 0;
}
```

Naming Your Variables

Variable names can consist of lower case and uppercase letters, digits, and underscore characters. A variable name must begin with either a lowercase or uppercase letter or underscore. Variable name cannot begin with a digit. Also, you cannot use a keyword as your variable name – because it has a special meaning for the system.

As we learned earlier, C is a case-sensitive language. Hence `Total` and `total` are two different variable names.

Practice Questions: -
6. Which among the following are valid variable names?
    1. totalscore1
    2. Total_score_1
    3. _total_score__1
    4. total score
    5. 1_total_score
    6. _
    7. 115
    8. _115
    9. int

              feedback@thebookofc.com

    10. Int
    11. __

If you are not sure about validity of any of the above variable names, it would be a good idea to declare them in a program and try running the program. If a variable name is invalid then system will flag it for you with a compilation error message.

As a good programming practice, you should always use descriptive names for your variables.

Variable name "average" will make your program much more readable as compared to variable name "a". Programming industry, by default, expects you to use descriptive variable names. Imagine a few million lines of code with variables names x, y, p, q, r. No one would know what any of it means and what to do with them. On the other hand variable names such as torque, acceleration, x_coordinate provide enough information about their intended purpose and make it much more easier to read and maintain a program.

As a variable naming convention in this book, we will use descriptive names. If a name consists of more than one word, then words would be separated by an underscore. For example,

```
top_score
smallest_element
first_name
```

Behind the Scenes

When you declare and initialize a variable, what really happens in the system?

Imagine system memory organized as an array of cells where each cell can store a fixed amount of data. Each cell has a unique address that can be used to access the cell to store or retrieve data from that cell.

Figure below shows a representation of memory with twenty one cells with addresses on top of each cell.

00	04	08	12	16	20	24

28	32	36	40	44	48	52

56	60	64	68	72	76	80

Additionally, system also maintains a special table (called *symbol table*) that stores the name of the variable and the address of the memory location that it refers.

When you declare a variable, system executes following actions:
1. It finds a memory location where this variable can be stored.
2. It updates its symbol table to store the variable name and its corresponding memory address.

After this point, whenever you store something in that variable, system looks up its symbol table, finds the address corresponding to the variable and stores the value at that address.

Whenever you use a variable, system looks up its table, finds the address corresponding to this variable, fetches the value stored at that address and uses this value in the statement where you used this variable.

Let's take an example.

Consider this program snippet

```c
int physics = 9;
int maths = 8;
int total_marks = 17;
printf ("Physics = %d, Maths = %d, Total = %d\n", physics,
maths, total_marks);
```

       feedback@thebookofc.com

When first statement is executed, system recognizes that you are trying to declare an integer variable called `physics` and you wish to store value 9 in it. So it looks for a memory location where it can store an integer. Let's say it finds memory address 32. System will update its symbol table to add this entry.

physics	32

Now that it has a location to store the value, it executes the initialization and updates the memory location 32 with value 9.

00	04	08	12	16	20	24

28	32	36	40	44	48	52
	9					

56	60	64	68	72	76	80

When system proceeds to second statement, it similarly adds a variable called `maths` and initializes it to 8. After this statement symbol table looks like as shown below

physics	32
maths	40

and memory looks like as shown below

00	04	08	12	16	20	24

28	32	36	40	44	48	52
	9		8			

56	60	64	68	72	76	80

Now let's look at the next statement

```
int total_marks = 17;
```

System again recognizes that you are trying to declare an integer variable called **total_marks** and you wish to initialize it to value 17. So it finds a memory location to store it, let's say it finds memory address 16, and initializes it to 17.

Consequently, symbol table and memory would now look like as shown below.

physics	32
maths	40
total_marks	16

00	04	08	12	16	20	24
				17		

28	32	36	40	44	48	52
	9		8			

56	60	64	68	72	76	80

Now let's see what happens when **printf** statement is executed

```
printf ("Physics = %d, Maths = %d, Total = %d\n", physics, maths, total_marks);
```

System finds the first format specifier, %d, and matches it to the first variable – **physics**. To get value of variable **physics**, system consults the symbol table and finds that value of **physics** variable is stored at location 32. It accesses memory address 32 and retrieves the value stored there.

As we can see in the above figure, memory address 32 stores value 9. Hence, value 9 is printed as the value for the first format specifier in the **printf** string.

   feedback@thebookofc.com

7. Trace retrieval of values for variables `maths` and `total_marks` in
    the `printf` statement in above example.

What happens when we declare a variable without initialising it? As
we discussed above, system would create a symbol table entry and
associate a memory address with the variable name. However,
system would not modify or update the contents of that memory
location. If there was some previous value written at that memory
location then now our variable holds that value. If we were to
mistakenly use that variable without first assigning it a value then this
pre-existing value would get used leading to unpredictable results.

Hence, we recommend that you always initialise your variables. If you
do not know what value shall be stored in a variable yet, initialise it
to 0. It will help you find programming errors sooner if you have a
consistent wrong value instead of a different random value during
each execution.

There is no good reason ever to leave your variables uninitialized.

Practice Questions : -
8. Which of the following statements are true.
    a. Initializing a variable is optional.
    b. All uninitialized variables are by default initialized to 0 by
        the system.
    c. It is mandatory to declare a variable before using it.
    d. A variable can be declared anywhere in a program.
    e. As a good programming practice, we should always
        initialize all our variables.

Operators

Remember this program from last chapter

```c
#include <stdio.h>

int main (int argc, char * argv[]) {
    int physics = 9, maths = 8;
    double average = 8.5;
    printf("physics is %d, math is %d, and average is
%f\n", physics, maths, average);
    return 0;
}
```

It is not much fun if we have to calculate the average ourselves. The whole purpose of programming is to make the computer do things for us. In this chapter, we will learn how to get some of these tasks done via a program.

Operators

Operator is a character or a sequence of characters that instructs the system to perform a specific operation on given data.

You have already used an operator '=', the assignment operator, that instructs the system to assign a value to a variable.

The values or variables on which an operator performs the operation are called **operands**.

In the expression,

```c
average = 8.5
```

= is the operator and average and 8.5 are the operands.

C provides you a rich set of operators. Let's start by learning a few that can be put to use right away.

Most relatable set of operators is the basic arithmetic operators set.

+ is the addition operator
- is the subtraction operator
* is the multiplication operator
/ is the divide operator
% is the modulus (or remainder) operator

These are the basic arithmetic operators that you can put to use to manipulate `int` and `double` variables.

Modulus (%) operator is supported only for integer type.

Let's examine a few expressions built using these operators.

Assume, `int x = 19, y = 5;`
`x + y` will evaluate to 24
`x - y` will evaluate to 14
`x * y` will evaluate to 95
`x / y` will evaluate to 3
`x % y` will evaluate to 4

Why did x/y evaluate to 3?

Answer lies in data types: x and y are both `int`. When you divide two `int` variables, the data type of the result is `int`. We already learned that an `int` can store integer values not fractions. Hence, result of the evaluation is the quotient from the division operation.

When you use an arithmetic operator on two integers, the data type of the result is always an integer.

What happens if you divide an `int` with a `double`? The result will be a `double`.

When you have different data type operands in an arithmetic operation, result is of the larger data type. Larger here refers to the larger range of values that a data type can store. `double` is can store a wider range of values as compared to an `int`.

We will discuss range of values that can be stored in a data type further ahead in this book.

Practice Questions : -

1. What is the value of variable z in following code snippets?

    a.
    ```c
    int x = 5;
    int y = 7;
    int z = x%y;
    ```

    b.
    ```c
    int x = 5;
    int y = 7;
    int z = x/y;
    ```

    c.
    ```c
    double x = 4.4;
    double y = 2.0;
    double z = x/y;
    ```

2. What will be the output of following program snippets?

    a.
    ```c
    int x = 5;
    double y = 2.5;
    printf ("x/y = %f\n", x/y);
    ```

    b.
    ```c
    double x = 5.0;
    int y = 2;
    printf ("x/y = %f\n", x/y);
    ```

    c.
    ```c
    int x = 5;
    double y = 2.5;
    printf ("x + y = %f\n", x+y);
    ```

3. Write a program that swaps value of two `int` variables.
4. Write a program the computes sum of two `int` variables.

Now let's rewrite our program to calculate average of two numbers.

          feedback@thebookofc.com

```c
#include <stdio.h>

int main (int argc, char * argv[]) {
    int physics = 9, maths = 8;
    double average = (physics + maths)/2;
    printf("physics is %d, maths is %d, and average is
%f\n", physics, maths, average);
    return 0;
}
```

Parentheses are used for grouping expressions that should be calculated first — very similar to regular arithmetic you learned in school.

Similar to arithmetic BODMAS (Bracket off, division, multiplication, addition, subtraction), C operators also have precedence rules that determine how an expression is evaluated. For now, we will not worry about operator precedence and continue using parentheses to make sure that our expressions are evaluated as we intend them to.

What do you think the above program will print?

Try running it, you should see

```
physics is 9, maths is 8, and average is 8.000000
```

What happened?

Let's examine the order of evaluation of this expression `average = (physics + maths)/2`

The first part that gets evaluated is `(physics + maths)`.

Both `physics` and `maths` are of type `int`. We learned that when you add two integers, the result is of type integer. Hence, this expression will evaluate to an integer with value 17.

Next part that gets evaluated is 17/2.

We learned that when you divide two integers, the result is an integer. Hence, this expression will evaluate to an integer with value 8.

Next part that get evaluated is the assignment, `average = 8`.

Since the double variable **average** is assigned value 8, when you print it, you see 8.000000 printed on your screen.

Unexpected results, like what we just saw, that are caused due to flaws in the program are called logical errors.

Logical errors are caused due to a flaw in the program or in the program's logic and they produce incorrect results but they do not cause a program to crash or terminate abnormally.

All errors in our code are called *bugs*.

Logical errors are a type of bug.

Process of finding a bug and fixing it is called *debugging*.

We will learn debugging in some detail later in the book.

Now that we understand, why we got average as 8.0 instead of 8.5, let's learn how to instruct computer to compute the right average.

Typecasting

Typecasting refers to changing the data type of a value or variable or expression.

There are two type of typecasting
- o   Implicit typecasting
- o   Explicit typecasting

Examine this statement closely,

```
double average = 8;
```

The right hand side of the assignment operator is an `int`. The left hand side is a `double`. When this statement is executed, system automatically converts the right hand side value to the left hand side data type: in this case, integer 8 will automatically be converted to double 8.0 and assigned to a `double` variable.

Automatic conversion of data type is called *implicit typecasting*.

Explicit typecasting refers to a programmer explicitly changing the data type.

You can perform an explicit typecasting by prepending the variable or value or expression with the target data type enclosed in parentheses. Applying explicit typecasting, the above statement would appear as

```
double average = (double)8;
```

Now let's revisit our average example.

Remember that if we divide two `int`, result is an `int`. However, if we divide an `int` and a `double`, result is a `double`. So in order to convert our result to a `double`, we need to convert either the numerator or the denominator to a `double`.

Let's try out explicit typecasting.

```
#include <stdio.h>

int main (int argc, char * argv[]) {
    int physics = 9, maths = 8;
    double average = ((double)(physics + maths))/2;
    printf("physics is %d, maths is %d, and average is
%f\n", physics, maths, average);
}
```

Voila, we now have a program to calculate average of two numbers. Try changing the values assigned to `physics` and `maths` variables and run the program again to see updated average.

There is another, and simpler, way to achieve the desired result in this case – simply convert the denominator to a double value.


```c
#include <stdio.h>

int main (int argc, char * argv[]) {
    int physics = 9, maths = 8;
    float average = (physics + maths)/2.0;
    printf("physics is %d, maths is %d, and average is
%f\n", physics, maths, average);
    return 0;
}
```

Note that we simply changed the denominator to 2.0 instead of 2. In this case implicit typecasting comes into play. Numerator is automatically typecast to a `double` and result of division operation is a `double` value. We will learn more about rules of implicit typecasting later in this book.

Practice Questions : -

5. Write a program to convert 15723 meters to kilometres.
6. Write a program to convert 42.2 degree Celsius to Fahrenheit.
7. Write a program to calculate area and circumference of a circle of radius 2 cm.

     feedback@thebookofc.com

Reading User Input Into Variables

Recall our program to compute average of marks in two subjects

```c
#include <stdio.h>

int main (int argc, char * argv[]) {
    int physics = 9, math = 8;
    float average = (physics + math)/2.0;
    printf("physics is %d, math is %d, and average is
%f\n", physics, math, average);
    return 0;
}
```

What happens if you had to compute average for your friend who scored 8 in physics and 10 in math? In order to compute the average, you will have to change scores in your source code, re-compile, and re-run the program. Wouldn't it be better if program would ask you to enter the score and tell you the average? It would in-effect become an average calculator program that could tell you average of any two numbers.

In order to do that, we need a way to read physics and math score from user and put them into variables `physics` and `math`.

This is where input statements are helpful – they let us place user input into variables. Let's see an example.

```c
#include <stdio.h>

int main (int argc, char * argv[]) {
    int physics = 0, maths = 0;
    float average = 0;
    printf("Enter physics score: ");
    scanf("%d", &physics);
    printf("Enter math score: ");
    scanf("%d", &maths);
    average = (physics + maths)/2.0;
    printf ("Average score is %f\n", average);
    return 0;
}
```

The new statement in this program is the scanf statement. It helps us read values input by the user and place them into variables. The format of scanf statement is very similar to a printf statement.

```
scanf("%d", &physics);
```

As in printf, format string is enclosed in double quotes, %d is the format specifier that tells the system that the value being input by the user is an integer. The value is stored in the first variable in the variable list – physics. Note that there is & operator in front of variable name. This is the "address of" operator.

Recall from previous chapter that all variables are simply names with associated memory address. & operator (called address of operator) in the above statement simply says, store the input value at the "address of" variable physics. Whatever value you input on the console would get stored at the address referred by variable physics.

For reading a double using scanf, we use %lf as the format specifier. Below is an example that reads in temperature in degrees Celsius and converts it into degrees Fahrenheit.

```
#include <stdio.h>

int main(int argc, char * argv[]) {
    double celsius = 0, fahrenheit = 0;
    printf("Enter temperature in celsius: ");
    scanf("%lf",&celsius);
    fahrenheit = ((celsius * 9)/5) + 32;
    printf("%f celsius = %f fahrenheit\n", celsius, fahrenheit);

    return 0;
}
```

Just as we could print multiple variables in a single printf statement, likewise we can read in multiple values in a single scanf statement. Here is an example.

```
scanf("%d %d",&math, &english);
```

                    feedback@thebookofc.com

Above statement reads in two `int` values. Using positional matching, first input value is placed in variable `math` and second input value is placed in variable `english`.

Practice Questions : -

1. Which of the following statements is/are true.
    a. `printf` format specifier for `double` is `%lf`
    b. We can read a `double` and an `int` in a single `scanf` statement.
    c. We can declare a `double` and an `int` in a single statement.
    d. `%d` is the format specifier for `int` for `printf` as well as `scanf` statements.
2. Consider this statement from above example.
    ```
    fahrenheit = ((celsius * 9)/5) + 32;
    ```
    Would following statement generate same output?
    ```
    fahrenheit = (celsius * (9/5)) + 32;
    ```
3. Write a program that reads height in inches and converts it into centimetres.
4. Write a program that reads three integers and prints their sum.
5. Write a program that reads length and breadth of a rectangle and prints its area and perimeter.
6. Write a program that reads radius of a circle and prints its area and circumference.
7. Write a program that reads in two angles of a triangle and prints the third angle.
8. Write a program that reads in principal amount, interest rate, and tenure of a deposit and computes simple and compound interest.
9. Write a program to convert number of days into years, weeks, and days. E.g. If user inputs 2000 days then program should print 5 years 25 weeks. Assume 365 days a year.

Flowcharts

Flowcharts are pictorial representation of logic of our programs. Flowcharts help us in writing logic in a graphical format that is universally understood. Flowcharts help us abstract away language specific syntax and constructs and focus solely on the logic required for solving the problem at hand. This gives us the flexibility of charting out the logic before we start worrying about expressing it in a programming language.

It is always a good idea to lay out the logic before you start coding it. As you write more and more programs, you would be able to lay down increasingly more complex logic in your head. Until such time, use flowcharts liberally for solving programming problems.

Key Building Blocks

A flowchart consists of blocks of various shapes connected via unidirectional arrows. Each block is a step in the logical process. Block shapes represent the type of action e.g. input/output or processing or decision etc. Details of the action such as what was input or output or what was the decision is written as text inside the block. Arrows indicate flow of logic. Actual action taken.

Let's begin by learning few basic shapes and then proceed to building flowcharts for the programs we have written.

     feedback@thebookofc.com

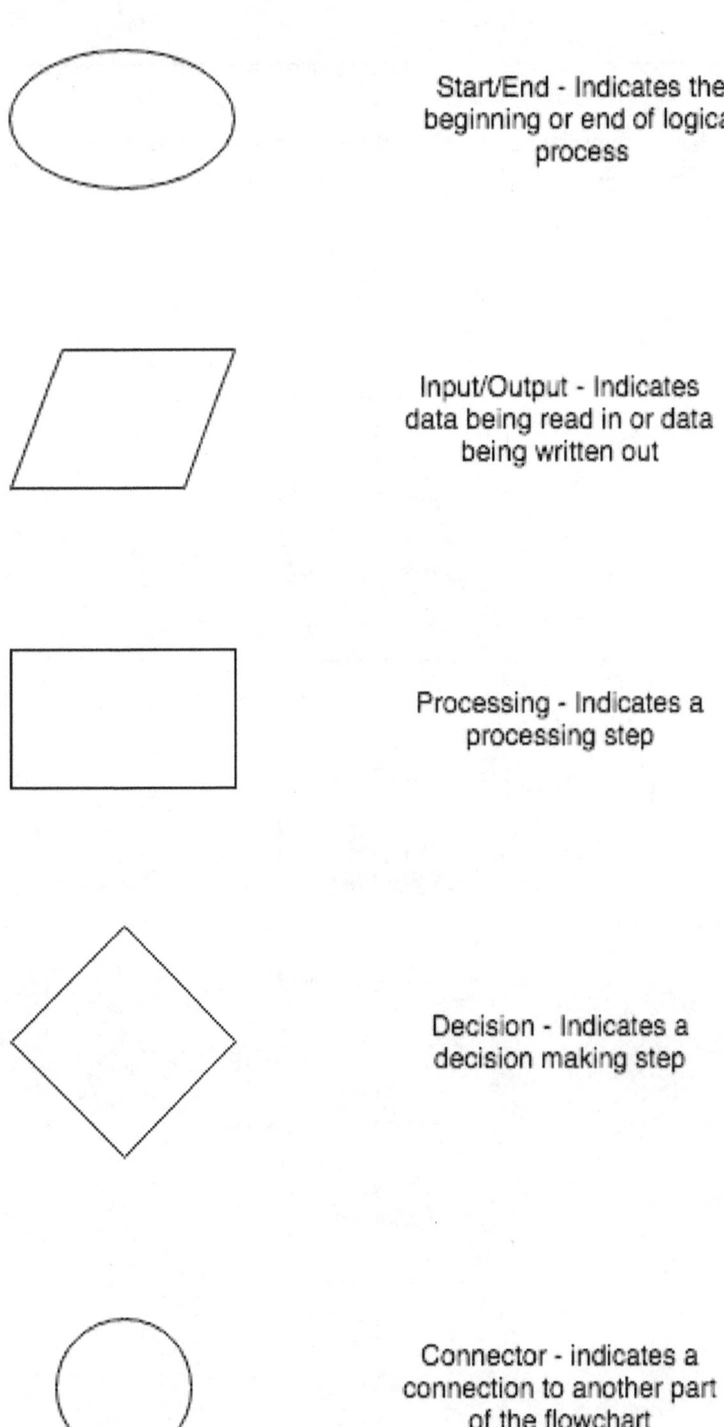

Start/End - Indicates the beginning or end of logical process

Input/Output - Indicates data being read in or data being written out

Processing - Indicates a processing step

Decision - Indicates a decision making step

Connector - indicates a connection to another part of the flowchart

In some texts ⬭ is also used for start/end blocks.

These five basic shapes shall suffice for the logic that we shall be building for now. Let's now study a flowchart for our example of converting temperature from Celsius to Fahrenheit.

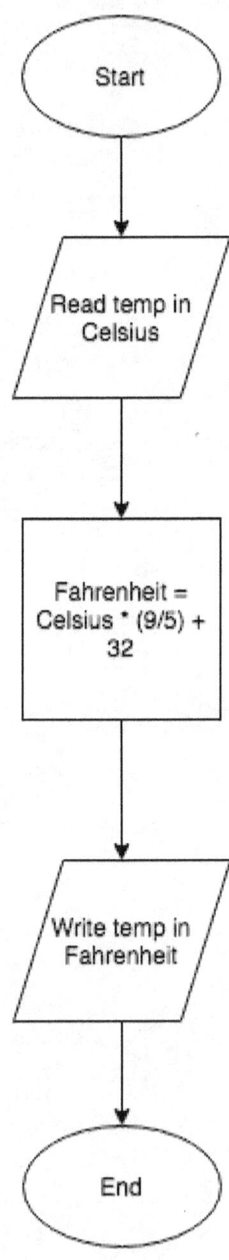

   feedback@thebookofc.com

Notice how graphical representation frees us up from language specific nuances such as `int` vs `double` arithmetic, syntax, format specifiers etc.

The flowchart itself is self-explanatory.

It consists of five steps:
1. Start
2. Read input – temperature in Celsius
3. Compute temperature in Fahrenheit
4. Write output - temperature in Fahrenheit
5. Stop

Arrows represent the flow of logic while shape of blocks indicate the type of operation. Since flow of logic is from one block to another, arrows in a flowchart will always be unidirectional.

There can be cases where control flows back to previous block. In such cases there will be another unidirectional arrow indicating such a jump. We shall be covering such flowcharts later in the book.

As another example, let's look at the flowchart for our earlier example computing average score of math and physics.

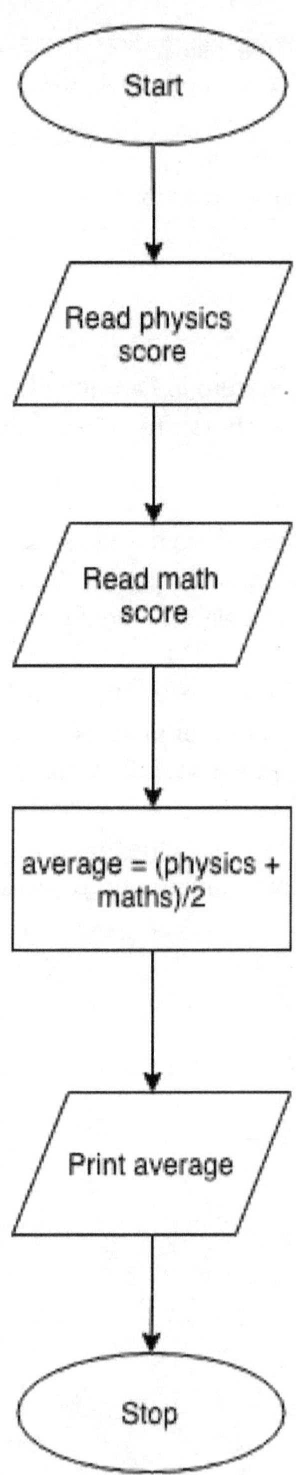

 feedback@thebookofc.com

<u>*Practice Questions : -*</u>

1. Which of the following statements is/are true
    a. Arrows in a flowchart can be bidirectional.
    b. Arrows indicate the flow of logic in a flowchart.
    c. There can be only one processing block in a flowchart.
2. Draw a flowchart for a program that reads three integers and prints their sum.
3. Draw a flowchart for a program reads in principal amount, interest rate, and tenure of a deposit and computes simple interest.

Making decisions – if–else

So far we have worked with programs where statements are executed in a sequential fashion, one after the other, without any jumps or omissions. In other words, all our programs so far had linear control flow.

> *Control flow* refers to sequence of execution of instructions in a program.

Now, we are going to learn how to make decisions and execute instructions selectively depending on result of our decisions.

What are decisions? Logically, decisions have two parts
1. Criteria or condition, and
2. The action to be performed when the condition is met.

For example, "If it is holiday today, I will go out to play". In this example "it is holiday today" is the condition/criteria for decision making. If condition is true, the action that is performed is "I will go out to play".

Such decision making can be represented using a simple flowchart shown in the figure below.

feedback@thebookofc.com

Notice that since decision can have two outcomes there are two outgoing arrows from the decision block, each labelled with the outcome that leads to that logic flow.

What if we want our C programs to develop intelligence to do similar 'decision making'? Then we need a way to define 'criteria or condition' and 'the action'. `if-else` construct helps us build decisions into our programs.

Let's begin by learning a few operators that will help us define the 'criteria or condition' for decision making.

Relational Operators

As the name indicates relational operators help you establish the relationship between their operands. You would have encountered them in your middle school. These operators are

==	Equal To
!=	Not Equal To
>	Greater Than
>=	Greater Than Or Equal To
<	Less Than
<=	Less Than Or Equal To

When you apply these operators to operands, you get a binary result – true or false.

```
Assuming int x = 5, y = 6
x == y is false
x != y is true
x > y is false
x >= y is false
x < y is true
x <= y is true
```

Note that equality operator is ==, while single equal sign is the assignment operator.

1. Assuming `int x = 5, y = 5` indicate which of the following expressions are true
    1. `x == y`
    2. `x != y`
    3. `x > y`
    4. `x >= y`
    5. `x < y`
    6. `x <= y`

In the discussion that follows, we refer to expressions evaluating to true or false but bear in mind that in C true and false are neither keywords nor predefined values. Internally, each of these expressions evaluates to an integer – 0 for false and 1 for true.

Since true and false are integers, what do other integers aside from 0 and 1 represent? Except 0, all integers are treated as true. We will test this piece of information in our programs later in the chapter.

The if Statement

`if` statement enables us to execute a block of statements based on result of an expression. `if` is a C language keyword.

Let's consider an example where we read marks scored from the user and if marks were 60+ we print a message saying they scored first class. Before termination we print a thank you message.

A flowchart representing the control flow of such a program is shown below. Notice the diamond shape which represents a decision. It has two possible outcomes and hence two paths leading out of it. If decision criterion evaluates to true, it prints that user achieved first class and then proceeds to thank you message. If decision criterion evaluates to false, it prints thank you message.

     feedback@thebookofc.com

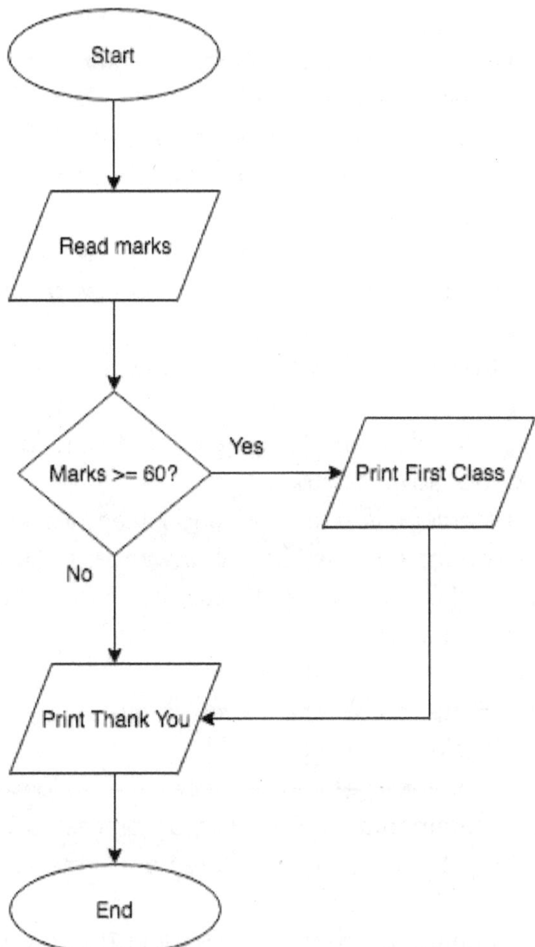

if statement helps us to program conditional execution of a block of statements. Let's examine source code of this example.

```
01: #include <stdio.h>

02: int main (int argc, char * argv[]) {
03:     int marks = 0;
04:     printf("Enter marks scored: ");
05:     scanf("%d", &marks);
06:     if (marks >= 60) {
07:         printf("You scored first class\n");
08:     }
09:     printf("Thank you for using grading program\n");
10:     return 0;
11: }
```

Here is how **if** statements work. First, the expression enclosed in parentheses immediately after the keyword **if** is evaluated. If that expression evaluates to true, statements in the following block (enclosed in braces {}) are executed, otherwise they are skipped.

The expression after **if** is also called controlling expression or simply control expression since its value controls the flow of execution.

Let's examine the control flow of the above example.

1. Integer variable marks is declared and initialized to 0 at line 03. Control advances to line 04.
2. Print statement is executed and `Enter marks scored:` is printed on the console. Control advances to line 05.
3. `scanf` reads user input. Let's say user input was 55. Control advances to line 06.
4. We encounter the **if** statement.
    a. First, control expression is evaluated, 55 >= 60. It evaluates to false.
    b. Since expression is false, the following block of statements in the pair of braces is skipped and control *jumps* to the statement immediately after this block to line 09.
5. Print statement is executed. Message `Thank you for using grading program` is printed on the console and program terminates.

Now let's examine the control flow if user had input 65

1. Integer variable marks is declared and initialized to 0 at line 03. Control advances to line 04.
2. Print statement is executed and `Enter marks scored:` is printed on the console. Control advances to line 05.
3. `scanf` reads user input. Let's say user input was 65. Control advances to line 06.
4. We encounter the **if** statement.
    a. First the control expression is evaluated, 65 >= 60. It evaluates to true.

     feedback@thebookofc.com

b. Since expression is true, the following block of statements in the pair of braces is entered. Control advances to line 07.

5. Print statement is executed and message `You scored first class` is printed.
6. Control reaches end of `if` block and advances to first statement after the `if` block, line 09.
7. Print statement is executed. Message `Thank you for using grading` program is printed on the console and program terminates.

Since execution of `if` block is conditional on expression being true, `if` is also referred to as conditional statement.

Let's use our new found power of `if` statement to determine whether our earlier assertion of "zero is false" and "non-zero is true" is indeed correct. Run the following program and observe its output.

```
01: #include <stdio.h>

02: int main (int argc, char * argv[]) {
03:      if (0) {
04:          printf("0 is true\n");
05:      }
06:      if (1) {
07:          printf("1 is true\n");
08:      }
09:      if (-1) {
10:          printf("-1 is true\n");
11:      }
12:      return 0;
13: }
```

You should see the following output.
```
1 is true
-1 is true
```

Practice Questions : -

2. What will be the output of below program for following user inputs
   1. -7
   2. 9
   3. 0

```c
#include <stdio.h>

int main (int argc, char * argv[]) {
    int number = 0;
    printf("Enter a number: ");
    scanf("%d", &number);
    if (number < 0) {
        printf("You entered a negative number\n");
    }
    if (number > 0) {
        printf("You entered a positive number\n");
    }
    printf("Good Bye!\n");
    return 0;
}
```
3. Draw a flowchart for above program.
4. What will be the output of below program.
```c
#include <stdio.h>

int main(int argc, char * argv[]) {
    int a = 100, b = 150, c = 200;

    if (a >= 100) {
        b = b + a;
        c = b + a;
    }

    if (c < 400) {
        a = 10;
    }

    printf ("%d %d %d\n", a, b, c);
}
```
5. What will be the output of below program for following user
    inputs
    1. 7
    2. 44
    3. 25

```c
#include <stdio.h>

int main (int argc, char * argv[]) {
    float temperature = 0;
    printf("Enter current temperature (deg C): ");
    scanf("%f", &temperature);
    if (temperature < 12) {
```

                    feedback@thebookofc.com

```c
        printf("It is getting cold.\n");
    }
    if (temperature > 35) {
        printf("It is hot!!\n");
    }
    printf("Good Bye!\n");
    return 0;
}
```

6. Draw a flowchart for above program.
7. Write a program that reads two numbers from the user and prints whether the numbers are equal or not.
8. Write a program that reads a number and prints whether the number is even or odd.
9. Write a program that reads two numbers and prints if the first number is a factor of second number or not.
10. Write a program that reads two numbers and prints if the sum of two numbers is greater than 0, equal to 0, or less than 0.
11. Write a program that reads total taxable income and computes tax liability based on following slabs.
    a. 0 – 300,000 : 0%
    b. 300,000 – 600,000 : 10%
    c. 600,000 – 10,000,000 : 20%
    d. 10,00,001 - : 30%
12. Write a program that reads the month number (1-12) from the user and prints the name of the month (January, February, etc.). If the user input is not in the range 1 – 12, program should print an error message.
13. Write a program that reads two numbers and prints the larger number.
14. Write a program that reads three numbers and prints the largest number.

The set of braces around an `if` block are optional. If braces are missing after `if`, only the first statement after `if` is considered to be part of `if` block.

Our program to determine a first class score could have been written as shown below.

```c
#include <stdio.h>

int main (int argc, char * argv[]) {
    int marks = 0;
    printf("Enter marks scored: ");
    scanf("%d", &marks);
    if (marks >= 60)
        printf("You scored first class\n");
    printf("Thank you for using grading program\n");
    return 0;
}
```

Notice that there are no braces around if block.

However, as a good programming practice, you should always enclose your if block within braces, even if it contains a single statement.

A common programming mistake that occurs when braces are omitted is that at a later date when programmer adds a statement to if block. This additional statement is treated as outside if block due to missing braces leading to a logical error.

Essential Programming Practice: Indentation

It is a truth of life that whatever programs you write, at a later date, you or someone else will have to read them too. In order to make the program readable, we use certain indentation guidelines.

Throughout this book, we will
1. Indent embedded code block 4 spaces to the right as compared to the outer block.
2. Keep the opening brace on the first line of the start of the block.
3. Keep the closing brace on a line by itself at the same indentation level as the start of first line of block of code.

This makes the program visually easy to read since all statements are neatly aligned and nesting of blocks is clearly visible.

 feedback@thebookofc.com

Let us examine a previous example to demonstrate the indentation style

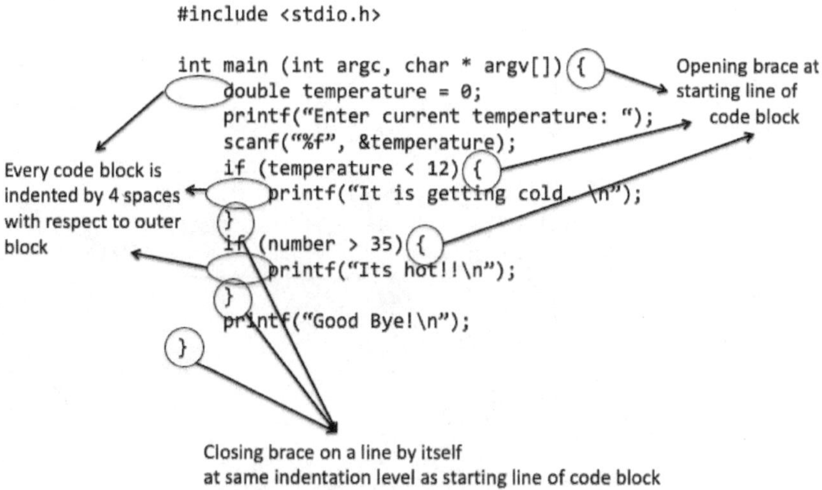

The Else Clause

Let's revisit one of the programming problems earlier in this chapter – determining if a number was even or odd. In situations like these, where we have two mutually exclusive courses of action depending on outcome of the same condition, else clause comes very handy.

An else clause is always attached to an if statement. If the control expression is true, if block is executed and else block is skipped. If the control expression is false, if block is skipped and else block is executed. Since they are mutually exclusive you will never see them both getting executed.

Flowchart below shows the logic flow when we solved the odd/even problem using just if construct.

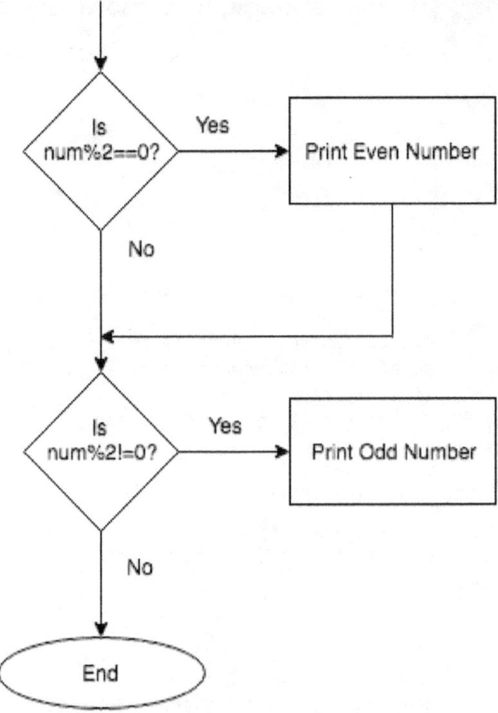

When we use only `if` we always end up evaluating two conditions when it is truly just one condition with two mutually exclusive action paths. Using an else clause, our solution gets simplified to the flowchart shown below.

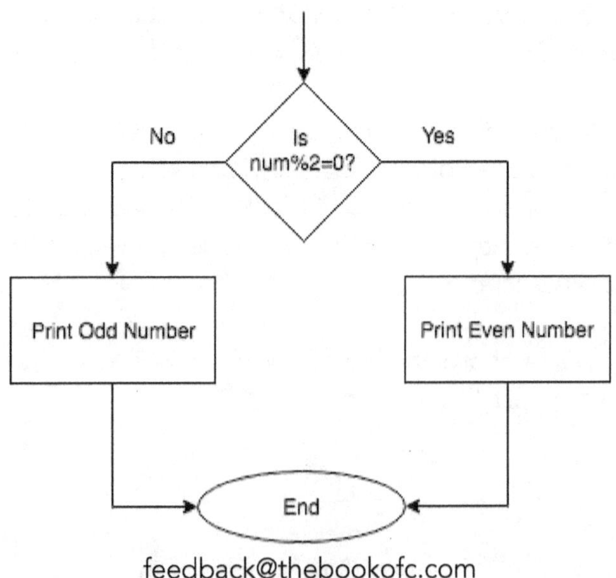

feedback@thebookofc.com

Now let's translate this flowchart to C code using `if-else` construct.

```
01: #include <stdio.h>

02: int main (int argc, char * argv[]) {
03:     int number = 0;
04:     printf("Enter a number: ");
05:     scanf("%d",&number);
06:     if (number % 2 == 0) {
07:         printf("You entered an even number\n");
08:     } else {
09:         printf("You entered an odd number\n");
10:     }
11:     printf ("Good Bye!\n");
12:     return 0;
13: }
```

Let's trace the control flow for user input 9.
1. After user input, control reaches line 06. `if` condition is evaluated.
    a. `9%2 == 0` evaluates to false.
    b. Control skips the `if` block and jumps to `else` block, line 09.
2. Print statement is executed and message You entered an odd number is printed.
3. Control reaches end of `else` block and advances to line 11.
4. Print statement is executed and message Good Bye! is printed.
5. Control reaches end of program and terminates.

Now, let's trace the control flow for user input 10.
1. After user input, control reaches line 06. `if` condition is evaluated.
    a. `10%2 == 0` evaluates to true.
    b. Control proceeds to `if` block, line 07.
2. Print statement is executed and message You entered an even number is printed.
3. Control reaches end of `if` block, skips `else` block and jumps to line 11.
4. Print statement is executed and message Good Bye! is printed.

5. Control reaches end of program and terminates.

Few things to note:
1. `else` is a C language keyword.
2. `else` clause is placed immediately next to closing brace of `if` block. There can be nothing between the closing brace of `if` and keyword `else`.
3. `else` clause cannot exist on its own. It has to be attached to an `if` statement.
4. Coding style of `else` block is same as `if` block, opening brace on the same line as `else` keyword, block indented by 4 spaces, and closing brace on a line by itself at the same indentation level as `else` statement.
5. Pair of braces around `else` block is also optional. If there is no opening brace after `else` then only next immediate statement is considered to be part of `else` block.

Practice Questions : -

15. Which of the following if else constructs are syntactically valid.

1.
```c
if (a>b) {
    a = a+2;
} else {
    b = b+2;
}
```

2.
```c
if (a>b)
    a = a+2;
else
    b = b+2;
```

3.
```c
if (a>b)
    a = a+2;
  else {
    b = b+2;
}
```

4.
```c
if (a>b) {
    a = a+2;
} else
    b = b+2;
```

          feedback@thebookofc.com

16. Trace the control flow of following program for following user
inputs
    1. 0
    2. 10
    3. 12
    4. 17
    5. 200
    6. -9

```
01: #include <stdio.h>

02: int main (int argc, char * argv[]) {
03:     int hour = 0;
04:     printf("Enter current hour of day (00-23): ");
05:     scanf("%d",&hour);
06:     if (hour < 12){
07:         printf("Its not noon yet.\n");
08:     } else {
09:         printf("Its past noon.\n");
10:     }
11:     printf("Have a good day!\n");
12:     return 0;
13: }
```

17. Use `if else` to write a program that reads a non-zero number from the user and prints whether the number is positive or negative.

18. Write a program that reads a number from the user and prints whether that number is a multiple of 7 or not.

19. Modify the program for finding largest of three numbers to use `if-else`.

20. What will be the output of following program.

```
#include <stdio.h>
int main (int argc, char * argv[]) {
    int a = 7, b = 9, c = 3, z = 0;
    if ((b + c) > z) {
        b = b * 2;
        z = b % a;
    } else {
        b = b / 2;
        z = a + b;
    }
    printf ("a=%d, b=%d, c=%d, z=%d\n", a, b, c, z);
    return 0;
}
```

Shorthand notation

C supports a shorthand notation for `if-else` construct. Instead of writing the complete `if-else` programming instructions, we can use the shorthand notation to compose same set of instructions, but in very concise form. Let's first understand the syntax of the shorthand notation.

```
condition ? true_evaluate: false_evaluate
```

where, characters "?" and ":" together are called the **conditional operator** or **ternary operator**. The word ternary signifies that it takes three operands.

Whole ternary operator expression evaluates to a single value – either `true_evaluate` or `false_evaluate`.

`condition` is the control expression. It must evaluate to either true or false.

If control expression evaluates to true then ternary operator evaluates to the value of `true_evaluate`.

If control expression evaluates to false then ternary operator evaluates to the value of `false_evaluate`.

We can assign the result of this conditional operation to a variable as shown below.

```
variable = condition?true_evaluate:false_evaluate
```

This is equivalent to writing

```
if (condition) {
   variable = true_evaluate;
} else {
    variable = false_evaluate;
}
```

     feedback@thebookofc.com

Let's consider an example to determine the greater of two numbers. A program using standard `if-else` construct can be written as shown below.

```c
#include <stdio.h>

int main(int argc, char* argv[]) {
    int number_1 = 0;
    int number_2 = 0;
    int greater_num = 0;

    printf("Enter first number: ");
    scanf("%d",&number_1);
    printf("Enter second number: ");
    scanf("%d",&number_2);

    if (number_1 > number_2){
        greater_num = number_1;
    } else {
        greater_num = number_2;
    }
    printf("The greater of two num is %d", greater_num);
}
```

Let us reconstruct above example in shorthand notation. Following will be the elements of the shorthand construct.

- `condition` is (number_1 > number_2)
- `true_evaluate` is number_1. greater_num is assigned value number_1 when the condition evaluates to true.
- `false_evaluate` is number_2. greater_num is assigned value number_2, when the condition evaluates to false.

Let us rewrite the above example using shorthand notation.

```c
#include <stdio.h>

int main(int argc, char* argv[]) {
    int number_1 = 0;
    int number_2 = 0;
    int greater_num = 0;

    printf("Enter first number: ");
    scanf("%d",&number_1);
    printf("Enter second number: ");
    scanf("%d",&number_2);

    greater_num = (number_1>number_2)?number_1:number_2;

    printf("The greater of two num is %d", greater_num);
}
```

Practice Questions : -

21. Which of the following code snippets are valid.
    1. ```c
       int a = 5, b = 7, c = 11;
       (a>b)?b=b+2;c=b*2:c=c*2;
       ```
    2. ```c
       int a = 0, b = 0, c = 0;
       a = (b+c > b-c)?b:c;
       ```

More Decisions, Mastering if-else

In previous chapter we learned how to make decisions involving up to two possible paths of action using a single criterion. While this is sufficient for simple programs, most real world scenarios are not that simplistic. For example, our initial example of "If it is holiday today, I will go out to play" is usually not that simplistic. If it is raining then you may not be able to go out to play. Or maybe there is a pending exam that requires you to study even if it is a holiday today.

Let's extend our knowledge of decisions and learn to write programs that include multiple action paths using multiple variables in decision making criteria.

Logical Operators

Many times our decisions involve more than one condition and more than one variable. As an example, consider a program to qualify if an student can apply for a scholarship. In order to apply, the candidate should have scored above 80% in the qualifying exam and should have at least 3 years of experience. Here our action path is dependent on value of two variables – score and years of experience.

This is where logical operators come in handy. They allow us to logically combine different conditions to get a true/false decision.

There are three logical operators.

Symbol	Operator
&&	AND
||	OR
!	NOT

AND Operator

&& is the AND operator. AND operator evaluates to true if both its operands are true. If any one or both operands are false, then AND will evaluate to false. This is same as saying operand 1 AND operand 2, both have to be true for operator to evaluate to true.

Below is a table that shows all possible combinations of operand values and result of AND operation.

A	B	A && B
True	True	True
True	False	False
False	True	False
False	False	False

Such a table that lists all scenarios is called truth table.

Let's see an example of **&&** operator in action.

```c
#include <stdio.h>

int main (int argc, char * argv[]) {
    double score = 0, years = 0;
    printf("Enter your score: ");
    scanf("%lf", &score);
    printf ("Enter years of experience: ");
    scanf("%lf", &years);
    if (score >= 80 && years >=3) {
        printf("You are eligible for scholarship\n");
    } else {
        printf("How about a student loan?\n");
    }
    return 0;
}
```

The `if` condition uses an **&&** operator. Hence it would be true only if both the conditions are true, i.e. `score >= 80` AND `years >= 3`. If any one or both the conditions are false, the `if` condition will evaluate to false.

We can also concatenate multiple conditions using **&&** operator. For example,

`if (score >= 80 && years >=3 && age <= 23)`

     feedback@thebookofc.com

The overall condition will be true only if all three AND conditions are individually true.

Practice Questions : -
1. Trace the flow of above example program for following user inputs
    1. score = 98.2, years = 2.3
    2. score = 88, years = 5
    3. score = 70, years = 10
    4. score = 79, years = 1.2
2. What would be the output of following program.

```c
#include <stdio.h>
int main(int argc, char * argv[]) {
    int copies_sold = 500000;
    double weeks_since_launch = 3.3;
    if (copies_sold > 5000 && weeks_since_launch < 1) {
        printf ("This is a bestseller\n");
    } else {
        printf("Not sure if this is a bestseller\n");
    }
}
```

3. Trace the control flow of following program for following user inputs
    1. 200
    2. 99
    3. 0

```c
01: #include <stdio.h>
02: int main (int argc, char * argv[]) {
03:     int runs = 0;
04:     printf("Enter runs scored by the batsman: ");
05:     scanf("%d", &runs);
06:     if (runs >= 200) {
07:         printf("You scored a double century\n");
08:     }
09:     if (runs >= 100 && runs < 200) {
10:         printf("You scored a century\n");
11:     }
12:     if (runs >= 50 && runs < 100) {
13:         printf("You scored a half century\n");
14:     }
15:     if (runs == 0) {
16:         printf("You got a duck\n");
17:     }
18:     printf("Good bye!\n");
19:     return 0;
20: }
```

4. What will be the output of following program
```c
#include <stdio.h>

int main (int argc, char * argv[]) {
    int a = 1, b = 2, c = 3, z = 0;
    if ( (a > (b - c)) && ((c - a) > (b - z)) ) {
        a = b - c;
        z = z + b;
    }
    if ((a <= z) && (b !=0)) {
        c = c * c;
    } else {
        z = a + b + c;
        b = z * 3;
    }
    printf("a=%d, b=%d, c=%d, z=%d", a,b,c,z);
    return 0;
}
```
5. Write a program that reads a number and prints whether the number has one digit, two digits, three digits, or more than three digits.

The OR Operator

|| is the OR operator. OR operator evaluates to true if at least one of its operands is true. If both operands are false, then OR will evaluate to false. This is same as saying either operand 1 OR operand 2 have to be true for the operator to evaluate to true.

Below is the truth table for OR operator

A	B	A || B
True	True	True
True	False	True
False	True	True
False	False	False

Let's take an example.

     feedback@thebookofc.com

```c
#include <stdio.h>

int main (int argc, char * argv[]) {
    int month = 0;
    printf("Enter the current month (1-12): ");
    scanf("%d",&month);
    if ((month < 1) || (month > 12)) {
        printf("You entered an invalid value\n");
    } else {
        printf("This computer has taught you well!\n");
    }
    printf("Good Bye!\n");
    return 0;
}
```

The condition (month < 1) || (month > 12) will be true only if
either value of month is less than 1 OR value of month is more than
12 – in both these cases the input value is invalid and hence we print
an error message.

You can concatenate multiple conditions using OR operator. For
example,

```c
if ((1 == month) || (3 == month) || (5 == month) || (7 ==
month) || (8 == month) || (10 == month) || (12 == month))
{
    printf ("Month has 31 days\n");
}
```

You can also use a combination of AND and OR operators. For
example,

```c
if ((transaction_value > 20000) && (account_balance >
100000 || income > 100000)) {
    printf("You are eligible for a discount\n");
}
```

In the above example, if condition is checking for customers who
are spending more than 20,000 and either have an account balance
of more than 100,000 or have income of more than 100,000 to select
them for a discount.

6. Assume `int a = 5, b = 7, c = 11, d = 13`. What is the result of following expressions.

    ```
    1.  a || b
    2.  (a && b) || (0 && d)
    3.  (1 || 0) && (b > c)
    4.  (d+b) > (a+c)
    5.  ((d+b) > (a+c)) && (0 || d<a)
    ```

7. Trace the control flow of the following program for user input values mentioned below

    ```
    1.  a = 5, b = -9, c = 2, d = 10, z = 0
    2.  a = 0, b = 7, c = 1, d = 3, z = -1
    3.  a = 0, b = 0, c = 0, d = 0, z = 0
    4.  a = 2, b = 2, c = 2, d = 2, z = 2
    ```

    ```c
    #include <stdio.h>

    int main (int argc, char * argv[]) {
        int a=0, b=0, c=0, d=0, z=0;
        printf("a = ");
        scanf("%d", &a);
        printf("b = ");
        scanf("%d", &b);
        printf("c = ");
        scanf("%d", &c);
        printf("d = ");
        scanf("%d", &d);
        printf("z = ");
        scanf("%d", &z);
        if ( (a<b) || ( ((c*d)<(b*b)) && ((a+b)<(c+d)) )){
            c = c + b;
            z = b * b;
            a = a + z;
            b = z - b;
        }
        if ( (a>b) || ((z+b)>(z-d)) ) {
            b = b + 20;
            c = z - b;
        }
        printf ("a=%d, b=%d, c=%d, d=%d, z=%d\n",
    a,b,c,d,z);
        return 0;
    }
    ```

8. Write a program that reads year from the user and then prints whether the input year is a leap year or not. Note that years divisible by 100 are not leap years unless they are divisible by 400. E.g. 1900 was not a leap year but 2000 was.

9. Write a program that reads in current time: hours (0-23) and minutes (0-59) separately from the user. Validate both inputs in a single control expression to make sure that the inputs are correct.

The NOT Operator

! is the NOT operator. NOT operator is a unary operator, i.e. it takes just one operand. NOT operator simply reverses the value of its operand – true becomes false and false becomes true. Truth table of NOT operator is shown below.

A	!A
False	True
True	False

Let's see ! operator in action.

```c
#include <stdio.h>

int main (int argc, char * argv[]) {
    double temperature = 0;
    printf ("Enter current temperature: ");
    scanf("%f", &temperature);
    if ( !(temperature<30) ) {
        printf ("Great weather for swimming\n");
    }
    return 0;
}
```

The condition (temperature<30) will be true for all values less than 30 and false for all values greater than or equal to 30. The NOT operator (!) in front of the condition will reverse the outcome - make it false for all values less than 30 and true for all values greater than or equal to 30.

10. What will be the output of following program

```c
#include <stdio.h>

int main (int argc, char * argv[]) {
    if (!0) {
        printf("NOT 0 is true\n");
    }
    if (!1) {
        printf("NOT 1 is true\n");
    }
    if (!-1) {
        printf("NOT -1 is true\n");
    }
    return 0;
}
```

Concatenating if else statements

Consider an example program to print a greeting appropriate for the time of the day.
- o Between 5 AM and 12 PM print good morning
- o Between 12 PM and 4 PM print good afternoon
- o Between 4 PM and 10 PM print good evening
- o Between 10 PM and 4 AM print good night

Partial flowchart for such a program is shown below.

          feedback@thebookofc.com

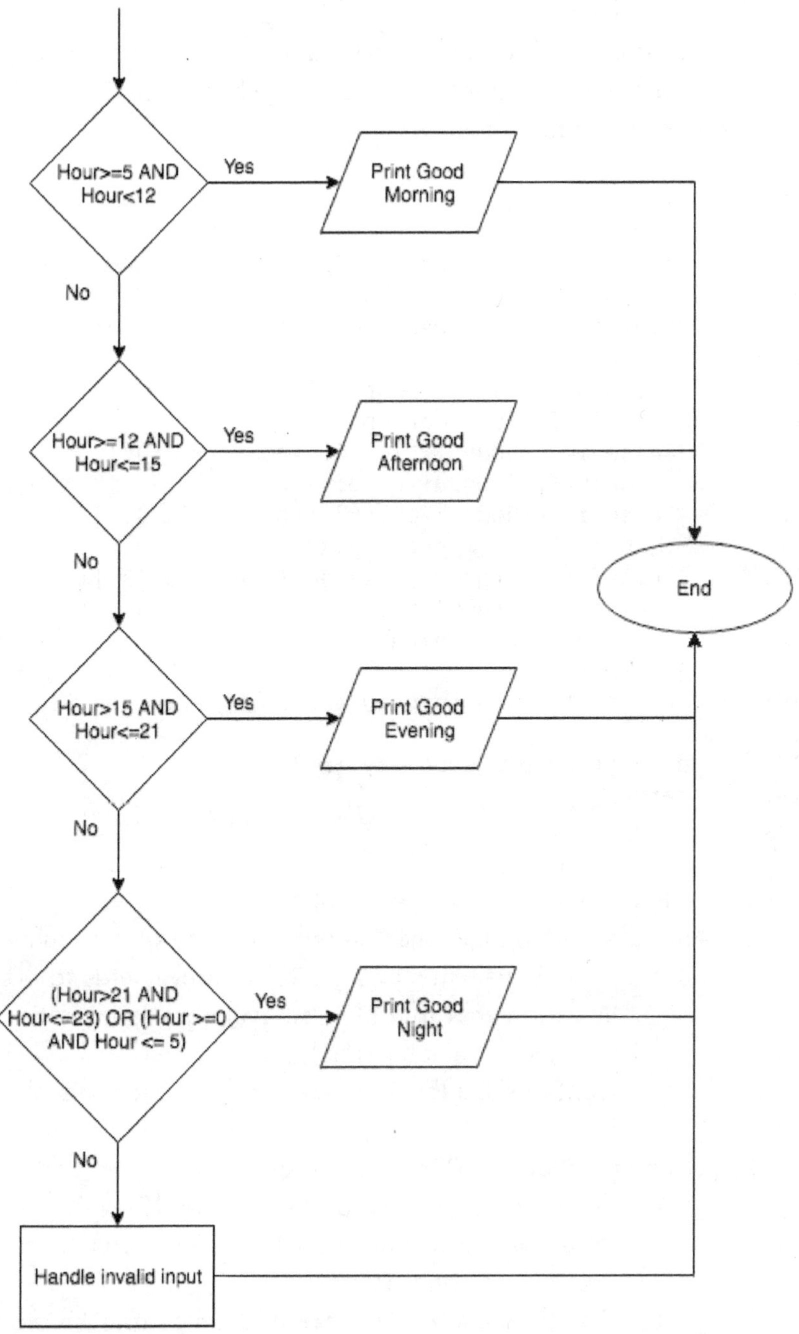

Here we have several successive conditions to be evaluated in case previous conditions evaluated to false. A single `if else` would not suffice to cover all possible control flows.

For solving problems like these, C allows us to concatenate multiple `if else` statements to create several mutually exclusive scenarios. Let's see source code for this example.

```c
01: #include <stdio.h>

02: int main (int argc, char * argv[]) {
03:     int hour = 0;
04:     printf("Enter current hour of day (00-23): ");
05:     scanf("%d",&hour);
06:     if ((hour > 5) && (hour < 12)){
07:         printf("Good morning!\n");
08:     } else if ((hour >= 12) && (hour <= 15)){
09:         printf("Good afternoon!\n");
10:     } else if ((hour > 15) && (hour <= 21)){
11:         printf("Good evening!\n");
12:     } else if ( ((hour > 21) && (hour <=23)) ||
13:                 ((hour >=0) && (hour <= 5)) ) {
14:         printf("Good night!\n");
15:     } else {
16:         printf("You entered the wrong input!\n");
17:     }
18:     printf("Have a good day!\n");
19:     return 0;
20: }
```

Let's trace the control flow for user input 16.
1. After the user input, first `if` statement (Line 06) is evaluated.
    a. 16 > 5 evaluates to true, 16 < 12 evaluates to false. We know that true && false evaluates to false. So `if` condition evaluates to false.
    b. Control skips the `if` block and jumps to `else` block, line 08.
2. `if` condition on line 08 is evaluated.
    a. 16 >= 12 evaluates to true, 16 <= 15 evaluates to false. We know that true && false evaluates to false. So `if` condition is false.
    b. Control skips the `if` block and jumps to `else` block, line 10.
3. `if` condition on line 10 is evaluated.

     feedback@thebookofc.com

a. 16 > 15 evaluates to true, 16 <= 21 evaluates to true. We know that true && true evaluates to true. So `if` condition is true.

b. Control enters the `if` block, line 11.

4. Print statement is executed and message Good evening! is printed.

5. Control skips the `else` block and jumps to end of `if-else`, line 17.

6. Print statement is executed and message Have a good day! is printed.

7. Control reaches end of program and terminates.

11. Trace the control flow of above program for following user inputs.

    1. 5
    2. 12
    3. 7
    4. 23
    5. 15

12. Rewrite the grading program using `if-else` statements that decides various grades based on marks?

    If marks >= 80 grade A

    If marks < 80 and marks > 60 grade B

    If marks < 60 and marks > 40 grade C

    If marks < 40 grade F

13. Write a program that reads the month number (1-12) and prints its equivalent name (January for 1, February for 2, and so on). Include input error checking in your program.

Nested If Else

Like any other statement, an `if` statement or an `if else` statement can be placed inside an `if` block or an `else` block. Placing an `if else` inside another is termed as nesting `if else`.

Below are some possible nested `if else` constructs.

1.
```
if ( ... ) {
    ...
    if (...) {      /*if nested inside if*/
        ...
    }
}
```

2.
```
if ( ... ) {
    ...
    if (...) {      /*if else nested inside if*/
        ...
    } else {
        ...
    }
}
```

3.
```
if ( ... ) {
    ...
} else {
    ...
    if (...) {      /*if else nested inside else*/
        ...
    } else {
        ...
    }
}
```

4.
```
if ( ... ) {
    ...
} else {
    ...
    if (...) {      /*if nested inside else*/
        ...
    }
}
```

Above constructs are just examples and by no means they represent the entire set of valid nested if else constructs. As long as our individual if else constructs are valid, we can nest them in any way required.

          feedback@thebookofc.com

Let's see an example of nested `if else` in action. Below is a partial program that reads the month and first day of the month (1 for Monday, 2 for Tuesday, and so on) from the user and prints the number of Sundays in that month.

```c
01: #include <stdio.h>

02: int main (int argc, char * argv[]) {
03:     int month = 0, date = 0, day = 0;
04:     printf("Enter the current month (1-12): ");
05:     scanf("%d", &month);
06:     printf("Enter first day of month (1-7): ");
07:     scanf("%d", &day);
08:     if ( month < 1 || month > 12 ||
09:             day < 1 || day > 7) {
10:         printf("Invalid input\n");
11:     } else {
12:         if (2 == month) {
13:             printf("Month has 4 Sundays\n");
14:         } else {
15:             if ((1 == month|| 3 == month||
16:                     5 == month|| 7 == month ||
17:                     8 == month || 10 == month ||
18:                     12 == month) && (5 == day ||
19:                         6 == day || 7 == day)) {
20:                 printf("Month has 5 Sundays\n");
21:             }
22:         }
23:     }
24:     printf("Good Bye!\n");
25:     return 0;
26: }
```

Let's trace control flow for user input month = 7 and day = 6.

1. After the inputs have been received, control reaches the first
    `if` statement, line 08.
    a. 7 < 1 is false, 7 > 12 is false, 6 < 1 is false, 6 > 7 is
        false. Since all conditions evaluate to false, OR of all
        will evaluate to false.
    b. Control skips the `if` block and jumps to the `else`
        block, line 11.
2. `if` statement Tuent on line 11 is executed.
    a. Condition 2 == 7 evaluates to false.

b. Control skips `if` block and jumps to `else` block – line 14.

3. `if` statement on line 14 is executed.

    a. Condition 1 == 7 is false, 3 == 7 is false, 5 == 7 is false, 7 == 7 is true, 8 == 7 is false, 10 == 7 is false, 12 == 7 is false. We know that OR evaluates to true if at least one of its operands is true. Hence the condition on left of **&&** evaluates to true.

    b. Let's evaluates the condition on the right of **&&**. Condition 5 == 6 is false, 6 == 6 is true, 7 == 6 is false. We know that OR evaluates to true if at least one of its operands is true. Hence the condition on right of **&&** evaluates to true.

    c. Since both left and right conditions are true, the **&&** and hence the overall condition evaluates to true.

4. Control enters the `if` block, line 15.Print statement is executed and message `Month has 5 Sundays` is printed.

5. End of `if` block is reached. Control advances to first statement outside the `if` block, line 17.

6. End of enclosing `else` (started on line 13) is reached. Control advances to first statement outside the `else` block, line 18.

7. End of outermost `else` (started on line 10) is reached. Control advances to first statement outside the `else` block, line 19.

8. Print statement is executed and message `Good Bye!` is printed.

9. Control advances to end of program and terminates.

We talked about indentation earlier in this chapter, and we highlighted that it makes the program more readable. At this stage, it would be instructive to revisit last few examples where concatenating `if` statement and nesting `if` statements have made the program a bit more complex than the sequential flow examples earlier in this book. You should be able to appreciate how indentation makes complex programs easier to read.

What we just saw was two levels of nesting, i.e. one `if else` nested inside another `if else`. There is no limit on levels of nesting. You nest an `if else` inside another which is nested inside another and so on.

        feedback@thebookofc.com

14. Trace the control flow of above program for following user inputs
    1. month = 13 day = 5
    2. month = 1 day = 9
    3. month = 3 day = 4
    4. month = 12 day = 7
    5. month = 6 day = 7
    6. month = 10 day = 2
15. Complete the above program to include calculations for all months and days
16. Which of the following nested `if else` constructs are valid.

    ```
    1.  if ( … ) {
            if ( … ) {
                else {
                    …
                }
            }
        }
    ```

    ```
    2.  if ( … ) {
            if ( … ) {
                if ( … ) {
                    if ( … ) {
                        …
                    }
                } else {
                    …
                }
            }
        }
    ```

    ```
    3.  if ( … ) {
            if ( … ) {
            } else {
                …
            }
        } else {
            if ( … ) {
                …
            }
        }
    ```

17. Write a calculator program that reads in two integers and an operator (+, -, *, /) from the user and prints the result of applying that operator to the numbers. For example, if the user entered

numbers 3 and 6 and operator -, your program should print -3 as result.

18. Write a program that reads the current hours and minutes from the user in GMT and converts them to current time IST. For doing so, you will have to add 5 hours 30 minutes to the entered time. If addition leads to change of day, just print the corresponding IST time for the following day. Make sure you validate the input values before using them.

Relational Operators with float[1] & double

Let's consider the following example.

```
01: #include <stdio.h>

02: int main(int argc, char * argv[]) {

03:     float f = 0.1;
04:     float sum = 0, product = 0;
05:     sum = f + f + f + f + f + f + f + f + f + f;
06:     product = f * 10;
07:     if (sum == product) {
08:         printf("Sum and product are same\n");
09:     } else {
10:         printf("Sum and product are not same\n");
11:     }
12:     printf("Sum is %.15f, product is %.15f\n", sum,
product);
13:     return 0;
14: }
```

In this example, we are using two different methods to compute value 1.0. At line 06, we have added 0.1 to itself 10 times, for which the result should be 1.0. At line 07, we have multiplied 0.1 by 10, which should again evaluate to 1.0. Hence logically, the comparison at line 08 should evaluate to true. However, the output of above program when executed is,

```
Sum and product are not same
Sum is 1.000000119209290, product is 1.000000000000000
```

---

[1] float and long double are floating datatypes, like double, discussed later in the book.

     feedback@thebookofc.com

What happened? Why didn't **sum** and **product** match? The answer lies in the precision of type `float` (or `double`). Remember our discussion about precision earlier in the book? When you derive the same value, but via different arithmetic operations, it may or may not lead to exact same value. Due to rounding errors, most floating-point numbers end up being slightly imprecise.

Also, note that the results you get may vary with compiler, CPU, and certain compiler settings. Also note, that compiler will not give any error for such a comparison. Although most modern compilers give a warning similar to the one below.

```
warning: comparing floating point with == or != is unsafe
```

What should we do when our decision making involves comparing floating point numbers? Instead of comparing with an exact number we can compare with a small range that could represent that number. That is, consider a small number epsilon such that

```
number - epsilon < number < number + epsilon
```

could represent **number** internally.

C standard guarantees minimum epsilon for `float` to be 1E-5, i.e. 1×10^{-5} or 0.00001. Hence any value that is greater than 0.99999 and less than 1.00001 is effectively 1.0.

Epsilon value for `double` and `long double` is defined to be at least 1E-9.

In our above example, if we compare the **sum** and **product** up to 5 digit precision, we should be able to successfully test for equality. Let's rewrite the above program to compare **sum** and **product** to match within defined epsilon range.

```c
01: #include <stdio.h>
02: int main(int argc, char * argv[]) {
03:     float f = 0.1;
04:     float sum = 0, product = 0;
05:     float epsilon = 0.00001;
06:     sum = f + f + f + f + f + f + f + f + f + f;
07:     product = f * 10;
08:     if ((sum - product < epsilon) || (product - sum <
epsilon)) {
09:         printf("Sum and product can be called
same\n");
10:     } else {
11:         printf("Sum and product are not same\n");
12:     }
13:     printf("Sum is %.15f, product is %.15f\n", sum,
product);
14: }
```

At line 05 we define a variable `epsilon`. The value of `epsilon` is defined according to the precision we want to use in our comparison.

At line 09, if difference of two variables is less than `epsilon`, we conclude that two variable are equal.

The output of above program is,

```
Sum and product can be called same
Sum is 1.000000119209290, product is 1.000000000000000
```

Things to note:
1. What we have learned above is the easiest way to handle imprecision in floating point data types. Detailed treatment of floating point numbers and their imprecision is outside the scope of this book.
2. In a practical implementation you would use value of epsilon defined on your system. We have not yet learned all the concepts to fully understand how to do that. Visit http://thebookofc.com/floating-point/comparing-floats-using-epsilon/ after you have read the book to learn how to use system defined epsilon.

     feedback@thebookofc.com

Even though above method of defining our own epsilon is not ideal or standard, it would work well for all of our learning needs for now.

Practice question :-
19. Run the above program with data type as `double` for f, sum and product. What is the magnitude of error you observe?

A Common Error

Let's create a grade evaluation program to include following scenarios.

- o   If your score is equal to 10, print "you are the best".
- o   If your score is between 6 to 10, print "you are good".
- o   If your score is less than equal to 6, print "you need to pull up your socks".

A sample implementation of such a program is provided below.

```
01: #include <stdio.h>

02: int main(int argc, char* argv[]) {
03:     int score = 0;
04:     printf ("Enter your score (0-10): ");
05:     scanf("%d",&score);
06:     if (score = 10) {
07:         printf("You are the best\n");
08:     }
09:     else if (score > 6) {
10:         printf("You are good\n");
11:     }
12:     else {
13:         printf("You need to pull up your socks\n");
14:     }
15:     return 0;
16: }
```

Let us execute this program with input `score` as "4". The expected output is `You need to pull up your socks`. But instead the program prints: `You are the best`.

What went wrong?

If you examine the code closely, answer lies in the control expression at line 06. Here, instead of ==, which is a relational operator, we have used =, which is an assignment operator. What happens when we erroneously use assignment operator in control expression?

Assignment operator evaluates to the value being assigned. In this case, since value being assigned is 10, control expression will evaluate to 10. Effectively the control expression becomes if (10), which is true. Remember, all non-zero numbers are true.

Let's rewrite the above program, where we also print the value of variable score to validate the same.

```c
#include <stdio.h>

int main(int argc, char* argv[]) {
    int score = 0;
    printf ("Enter your score: ");
    scanf("%d",&score);
    if (score = 10) {
        printf("You are the best, score %d\n", score);
        }
    else if (score > 6) {
        printf("You are good, score %d\n", score);
    }
    else {
        printf("You need to pull up, score %d\n", score);
    }
    return 0;
}
```

Since the input value of score is always overwritten with value 10 at line 06, irrespective of whatever is the user input to the above program, the output will always be You are the best, score 10.

In most cases, using assignment operator in control expression is an unintentional mistake. While compiler does not flag score = 10 as an error, almost all recent compilers would give you a warning. Review the warnings you might have received while compiling the above example.

     feedback@thebookofc.com

22. What will be the output of following program.

```c
#include <stdio.h>
int main(int argc, char* argv[]) {
    int a = 0;
    if (a == 0) {
        printf("The expression a == 0 is true\n");
    }
    if (a = 0) {
        printf("The expression a = 0 is true\n");
    }
    return 0;
}
```

A common industry practice to avoid this error is to write the variable as right operand and literal as the left operand. In above example, the intention was to write `if (score == 10)`, hence it is better programming practice to write `if (10 == score)` instead. If we unintentionally use assignment operator instead of relational one, that is if we write `if (10 = score)`, compiler will throw the following error.

```
main.c:6:12: error: lvalue required as left operand of
assignment
        if (10  = score) {
            ^
```

Remember the '^' sign? It indicates the exact location of compiler error. However, we are introduced to a new term, lvalue in compiler error. Let's deviate for a minute and understand what is lvalue and rvalue.

lvalue and rvalue

Every expression that we have talked about in this book, is either an lvalue or an rvalue. In simple terms, lvalue is an expression which can store a value. This also means that the lvalue can be used to retrieve the stored value anytime later in the program. Variables are a good example of lvalue.

rvalue is an expression which evaluates to a valid value, and hence can be assigned to lvalue. All valid arithmetic expressions are rvalues.

```c
int count = 5*10+2;
```

Here count is the lvalue, and 5*10+2 is the rvalue. Note that rvalue can also be a variable, or an expression including one or more variables.

```c
int science = 76, maths = 82;
int average = (science+math) / 2;
```

Here, average is lvalue and (science+math) / 2 is rvalue.

In an assignment operation in C, the left hand operand has to store values, which can be retrieved at a later stage. Hence the left hand operand of an assignment operator should always be a lvalue.

Let's understand the concept with some examples.

```c
printf ("Hello world!") = 0;
```

This piece of code will give following error while compiling:

```
main.c:5:27: error: lvalue required as left operand of assignment
        printf("Hello World") = 0;
```

Here as you can see, the left hand side of assignment operator is a print statement. It is not an expression that can hold an integer value

Similarly, observe this code:

```c
int a + 4 = 10;
```

On compiling this, you will get the following error:

```
main.c:5:15: error: lvalue required as left operand of assignment
        int a + 4 = 10;
```

The left hand operand here as well is not an lvalue, hence not a valid operand for assignment operator.

Switch Case

Let's revisit the programming exercise in last chapter to create a program that reads the month number from the user and prints the name of the month. This program will contain a series of `if` statements – all testing for mutually exclusive cases on the same variable.

The logic flow of this program is shown in the flowchart below.

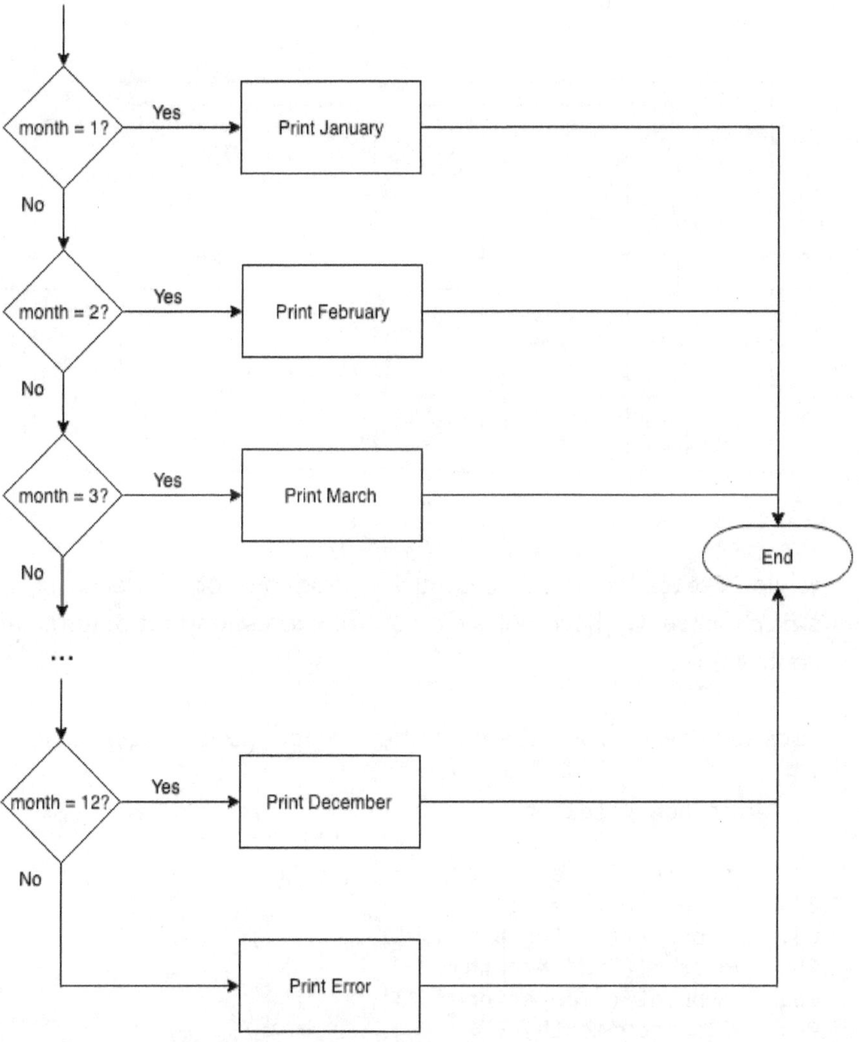

It is a sequence of checks for value of month and actions based on results of these checks.

In such scenarios where we have multiple control flow paths depending on the value of an integer variable or expression, we can use `switch case` statement.

Same program written using `switch case` would have logical flow as shown below.

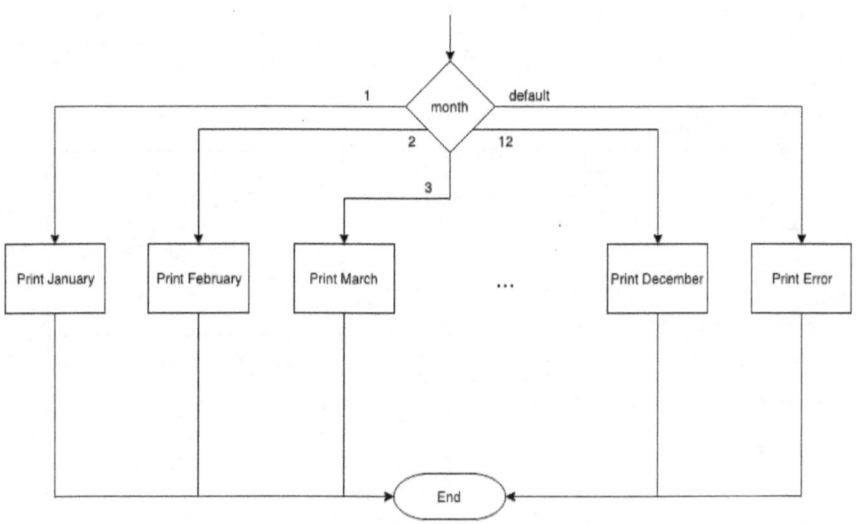

While `if-else` had multiple control expressions, one for each `if`, in `switch case`, we have only one control expression that determines control flow.

Let's see how we can write the same program using `switch case`.

```
01: #include <stdio.h>

02: int main (int argc, char * argv[]) {
03:     int month = 0;
04:     printf("Enter a month[1-12]: ");
05:     scanf("%d",&month);
06:     printf("You entered ");
07:     switch(month) {
08:         case 1:
```

          feedback@thebookofc.com

```c
09:            printf("January\n");
10:            break;
11:        case 2:
12:            printf("February\n");
13:            break;
14:        case 3:
15:            printf("March\n");
16:            break;
17:        case 4:
18:            printf("April\n");
19:            break;
20:        case 5:
21:            printf("May\n");
22:            break;
23:        case 6:
24:            printf("June \n");
25:            break;
26:        case 7:
27:            printf("July \n");
28:            break;
29:        case 8:
30:            printf("August \n");
31:            break;
32:        case 9:
33:            printf("September\n");
34:            break;
35:        case 10:
36:            printf("October\n");
37:            break;
38:        case 11:
39:            printf("November\n");
40:            break;
41:        case 12:
42:            printf("December\n");
43:            break;
44:        default:
45:            printf("invalid input\n");
46:    }
47:    return 0;
48: }
```

Let's examine this example closely starting with the syntax.

switch and case, both are C language keywords.

`switch case` construct has one `switch` statement followed by one or more `case` statements. All cases after `switch` are enclosed in a pair of braces and hence are indented by 4 spaces.

Variable or expression whose value is being used to decide the control flow is placed in parentheses right after the keyword `switch`. Similar to `if else`, `switch` expression is also called controlling expression or control expression. Control expression should be an integer or it should evaluate to an integer.

Keyword `case` is followed by the specific value (integer constant expression) for which this case has to be executed, followed by a colon. This value is called case label since it serves as a label to identify the control expression value that would lead to execution of its `case` construct.

As a good programming practice, statements within a `case` are indented by 4 additional spaces. They do not require enclosing braces.

We also introduced another keyword; `break`, in the above example.

`break` tells the system that control should jump to the first statement outside the current block. Recall that end of block is indicated by first closing brace after the statement - which in this case is the closing brace of the `switch case` construct.

`switch` statement works by first evaluating the control expression enclosed in the parentheses. Then it matches the result with all `case` values. Control enters the `case` construct for the `case` value that matches. Note that `case` values cannot be duplicates. Hence, at most one `case` value would match.

After executing the matched `case` construct, control continues execution through all cases listed after the matching `case` until either the end of `switch case` or until a `break` statement is encountered. `break` statement forces the control to jump outside the current `switch case`.

          feedback@thebookofc.com

The labels used in `switch case` should be integers.

Lastly, notice the last case in the example. It contains another C language keyword: `default`.

If no `case` values match the switch expression, `default` is executed. `default` is an optional case. You can write a `switch case` without `default`. In a program without `default`, if no `case` statements match then nothing will get executed and control will advance to end of `switch case`.

`default` can be placed anywhere inside the `switch case` though as a convention it is typically the last case in a `switch case`.

`switch case` control flow is easily understood by the flowchart below

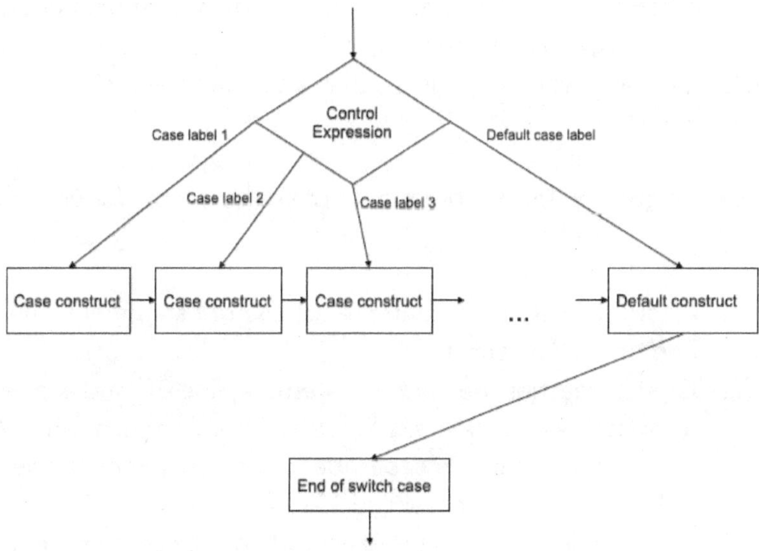

Summary of things to remember about `switch case`:
1. Depending on value of `switch` control expression, control jumps to matching `case` construct.
2. If no `case` matches and `default` is present then control jumps to `default` else control jumps to end of `switch case`.

3. Once matched **case** is executed, control advances to next **case** in the order listed in your program unless a **break** statement is encountered.
4. Encountering a **break** statement makes the control jump to end of **switch case**.
5. Note that there is no defined order in which **case** labels are matched. Each implementation is free to choose any order or technique as long as above behaviour is guaranteed.

Since **switch case** does not impose linear evaluation of **case** labels, compilers usually optimise the matching operation resulting in more efficient execution. The nature of these optimisations is outside the scope of this book. You can find some more details about such optimisations at http://thebookofc.com/switch-case/jump-table/.

It is important to note that any efficiency gain is implementation dependent. However, in general, on most systems **switch case** would perform fewer comparisons than equivalent series of **if else** statements.

Let's trace control flow for our month of year example for user input 3.

    1. After the user input, control reaches print statement, line 06, and prints **You entered** .
    2. Control reaches the **switch** statement, line 07, and evaluates its control expression, the value of variable **month**, which has value 3. This matches **case** label 3. Control jumps to line 14.
    3. Control enters the **case**, line 15.
        a. Print statement is executed and **March** is printed.
        b. Control advances to next statement, line 16, which is **break**. Control jumps outside the **switch case**, line **46.**
    4. Control reaches the end of the program and terminates.

Now let's trace the control flow of the same program for user input 39.

feedback@thebookofc.com

1. After the user input, control reaches print statement, line 06, and prints You entered .
2. Control reaches the switch statement, line 07, and evaluates its control expression, the value of variable month, which has value 39. It does not match any case labels. However, a default is present. Control jumps to default, line 44.
3. Control enters default case. Print statement is executed, line 45, and invalid value is printed.
4. Control advances to end of switch case, line 46, and then to end of program and terminates.

Practice Questions : -

1. Which of the following statements are true.
    a. Every switch statement requires a default case.
    b. switch(4.2 > 3.14) is a valid switch control expression.
    c. break makes the control jump out of current code block.
    d. break can be used to terminate a program.
    e. If control expression matches a case label then control will jump to that case and then to default case since default matches everything.
2. Write a program using switch case that takes day of the week (1-7) as user input and prints the name of the day, Monday for 1, Tuesday for 2, and so on. In case user input is outside the range 1-7, program should print an error message using default case.
3. Write a program using switch case that takes year as input and prints the name of cricket world cup winning country for that year,

    a. 1975: West Indies
    b. 1979: West Indies
    c. 1983: India
    d. 1987: Australia
    e. 1992: Pakistan
    f. 1996: Sri Lanka
    g. 1999: Australia
    h. 2003: Australia
    i. 2007: Australia
    j. 2011: India
    k. 2015: Australia

If world cup was not played in the year entered by the user, program should print an error message.

As we discussed earlier in this chapter, once a **case** statement matches, control flow continues through the **case** statements until a **break** statement is encountered or control flow reaches end of **switch case** construct. That implies, if a **break** statement is not present in a **case** construct and control enters that construct then control flow will enter the next **case** construct as well.

Let's consider an example.

```
01: #include <stdio.h>

02: int main (int argc, char * argv[]) {
03:     int test = 0;

04:     printf("Enter a value (1-3): ");
05:     scanf("%d",&test);

06:     switch(test) {
07:         case 1:
08:             printf("I ");
09:         case 2:
10:             printf("am ");
11:         case 3:
12:             printf("C Champion!");
13:     }
14:     return 0;
15: }
```

Let's trace the control flow of this program for user input 1.

1. After the user input, control reaches the **switch** statement, line 06.
2. **switch** control expression is evaluated, value of variable test which has value 1. This matches a **case** label. Control jumps to matching **case**, line 07.
3. Control enters the **case** construct and advances to line 08.
4. Print statement is executed and **I** gets printed on the console. Control advances to line 09, which is next **case** statement. Since there was no **break** statement, control

               feedback@thebookofc.com

enters the next case and advances to line 10. Note that no case value matching took place. It was just the absence of break that allowed the control to enter next case construct.

5. Print statement is executed and am gets printed on the console. Control advances to line 11. Again, no case matching, control simply advances to line 12.

6. Print statement is executed and C Champion! gets printed on the console. Control advances to line 13, end of switch case and then to end of program.

Practice Questions : -

4. Trace the control flow of following program for user inputs listed below.
    1. 4
    2. 5
    3. 9
    4. 11
    5. 3

```
01: #include <stdio.h>

02: int main (int argc, char * argv[]) {
03:     int test = 0;
04:     printf("Enter a value[1-9]: ");
05:     scanf("%d",&test);
06:     printf("You entered ");
07:     switch(test) {
08:         case 9:
09:             printf("9\n");
10:           break;
11:         case 3:
12:             printf("3\n");
13:         default:
14:             printf("Default\n");
15:         case 4:
16:             printf("4\n");
17:         case 5:
18:             printf("5\n");
19:           break;
20:         case 6:
21:             printf("6\n");
22:           break;
23:     }
24:    return 0;
25: }
```

5. Trace the control flow of the program below for following user
    inputs
    1. 99
    2. 100
    3. 7
    4. 49

```
01: #include <stdio.h>

02: int main (int argc, char * argv[]) {
03:     int percentile = 0;
04:     printf("Enter your percentile [1-99]: ");
05:     scanf("%d",&percentile);
06:     switch(percentile/10) {
07:         case 9:
08:             printf("Wow, you are among top 10% \n");
09:             break;
10:         case 8:
11:             printf("Good job, among top 20% \n");
12:             break;
13:         case 7:
14:             printf("Decent show, among top 30% \n");
15:             break;
16:         case 6:
17:         case 5:
18:             printf("Pull up your socks \n");
19:             break;
20:         case 4:
21:         case 3:
22:         case 2:
23:         case 1:
24:         case 0:
25:             printf("You should attempt again \n");
26:             break;
27:         default:
28:             printf("Value out of range\n");
29:     }
30:     return 0;
31: }
```

6. Rewrite the world cup winning team program such that there is
    only one print statement for each winning country.

Nested switch case

Just as we could nest if else statements, switch case too can be nested, i.e. we can have one switch case inside another. Nested switch case is useful where you have to make decisions depending on different values of more than one variable. Let's see an example.

```
01: #include <stdio.h>
02: int main(int argc, char * argv[]) {
03:     int temperature = 0, coolant_level = 0;
04:     printf("Enter reactor temperature [1]hot [2]warm [3]cold ");
05:     scanf("%d", &temperature);
06:     printf("Enter coolant level [1]high [2]medium [3]low ");
07:     scanf("%d", &coolant_level);
08:    switch (temperature) {
09:         case 3:
10:             printf("Kick back and have a coffee!");
11:             break;
12:         case 2:
13:             printf("Keep eyes open for any changes");
14:             break;
15:         case 1:
16:             switch (coolant_level) {
17:                 case 1:
18:                     printf("Good job. Keep it full");
19:                     break;
20:                 case 2:
21:                     printf("Quick, fill up the coolant");
22:                     break;
23:                 case 3:
24:                     printf("Run for your life");
25:                     break;
26:                 default:
27:                     printf("Invalid input");
28:                     break;
29:             }
30:             break;
31:         default:
32:             printf("Invalid input");
33:             break;
34:     }
35:     return 0;
36: }
```

Let's trace control flow of the program for user input 1 and 2 for `temperature` and `coolant_level` respectively.

1. After reading the input values control flow reaches the `switch` statement, line 08.
2. `switch` control expression evaluates to value of variable `temperature`, which has value 1. This matches a `case` label. Control jumps to matching `case`, line 15.
3. Control enters the `case` construct, line 16.
4. Line 16 is nested `switch` `case` construct. `switch` control expression evaluates to value of variable `coolant_level`, which has value 2. This matches a `case` label. Control jumps to matching `case`, line 20.
5. Control enters the `case` construct, line 21.
6. Print statement is executed. Message `Quick, fill up the coolant` is printed on console. Control advances to line 22.
7. Line 22 is a `break` statement which tells the control to jump to end of current block. Control jumps to end of nested `switch` `case`, line 29. Control advances to line 30.
8. Line 30 is another `break` statement which tells the control to jump to end of current block. Control jumps to end of outer `switch` `case`, line 34.
9. Control reaches end of program and terminates.

Practice Questions : -

7. Trace control flow of above program for following user inputs
    1. `temperature = 3 and coolant_level = 4`
    2. `temperature = 1 and coolant_level = 4`
    3. `temperature = 1 and coolant_level = 3`

    feedback@thebookofc.com

Data Types – The Sequel

So far, we have learned about `int` and `double` data types. C provides us several other in-built data types. Let's expand our horizon and learn more native C data types and what we can do with them.

short int

A `short int` or just `short`, as the name indicates, is a smaller version of `int` type that we have learned.

We can declare and initialize a `short` variable as shown below:

```
short height = 182;
short int height = 182;
```

Both the declarations above are equivalent.

Note that `short` is a C language keyword.

In order to print a `short` value we can use **%hd** as format specifier in our `printf` statement. In order to read a `short` value we can use **%hd** as format specifier in our `scanf` statement.

Let's see source code of a program that reads in weight and height and tells appropriateness of weight based on BMI. Since height and weight would typically be small integers we can use `short` instead of `int` as data type.

```c
#include <stdio.h>

int main(int argc, char * argv[]) {
    short weight = 0, height = 0;
    double bmi = 0;

    printf("Enter your height in cms: ");
    scanf("%hd",&height);
    printf("Enter your weight in kgs: ");
    scanf("%hd",&weight);

    bmi=weight/((height/100.0) * (height/100.0));
```

```c
    if (bmi < 18.5) {
        printf("Weight of %hd kgs for height of %hd cms
is too less\n",weight, height);
    } else if (bmi > 24.9){
        printf("Weight of %hd kgs for height of %hd cms
is too high\n",weight, height);
    } else {
        printf("You have the right balance of height and
weight\n");
    }
    return 0;
}
```

Practice Questions : -

1. Which of the following declaration statements are valid.
   ```c
   1.  short int radius, double area;
   2.  short int radius = 0, double area = 0.0;
   3.  short math, science = 0;
   4.  short math, int total;
   5.  short int age = 19;
   6.  short num_countries_in_UN = 193;
   ```
2. Trace control flow of above program for following user inputs
   ```c
   1.  weight = 87, height = 168
   2.  weight = 59, height = 172
   ```

What exactly does being a smaller version of int type mean?

As we have learned, all variables store data at some memory location. At the assigned location they are assigned a fixed number of bytes[2] to store data. The number of bytes that are assigned depends on the data type of the variable. Data types that store a larger range of values would need more space as compared to other data types.

In this case, a short int can store a smaller range of values and hence takes up less space compared to an int.

Let's find out how much space does a variable of any data type takes.

---

[2] A byte refers to memory space for storing 8 bits.
A bit is a single binary value that can store 0 or 1

                    feedback@thebookofc.com

sizeof

`sizeof` is a unary C operator, i.e. it takes one operand. It tells us the number of bytes taken up by a data type. `sizeof` is also a C language keyword. `sizeof` can take a data type as well as a variable as its operand. When used with a variable, it tells us the size of the data type of that variable. The result of `sizeof` operator is of integer type[3].

Let's see an example.

```c
#include <stdio.h>

int main(int argc, char * argv[]) {

    int integer_value = 100;
    short int short_value = 100;

    printf("size of int = %d\n",sizeof(int));
    printf("size of integer_value =
%d\n",sizeof(integer_value));

    printf("size of short = %d\n",sizeof(short int));
    printf("size of short_value =
%d\n",sizeof(short_value));

    return 0;
}
```

Run the above program and you should see identical values for size of `int` data type and size of `int` variable. Likewise, size of `short int` data type and size of `short int` variable would also be identical.

Few things to note:
1. Operand of `sizeof` operator is enclosed in a pair of parentheses. If operand is a variable then it is not necessary to use parentheses. However, for readability we recommend that you always use parentheses with `sizeof`.
2. The actual size of data type depends on the implementation, i.e. on the system that you are running. C does not dictate a

---

[3] We will refine this understanding as we proceed further

fixed size for any data type except `char` which we will learn later in this chapter.

Several books incorrectly suggest size of integer to be 2 or 4 bytes. Making any such assumption while writing code is dangerous. It reduces portability of your program and is very likely to make your program behave incorrectly on some systems.

`sizeof` operator can also be applied to expressions. In such case, `sizeof` will evaluate to size of data type of the result of the expression.

Practice Questions : -

3. Which of the following statements are true.
    1. `sizeof` is a C language keyword.
    2. `sizeof` is a C language operator.
    3. `sizeof` evaluates to number of bits required to store the value of its operand.
    4. `sizeof` evaluates to number of bytes required to store the data type of its operand.
4. Assume `int a = 2` and `int b = 100000`, which of the following statements are true
    1. `sizeof(a)` is equal to `sizeof(b)`.
    2. `sizeof(a)` is less than `sizeof(b)`.
    3. `sizeof(a)` is equal to `sizeof(int)`.
5. Write a program to print size of `double`.
6. Assume that size of `double` is 8, size of `int` is 4. Given, `int a = 4` and `double b = 2.0`, what would be the result of `sizeof(a/b)`.

long int

`long` is another C language keyword and a native data type. Similar to `short` `int` which was a smaller integer, a `long` `int` is a larger integer data type.

We can declare and initialize a `long` variable as shown below:

```
long phone_memory = 8589934592;
long int phone_memory = 8589934592;
```

Both the declarations above are equivalent.

In order to print a `long` value we can use `%ld` as format specifier in our `printf` statement. In order to read a `long` value we can use `%ld` as format specifier in our `scanf` statement. Let's see an example where we read in amount of memory used in a phone and print a cleanup memory prompt if more than 90% memory has been used up.

```c
#include <stdio.h>

int main(int argc, char * argv[]) {
    long phone_memory = 8589934592;
    long memory_used = 0;
    double percent_used = 0;

    printf("Enter memory used: ");
    scanf("%ld", &memory_used);
    percent_used = (memory_used*100.0)/phone_memory;

    if (percent_used > 90) {
        printf("Running out of storage, cleanup now\n");
    } else {
        printf("Still have %ld bytes free",phone_memory-
memory_used);
    }

    return 0;
}
```

Practice Questions : -

7. Which of the following are valid declarations?
    1. `int long count = 222222;`
    2. `long int count = 222222;`
    3. `short long count = 22;`
    4. `short long int count = 22;`
    5. `long count = 222222;`
8. Write a program to print size of `long`.
9. Modify the above example to check for erroneous input such that memory_used is less than zero or is more than phone_memory.

long long

As you must have been able to guess, `long long` is an even larger integer.

We can declare and initialize a `long long` variable as shown below:

```
long long disk_bytes = 986503245630389;
long long int disk_bytes = 986503245630389;
```

Both the declarations above are equivalent.

In order to print a `long long` value, we can use %lld as format specifier in our `printf` statement. In order to read a `long long` value, we can use %Ld as format specifier in our `scanf` statement. Note that format specifier for `printf` and `scanf` are different for a `long long`.

Let's see an example.

```c
#include <stdio.h>

int main(int argc, char * argv[]) {
    long long light_year_to_km = 9460730472580;
    long long distance = 0;
    int light_years = 0;

    printf("How many light years to your planet: ");
    scanf("%d",&light_years);
    distance = light_years * light_year_to_km;

    printf("Welcome to earth!\n");
    printf("You are %lld kms from home\n", distance);

    return 0;
}
```

Practice Questions : -

10. Write a program to print size of `long long`.

    feedback@thebookofc.com

float

float is another numeric data type that can hold decimal numbers. The difference between float and double is their size. double is larger than float and hence can store a wider range of values than a float.

We can declare and initialize a float variable as shown below:

```
float pi = 3.14;
```

In order to print a float value, we can use %f as format specifier in our printf statement. In order to read a float value, we can use %f as format specifier in our scanf statement.

Let's see an example of float in action. Below program reads in percent score and class average score and qualifies all above average scores for taking up a scholarship exam.

```
int main(int argc, char * argv[]) {
    float percent = 0, average = 0;
    printf("Enter your percent score: ");
    scanf("%f",&percent);
    printf("Enter class average score: ");
    scanf("%f",&average);

    if (percent > average) {
        printf("You qualify for scholarship exam\n");
    } else {
        printf("You don't qualify for scholarship
exam\n");
    }
    return 0;
}
```

Practice Questions : -

11. Which of the following are valid declarations?
    1. float pi = 3.14;
    2. Float pi = 3.14;
    3. double float pi = 3.14;
    4. float int = 3.14;
    5. float double pi = 3.14;
    6. float pi;

12. Modify the above program to include invalid input value checks, percent and average should be between 0 and 100.
13. Further enhance the program to qualify students that have scored above average and a minimum of 80%.
14. Write a program to print size of float.

long double

As the name indicates, `long double` is a larger version of `double`.

We can declare and initialize a `long double` variable as shown below.

```
long double earth_circumference_kms = 40075.34890123456;
```

In order to print a `long double` value, we can use %Lf as format specifier in our `printf` statement. In order to read a `long double` value, we can use %Lf as format specifier in our `scanf` statement.

Let's see an example using `long double`. The program below reads in breadth of a slice of a microscopic sample and determines if slice is thinner or thicker than a typical human hair.

```
#include <stdio.h>
int main(int argc, char * argv[]) {
    /* Typical human hair is 17um to 181um thick */
    long double hair_min = 17e-06;
    long double hair_max = 181e-06;
    long double sample = 0;
    printf("Enter breadth of slice: ");
    scanf("%Lf",&sample);
    if (sample < hair_min) {
        printf("This sample is thinner than human
hair\n");
    } else if (sample > hair_max) {
        printf("This sample is thicker than human
hair\n");
    }
    printf("Sample breadth %Le",sample);
    return 0;
}
```

          feedback@thebookofc.com

Notice the initialization statement.

```
long double hair_min = 17e-06;
```

17e-06 is equivalent to 17×10^{-6}. The character e separates exponent from decimal value. You can also use exponent representation for input values. Try entering 1e-10 as input to the program.

In order to print a **long double** in exponent notation, use format specifier **%Le**.

You can use **%e** to print a **float** or a **double** in exponent notation.

Practice Questions : -

15. Modify the above program to print input sample width. Use a very small value $< 1 \times 10^{-10}$. Print it using **%Lf** as well as **%Le** format specifier and observe the difference in readability.
16. Write a program to print size of **long double**.

Literals

We have been using literals for a while without defining the term.

A *literal* is a value expressed as itself.

In other words, when we write a value as is in a program, it is called a literal. Our "Hello World!" was a literal, so was the value 3.14 that we assigned to a **float** in an example earlier in this chapter.

char

char data type stores one character. Let's see an example of how we declare, initialise and print a **char**.

```c
#include <stdio.h>
int main(int argc, char * argv[]) {
    char grade = 'A';
    printf("Your grade is %c", grade);
    return 0;
}
```

Things to note about using char:
1. The character literal used for initialisation is enclosed in single quotes. All character literals are enclosed in single quotes.
2. Format specifier %c is used to print a char value.
3. Format specifier %c is used to read a char value using scanf.
4. '\n' is also a character literal - it represents a single character - the newline character.
5. sizeof(char) is always 1. Unlike data types we have learned so far, size of char data type is defined by C standard.

char data type is internally stored as an integer value. What that means is that internally system would store an integer code for every character value that can be stored in a char.

Most common char encoding is called 7-bit US ASCII. However, as far as possible, you should not assume any encoding in your programs. Below is a table of all characters in 7-bit US ASCII encoding. Encoding values are in decimal (base 10).

ASCII Value	Character
0	NUL – '\0' NULL
1	SOH – Start of heading
2	STX – Start of text
3	ETX – End of text
4	EOT – End of transmission
5	ENQ – Enquiry
6	ACK – Acknowledge
7	BEL – '\a' BELL
8	BS – '\b' Backspace
9	HT – '\t' Horizontal tab
10	LF – '\n' New line
11	VT – '\v' Vertical tab
12	FF – '\f' Form feed
13	CR – '\r' Carriage return
14	SO – Shift out
15	SI – Shift in
16	DLE – Data link escape

     feedback@thebookofc.com

17	DC1 – Device control 1
18	DC2 – Device control 2
19	DC3 – Device control 3
20	DC4 – Device control 4
21	NAK – Negative acknowledgement
22	SYN – Synchronous idle
23	ETB – End of transmission block
24	CAN – cancel
25	EM – End of medium
26	SUB – Substitute
27	ESC – Escape
28	FS – File separator
29	GS – Group separator
30	RS – Record separator
31	US – Unit separator

ASCII Value	Character	ASCII Value	Character
32	Space	80	P
33	!	81	Q
34	"	82	R
35	#	83	S
36	$	84	T
37	%	85	U
38	&	86	V
39	'	87	W
40	(	88	X
41	)	89	Y
42	*	90	Z
43	+	91	[
44	,	92	\
45	-	93	]
46	.	94	^
47	/	95	_
48	0	96	`
49	1	97	a
50	2	98	b
51	3	99	c
52	4	100	d

Decimal	Character	Decimal	Character
53	5	101	e
54	6	102	f
55	7	103	g
56	8	104	h
57	9	105	i
58	:	106	j
59	;	107	k
60	<	108	l
61	=	109	m
62	>	110	n
63	?	111	o
64	@	112	p
65	A	113	q
66	B	114	r
67	C	115	s
68	D	116	t
69	E	117	u
70	F	118	v
71	G	119	w
72	H	120	x
73	I	121	y
74	J	122	z
75	K	123	{
76	L	124		
77	M	125	}
78	N	126	~
79	O	127	Delete

Note that some characters in the above table consist of multiple characters with backslash (\) as the first character. For example, new line (\n) and horizontal tab (\t). In C backslash is the escape character, i.e. if system encounters backslash then interpretation of following character is modified. Hence, when system encounters n after \, it interprets it as new line instead of simply character n.

Escape character is also used in `printf` format string to print characters that have predefined interpretation in format string, e.g. double quote and backslash itself. Following `printf` statements print a double quote and backslash character.

     feedback@thebookofc.com

```c
printf("This is a double quote \" ");
printf("This is a backslash \\ ");
```

In first statement backslash (\) modifies the interpretation of double quote ("). Instead of treating it as terminating double quote for format string, system treats it as double quote character itself.

In second statement (\) modifies the interpretation of following backslash (\). Instead of treating it as escape character, system treats it as backslash character itself.

Practice Questions : -

17. Which of the following are valid char declarations
    ```c
    1.  char flag = "A";
    2.  char flag = 'A';
    3.  char flag;
    4.  char flag = '"';
    5.  char flag = '\\';
    6.  char flag = '\';
    ```
18. Write a program incorporating the following `printf` statements and observe the output.
    ```c
    printf("This is a double quote \" ");
    printf("This is a backslash \\ ");
    ```
19. Write a program to print string given below, including the quotes
    "In C \\ prints \ on console"

Since `char` is internally stored as `int` value, we can use relational operators on char just like we use them on `int`. Let's see an example.

```c
#include <stdio.h>

int main(int argc, char * argv[]) {
    char small = 'a';
    char big = 'A';

    if (big > small) {
        printf ("'A' is bigger than 'a'");
    } else {
        printf ("'a' is bigger than 'A'");
    }
    return 0;
}
```

20. Using the ASCII table above for encoding characters, what will
    be the output of above program?

char Vs int Values

Consider the following program.

```c
#include <stdio.h>

int main(int argc, char * argv[]) {
    char char_one = '1';
    int int_one = 1;
    if (char_one == int_one) {
        printf("They are same - %c %d", char_one,
int_one);
    } else {
        printf ("They are different - %c %d", char_one,
int_one);
    }
    return 0;
}
```

The output of the above program is shown below.

```
They are different - 1 1
```

Why? Both of them are printed as '1', and yet output indicates that
the two are different.

Answer lies in the fact that character variables store the encoded
integer value instead of the character itself. We saw these encodings
in the ASCII table earlier in this chapter.

Note from the ASCII table above that on a system using ASCII
encoding, character variable with value '1' has integer value 49
stored in it. In other words, character value '1' and integer value 1
are not equal. char value '1' is equal to int value 49.

When we use %c as format specifier to print the value of a character variable, the translation from ASCII code to character representation is done and printed.

To figure out the encoding value of a character on your system, you can print it as an integer. For example, to print encoding of character '1', you could use following snippet.

```
char c = '1';
printf("%d", c); /* Print char as int */
```

Internal representation as integer code also means that arithmetic operators can work on char data type. However, it is not recommended unless you are really using char to store integers. Using arithmetic operators on char variables is confusing and error prone.

There are exceptions to this guideline, e.g. if you have to write a program that needs to iterate over a range of characters, let's say 'a' to 'z'. We will see an example of this when we learn more about iteration and loops.

Switch Case with char

So far, we have used integers in our switch case examples. Since char is internally stored as an integer, we can use char data type with switch case. Let's see an example program where we read in a character and tell whether it a vowel or not.

```
01: #include <stdio.h>

02: int main (int argc, char * argv[]) {
03:     char test = 0;
04:     printf("Enter a small case alphabet [a-z]: ");
05:     scanf("%c",&test);

06:     switch(test) {
07:         case 'a':
08:         case 'e':
09:         case 'i':
10:         case 'o':
```

```
11:          case 'u':
12:              printf("You entered a vowel\n");
13:              break;
14:          default:
15:              printf("You did not enter a vowel\n");
16:      }
17:      return 0;
18: }
```

Practice Questions : -

21. Trace the control flow of above program for following user inputs
    a. 'r'
    b. 'E'
    c. 'e'
    d. '%'

22. Write a calculator program using `switch case`. Program should read in two integers and an operator (+,-,*,/) and print the result of the operation.

Signed and Unsigned Variants

We have learned quite a few data types by now. It would be meaningful to learn about their variants at this time - `signed` and `unsigned`.

Note that these variants apply only to `char`, `int`, `short`, `long`, and `long long`.

When we store an integer type, system provides memory that is sufficient for a range of values, from lowest negative to highest positive, that such data type has to support. In order to support negative values in a data type, system reserves one bit - called the sign bit - which simply stores the sign of the value.

What if you knew you would never store negative values, e.g. cupboard height, age, rotations per minute, size of a data type and lot of other things in practice can never be negative. When you know there won't be any negative values, you can utilise the sign bit to

          feedback@thebookofc.com

store data and hence increase the range of useful positive values for your program[4].

unsigned data types allow you to utilise the sign bit to store additional data. Note that `signed` and `unsigned` are C language keywords.

By default, `int`, `short`, `long`, and `long long` type declarations are signed integers. Default for `char` type declaration is implementation defined, i.e. when you declare a `char` type variable, it can be `signed` or `unsigned` depending on the system you are running.

```
int marks = 92;
```

and

```
signed int marks = 92;
```

are equivalent declarations.

In order to print an unsigned integer type, simply replace d in your format specifier with u. Thus, `%lld` that was used to print a `signed long long int` becomes `%llu` to print an `unsigned long long int` and so on.

What about `unsigned char`? You can use format specifier %c to print an `unsigned char`. In fact %c is really the format specifier for `unsigned char`.

Table below provides a ready reference of `printf` and `scanf` format specifiers for all data types that we have learned so far.

---

[4] We will learn more about bits and internal representations in later chapters when we learn bitwise operators.

Data Type	printf Format Specifier	scanf Format Specifier
int	%d	%d
unsigned int	%u	%u
char	%c	%c
unsigned char	%c	%c
signed char	%c	%c
short	%hd	%hd
unsigned short	%hu	%hu
long	%ld	%ld
unsigned long	%lu	%lu
long long	%lld	%Ld
unsigned long long	%llu	%Lu
float	%f,%e	%f
double	%f,%e	%lf
long double	%Lf,%Le	%Lf

If you wish to learn more about printf and scanf format string and other things you can do with them, refer to your system documentation or an online man page.

Note that it is up to you, the programmer, to make sure that format specifier and variable positions are matched correctly. Further, it is up to the user to input values of correct type for each variable. Mismatched positions or incorrect input can lead to logical errors or in some cases undefined behaviour.

Later in this book we will learn more robust input techniques that help prevent errors and detect input data issues and handle them safely.

          feedback@thebookofc.com

23. Write a program to print size of following data types
    1. `unsigned char`
    2. `unsigned int`
    3. `unsigned short`
    4. `unsigned long`
    5. `unsigned long long`

24. Write a program in which you assign a negative value to an unsigned integer. Observe the warnings issued by the compiler. Compiler warnings are your friend that can help you avoid mistakes.

25. Which of the following statements are true
    1. `sizeof(int)` is greater than `sizeof(unsigned int)`
    2. Max value stored in `unsigned int` is greater than max value stored in `int`

26. Which of the following declarations are equivalent to `long int a = 5;`
    1. `int a = 5;`
    2. `signed long a = 5;`
    3. `signed long int a = 5;`
    4. `unsigned long a = 5;`
    5. `long a = 5;`

sizeof Result Data Type

Now that we have learned unsigned integers, let's revisit `sizeof` operator. Recall that we had learned that `sizeof` operator gives us an integer type result. Since size of a data type cannot be negative, actual data type of `sizeof` result is an unsigned integer type, usually an `unsigned int` or an `unsigned long`.

You could be seeing some compiler warnings about mismatch in format specifiers and argument types in programs where we printed size of data types. Fix them by using appropriate format specifiers for unsigned integer type as indicated in the warning message.

Underflow and Overflow

No matter what data type you choose, it will have only finite capacity to store data. If you try to fit in a value larger than its highest range or smaller than its lowest range then you will encounter issues.

When the value assigned to a variable is larger than the highest value it can store the error is called **overflow error**

When the value assigned to a variable is smaller than the smallest value it can store the error is called **underflow error**

The system behaviour in either case is undefined. That means, C standard does not impose any requirements on the system for handling such code or data. System can silently ignore it, or it can give you an erroneous result for your expression, or give an error, or handle it any other way it wants.

Hence, it is very important to choose the right data type for your data.

This leads to two questions:
1. How can we figure out what is the largest value that can be stored in a data type?
2. How can we guard against overflow and underflow errors?

We haven't yet learned all the concepts to fully understand the answers to these questions. Once you have finished reading this book, visit the following links to find answers to these questions.

http://thebookofc.com/datatypes/finding-range-of-a-data-type/

http://thebookofc.com/best-practices/avoiding-overflow-and-underflow/

For the meanwhile, below table provides you the minimum range of values each data type supports as required by the C standard. Appropriate choice of data type will help you avoid underflow and overflow for now.

                    feedback@thebookofc.com

Data Type	Minimum Low Range	Minimum High Range
`signed char`	-127	+127
`unsigned char`	0	+255
`short`	-32767	+32767
`unsigned short`	0	+65535
`int`	-32767	+32767
`unsigned int`	0	+65535
`long`	-2147483647	+2147483647
`unsigned long`	0	+4294967295
`long long`	-9223372036854775807	+9223372036854775807
`unsigned long long`	0	+18446744073709551615
`float`	1E-37	1E+37
`double`	1E-37	1E+37
`long double`	1E-37	1E+37

Few things to note:

1. The values in the table above represent the MINIMUM range that all standard implementations are required to support. Your specific implementation can support a wider range as well.
2. The range for floating point types represents the smallest positive to the largest positive number that a given data type should support. In other words, C standard enforces a minimum precision. We will discuss precision next.

3. In order to find out the ranges on your system refer to the links above.

Precision

We have learned that each data type has a finite memory allocated to it and hence it can store finite range of data. In case of floating point numbers memory utilisation includes another parameter - precision.

In simple terms, precision is a measure of accuracy. For example, 3.14 and 3.14285714 are both values of pi. However, 3.14285714 is a more precise value of pi, or in other words it has higher precision. You would need more memory to store all the extra digits in 3.14285714.

Let's run below program to illustrate the concept.

```c
#include <stdio.h>

int main(int argc, char * argv[]) {
    double pi = 22.0/7;
    float float_pi = 22.0/7;
    printf ("%.40f\n%.40f\n", pi, float_pi);
}
```

The `.40` in the middle of %f tells the system to print the value up to 40 decimal places. Here is the output from a sample run.

```
3.1428571428571427937015414499910548329353
3.1428570747375488281250000000000000000000
```

Results on your system can be slightly different. If you see identical values for `pi` and `float_pi`, increase the number of decimal places until you start seeing a difference.

As you can see in the results, value of `float_pi` was padded with zeros because `float` has lesser size and lesser precision than `double` and hence it could only store a less precise value compared to a `double`.

                feedback@thebookofc.com

Typecasting Revisited

Whenever you typecast a variable or a value or an expression to a larger data type, there is no loss of precision. However, when you typecast to a smaller data type, there could be a loss of precision – simply because the smaller data type is not large enough to hold all the data that could have been held in a larger data type.

We already know that `double` is larger than `float`, and `float` is larger than `int`. This means that typecasting from `int` to `float` and from `float` to `double` will not lead to loss of precision. However, typecasting from `double` to `float` and from `float` to `int` might lead to loss of precision.

Let's see an example.

```c
#include <stdio.h>

int main(int argc, char * argv[]) {
    double pi = 22.0/7;
    float float_pi = pi;
    int int_pi = float_pi;
    printf ("%.40f\n%.40f\n%d\n", pi, float_pi, int_pi);
}
```

Here is output from a sample run.

```
3.1428571428571427937015414499910548329353
3.1428570747375488281250000000000000000000
3
```

As you can see `double` had more precise value of pi. When we converted it to a `float`, we lost some precision. Further conversion of `float` to `int` led to further loss of precision.

Note that when a floating type is typecast to an integer type the fraction part is discarded. It is not a rounding operation. You should always be mindful of precision loss whenever you are typecasting.

In some texts, typecasting to a larger data type is called *upcasting* and typecasting to a smaller data type is called *downcasting*.

Remember implicit typecasting that we introduced earlier in this book? One of the instances where implicit typecasting occurs is when an arithmetic operand has operands of two different data types, let's say `int` and `float`.

In such cases system automatically upcasts the lower rank data type to higher rank data type. Table below gives the rank order of data types for typecasting from highest to lowest.

`long double`
`double`
`float`
`signed long long, unsigned long long`
`signed long, unsigned long`
`signed int, unsigned int`
`signed short, unsigned short`
`signed char, unsigned char, char`

Above table should serve you well to identify implicit typecasting in expressions in your program.

Practice Questions : -

27. Run the following program and explain its output.

```c
#include <stdio.h>

int main(int argc, char * argv[]) {
    double double_var = 3.142;
    int int_var = 5;

    printf("%u %u %u \n",
sizeof(double_var),sizeof(int_var),sizeof(double_var+int_
var));
}
```

              feedback@thebookofc.com

28. What will be the data type of result of following expressions.
    Assume `int i; float f; double d; char c; unsigned int
    ui; short s; long double ld;`
    1. (ld + f)
    2. (ld + f)/s
    3. (i * c)/f
    4. (i + ui)/d

Constants

There are times when you want value stored in a certain variable to remain constant throughout the program. Examples of such values could be pi, gravitational constant, distance to moon etc. In such cases, you would not want yourself or anyone else editing the program to be able to overwrite these value. This is where constants come in handy.

const keyword is used while declaring a constant and tells the system that value at this location cannot be overwritten. Let's see an example.

```c
#include <stdio.h>

int main(int argc, char * argv[]) {
    const double pi = 3.142;
    float radius = 2.7;
    printf ("Area of circle = %f\n", pi*radius*radius);
}
```

Notice declaration of pi in above example. Declaration starts with keyword const telling the system that what is to follow is a constant, followed by data type, followed by name of constant and finally the value to be assigned to the constant.

Notice that constant and literal are two different things. In our constant declaration in above example, 3.142 was a literal and pi was a constant. Literals are constant values but they do not have a name assigned to them.

When should you use constants?

You should use constants when you do not want the value to change during execution, you want to signal readers and future maintainers of your program that you intend for this value to remain constant, and you want to protect against any unintentional value overwrites in future.

<u>**Practice Questions : -**</u>

29. Try overwriting the value of `pi` in the above example by adding an assignment statement assigning value 9.9 to `pi`. What error do you observe?

     feedback@thebookofc.com

Operators Revisited

Over last few chapters we have expanded our horizons and learned quite a few operators and data types. Now would be a good time to understand how operators interact and how expression evaluation actually works.

Let's begin with an example to show why this is a very important concept to understand and what it does for us.

What would be the value of expression 5/3/4?

If we interpret it as (5/3)/4 then it evaluates to 0 - remember integer division evaluates to quotient. Hence 5/3 gives us 1 and 1/4 gives us 0.

If we interpret it as 5/(3/4) then it evaluates to infinite or in programming terminology, NaN (Not a Number). 3/4 gives us 0 and 5/0 is a divide by zero operation.

The way an expression with multiple operators is interpreted makes significant difference to the value of that expression. As another example, assume unsigned char data type with range 0 to 255 for following expression:

10 + 250 - 20

If this expression is treated as (10 + 250) - 20 then 260 cannot be stored in unsigned char data type and will lead to overflow error and undefined behaviour.

However, if this expression is treated as 10 + (250 - 20) then it has a well defined behaviour with result 240.

Above examples underscore two very important points:
1. Our good coding practice of writing unambiguous expressions using parentheses make the program very readable and less prone to errors.

2. Understanding how expressions are evaluated is critical to develop our programming strength in professional capacity. If we do not understand expression evaluation, we would find it very hard to comprehend expressions. As a result, working with even a reasonable size code base of few ten thousand lines would be very hard.

Expression evaluation is interplay of two major concepts - operator precedence and operator associativity.

Operator Precedence

Operator precedence refers to the order in which different operators are evaluated in an expression.

This concept is similar to BODMAS (Bracket Off, Division, Multiplication, Addition, Subtraction) that you may have learned in early arithmetic classes. BODMAS told us that in 5 + 4 * 3, multiplication has higher precedence than addition and hence expression would be interpreted as 5 + (4 * 3) and will evaluate to 17.

Table below provides the precedence order of all C operators in descending order from highest to lowest precedence. You are already familiar with a some of these operators. We will learn all of them by the end of this book. All operators in the same cell of the table below have same precedence.

Operator	Description	Associativity
( )	Parentheses or function call	
[ ]	Array subscript	
.	Member selection via object name	
->	Member selection via pointer	Left to Right
++	Postfix increment	
--	Postfix decrement	

　feedback@thebookofc.com

Operators	Description	Associativity
++ -- + - ! ~ (type) * & sizeof	Prefix increment Prefix decrement Unary plus Unary minus Logical NOT Bitwise complement Type cast Pointer dereference Address of Size of operand in bytes	Right to Left
* / %	Multiplication Division Modulo/remainder	Left to Right
+ -	Addition Subtraction	Left to Right
<< >>	Bitwise left shift Bitwise right shift	Left to Right
< <= > >=	Less than Less than or equal to Greater than Greater than or equal to	Left to Right
== !=	Is equal to Is not equal to	Left to Right
&	Bitwise AND	Left to Right
^	Bitwise XOR	Left to Right
|	Bitwise OR	Left to Right
&&	Logical AND	Left to Right
||	Logical OR	Left to Right
? :	Ternary conditional operator	Right to Left

Operator	Description	Associativity
=	Assignment	Right to Left
+=	Addition assignment	
-=	Subtraction assignment	
*=	Multiplication assignment	
/=	Division assignment	
%=	Modulo assignment	
&=	Bitwise AND assignment	
^=	Bitwise OR assignment	
|=	Bitwise XOR assignment	
<<=	Bitwise left shift assignment	
>>=	Bitwise right shift assignment	
,	Comma	Left to Right

Note that parentheses have highest priority. When we embed part of an expression in a pair of parentheses, we unambiguously instruct the system to evaluate that part first. We have been using parentheses for disambiguating our expressions so far and shall continue using them for readability purpose.

If we have an expression with nested parentheses, e.g. (5 * (2 - (9*2))) then order of evaluation of nested parentheses is from innermost to outermost.

Practice Questions : -
1. What would be the value of following expressions.
    1. 6 * 9 + 2
    2. 4 + sizeof(int) * 5
    3. val = a+b>a+c: sizeof(long double)/4+5? sizeof(long double)*4+5 //Assume a=3, b=5, c=1

Let's return to our earlier example of 5/3/4. Here we have two division operators. Since we have two operators with same precedence, operator precedence cannot be used to determine the order of evaluation. In situations like these, operator associativity is used.

          feedback@thebookofc.com

Operator Associativity

Operator associativity defines the order of evaluation when we have two or more operators of same precedence in an expression. Note that in the precedence table we had a column called "Operator Associativity". This column defines the evaluation order of operators of same precedence.

Coming back to our example of 5/3/4, we see that division operator has "Left to Right" associativity. This means operators would be evaluated from left to right, i.e. (5/3)/4 is the right interpretation of our expression.

Note that all operators of same precedence have same associativity. This ensures unambiguous interpretation of expressions.

Practice Questions : -
2. What is the value of following expressions
    1. 4*3/5+9
    2. sizeof(int)+sizeof(float)*5.0/2
    3. (float)100/12/4

Now that we understand how expression evaluation works, let's expand our horizons a little bit more and learn a few more operators.

Assignment Operators

So far we have learned just one assignment operator =. C provides us few more assignment operators that perform an operation and then assign the value.

One such operator is +=. It takes two operands, adds them, and assigns the sum to the left operand.

```
a += b;
```

is equivalent to

```
a = a + b;
```

Table below lists some more assignment operators that C provides with an example of each. Below table assumes a = 4 and b = 2.

Operator	Sample Statement	Equivalent to	Result
+=	a += b	a = a+b	a = 6, b = 2
-=	a -= b	a = a-b	a = 2, b = 2
*=	a *= b	a = a*b	a = 8, b = 2
/=	a /= b	a = a/b	a = 2, b = 2
%=	a %= b	a = a%b	a = 0, b = 2

From precedence table we can see that all of these assignment operators have same priority and right to left associativity. That means, if a = 2, b = 4, c = 6 then,

```
a += b *= c
```

would be treated as

```
a += (b *= c)
```

which is equivalent to

```
b = b * c
a = a + b
```

which evaluates to a = 26, b = 24, c = 6.

As with corresponding arithmetic operators, these assignment operators also work with integer data types.

Practice Questions : -

3. What are the values of a, b, and c after execution of following expressions, assuming they are int with a = 5, b = 7, c = 11
   ```
   1.  a -= b /= c
   2.  a - b/= c
   3.  a -= (b+c)/a
   ```

          feedback@thebookofc.com

4. Write a program that reads in scores of five subjects for a student and prints their total and percentage score.

Unary + and -

While we have not called out these operators by name, we have used them a few times by now. Unary + evaluates to value of its operand while unary - evaluates to negative of value of its operand. For example,

```
int a = 2;
a = -a; //-a evaluates to -2
printf("%d\n", a);
```

First statement assigns value 2 to integer variable a. Since unary - evaluates to negative of value of its operand, -a evaluates to -2 and this value gets assigned to a. Printing value of a would print -2 on the console.

Note that unary + operator evaluates to value of its operand. It does not convert a negative operand value to positive. For example,

```
int a = 2;
a = -a; //-a evaluates to -2
a = +a; //since value of a is -2, +a evaluates to -2
printf("%d\n", a);
```

Note the third statement above, a = +a. When control reaches third statement, a contains value -2. Since unary + evaluates to value of its operand, +a evaluates to -2 and this value is assigned back to a. Printing value of a would print -2 on the console.

Since unary + has no impact on value of its operand, it is almost never seen in real code.

<u>Practice Questions : -</u>
5. What are the values of a, b, and c after execution of following expressions, assuming they are int with a = 2, b = 4, c = 8
   1. a -= b /= -c
   2. a -= +(b+c)/-a

Postfix Increment and Decrement

Postfix increment and decrement are also unary operators.

Postfix increment operator, represented by ++, evaluates to value of its operand and **post** (after) evaluation it increments the value of its operand by one.

Let's see an example.

```
01: #include <stdio.h>

02: int main(int argc, char * argv[]) {
03:     int a = 2, b = 0;
04:     b = a++;
05:     printf("a=%d b=%d\n", a, b);
06: }
```

Note that postfix increment operator is placed **after** its operand.

After execution of line 03, a and b hold values 2 and 0 respectively. As we just learned, postfix increment operator evaluates to value of its operand. On line 04, a++ evaluates to value of a, i.e. 2. This value gets assigned to variable b. Post evaluation, postfix increment operator increments the value of its operand, i.e. value of a increases by 1 and becomes 3.

As a result, print statement prints a=3 b=2.

It is not necessary to assign value of increment operator to another variable.

a++;
is a perfectly valid statement that simply increases the value of variable a by 1.

Postfix decrement operator behaves similar to postfix increment operator, only difference being that it decrements the value of its operand instead of incrementing it. Postfix decrement operator is represented by --.

          feedback@thebookofc.com

```
01: #include <stdio.h>

02: int main(int argc, char * argv[]) {
03:     int a = 2, b = 0;
04:     b = a--;
05:     printf("a=%d b=%d\n", a, b);
06: }
```

On line 04, a-- evaluates to value of a, i.e. 2. This value 2 is assigned to b and value of a is decremented to 1. As a result, print statement prints a=1 b=2.

Prefix Increment and Decrement

Prefix increment and decrement are also unary operators.

Prefix increment operator increments the value of its operand **pre** (before) evaluation. Prefix increment operator evaluates to the incremented value of its operator.

Let's see an example.

```
01: #include <stdio.h>

02: int main(int argc, char * argv[]) {
03:     int a = 2, b = 0;
04:     b = ++a;
05:     printf("a=%d b=%d\n", a, b);
06: }
```

Note that prefix increment operator has the same symbol as postfix increment operator. However, it is placed **before** its operand as opposed to postfix increment operator that is placed **after** its operand.

After execution of line 3, a and b are assigned values 2 and 0 respectively. As we just learned, prefix increment operator increments the value of its operand and evaluates to the incremented value. On line 04, ++a increments the value of a to 3. Operator evaluates to this incremented value, 3, which gets assigned to variable b.

As a result, print statement prints a=3 b=3.

Prefix decrement operator behaves similar to prefix increment operator, only difference being that it decrements the value of its operand instead of incrementing it.

```
01: #include <stdio.h>

02: int main(int argc, char * argv[]) {
03:     int a = 2, b = 0;
04:     b = --a;
05:     printf("a=%d b=%d\n", a, b);
06: }
```

Again, note that prefix decrement operator has same symbol as postfix decrement operator. However, it is placed **before** its operand as opposed to postfix decrement operator that is placed **after** its operand.

On line 04, --a decrements the value of a to 1 and evaluates to this decremented value of a, i.e. 1. This value 1 is assigned to b. As a result, print statement prints **a=1 b=1**.

Similar to a++ or a--, ++a or --a are also perfectly valid statement by themselves.

Sequence Points

What would be the output of following program?

```
#include <stdio.h>

int main(int argc, char * argv[]) {

    int a = 2;
    a=a++ + ++a;
    printf("a=%d\n", a);
    return 0;
}
```

                  feedback@thebookofc.com

Let's focus on expression a++ + ++a

If we follow operator precedence order then postfix increment has higher priority and would get executed first. Which means a++ would evaluate to 2 and increment the value of a to 3. Next in precedence order is prefix increment; ++a. What is the value of a when prefix increment is evaluated? Has it already been incremented to 3 or is it still 2?

Answer is undefined. C standard does not force an implementation to fully execute each sub-expression at every step of evaluation. It is perfectly legal for an implementation to have incremented the value of a before evaluating prefix operator or to have left it at original value and postponed the increment for later.

C standard defines specific sequence points in a program. A sequence point is a point in program at which all instructions up to then should have been fully executed and no instruction beyond that point should have started execution. What does this mean?

Actual execution of a statement can consist of multiple operations. System is free to optimise its execution by ordering these operations in any order suitable as long as results are guaranteed as per the standards. A sequence point enforces that all operations up to that point have been fully executed and no new operations have been started.

End of a statement or end of a full expression is a sequence point. However, in this case, we are modifying value of variable a more than once between two sequence points. Hence the behaviour is undefined.

Note that if you run the above program you are likely to get some output on console. However, that output is not guaranteed to be the same on every system or even be the same for multiple runs on the same system. It is undefined. Most compilers would provide you warning about such statements. These warnings should never be ignored.

For a complete list of all sequence points in C visit
http://thebookofc.com/c11-standard/sequence-points/.

<u>**Practice Questions : -**</u>

6. What are the values of a, b, and c after execution of following
    code snippets, assuming they are `int` with a = 2, b = 4, c = 8

    ```
    1.  b += (
    2.  a -= +(b+c)/-a
    ```

            feedback@thebookofc.com

Loops

Oftentimes we need to perform the same action repetitively, e.g. consider printing numbers from 1 to 100 in a C program. With the C language constructs that we have learnt so far, we will have to print each number individually; even though the task is repetitive – print and increment a number 100 times.

The repetitive nature of task can be easily observed from the flowchart below.

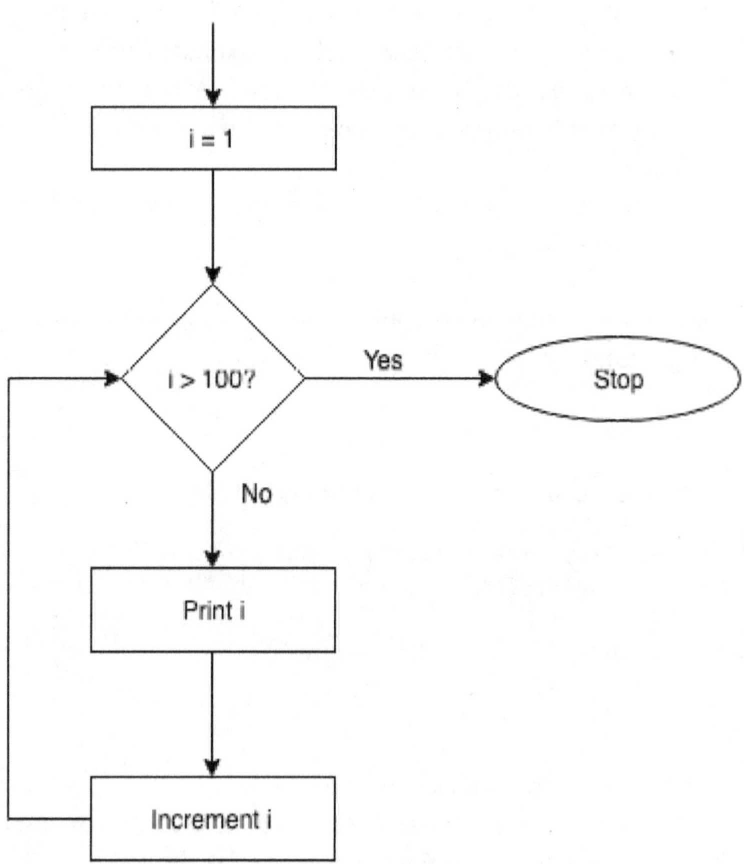

Fortunately C provides us loop constructs to write such repetitive instructions in an elegant and concise manner.

For Loop

Let's dive into our first loop construct – the `for` loop.

Here is an example of `for` statement.

```
for(a=0; a<10; a++)
```

`for` is a C language keyword. It is followed by parentheses enclosing three statements:
1. The loop initialization `a=0`, which is executed only once when the loop is first entered.
2. The loop control condition `a<10`, which is evaluated every time loop begins an iteration. Loop executes again and again as long as this condition is true. When this condition evaluates to false, control jumps to the first statement outside the loop.
3. The loop tail statement `a++`, which is executed at end of every loop iteration.

Let's understand the functioning of a `for` loop with the help of following program.

```
01: #include <stdio.h>

02: int main (int argc, char * argv[]) {
03:     int i=0;
04:     for(i=1; i<=3; i++) {
05:         printf("%d\n", i);
06:     }
07:     printf("Have a good day!\n");
08:     return 0;
09: }
```

Let's trace the control flow for this program.
1. Integer variable `i` is declared and initialized to 0 at line 03.
2. Control reaches the `for` loop at line 04.
    a. Upon entry, initialization statement, `i=1`,is executed. Value of variable `i` is set to 1.
    b. Loop control condition is evaluated, 1<=3, condition evaluates to true. Control enters the loop block.

     feedback@thebookofc.com

3. Control reaches `printf` statement at line 05, value of `i`, i.e. 1, is printed.

4. Control reaches end of loop block, tail statement, `i++`, is executed. Value of `i` becomes 2.

5. Control now goes back to the beginning of `for` loop at line 04. Note that after hitting the end of the loop block, control will always go back to the beginning of `for` loop to evaluate loop control condition.

6. Next iteration of loop begins - loop control condition is evaluated, 2<=3, condition evaluates to true. Control enters the loop block. Note that the initialization statement is not executed again.

7. Control reaches `printf` statement at line 05, value of `i`, i.e. 2, is printed.

8. Control reaches end of loop block, tail statement, `i++`, is executed. Value of `i` becomes 3.

9. Once again control goes back to the beginning of `for` loop at line 04.

10. Next iteration of loop begins - loop control condition is evaluated, 3<=3, condition evaluates to true. Control enters the loop block.

11. Control reaches `printf` statement at line 05, value of `i`, i.e. 3, is printed.

12. Control reaches end of loop block, tail statement, `i++`, is executed. Value of `i` becomes 4.

13. Once again, control goes back to the beginning of `for` loop at line 04.

14. Next iteration of loop begins - loop control condition is evaluated, 4<=3, condition evaluates to false. Control jumps to the first statement outside loop block, that is line 07.

15. Message `Have a good day!` is printed.

16. Control reaches the end of the program and terminates.

Let's represent the above example in a flowchart and identify different elements of `for` loop. The statements that are part of `for` loop are shaded in the flowchart.

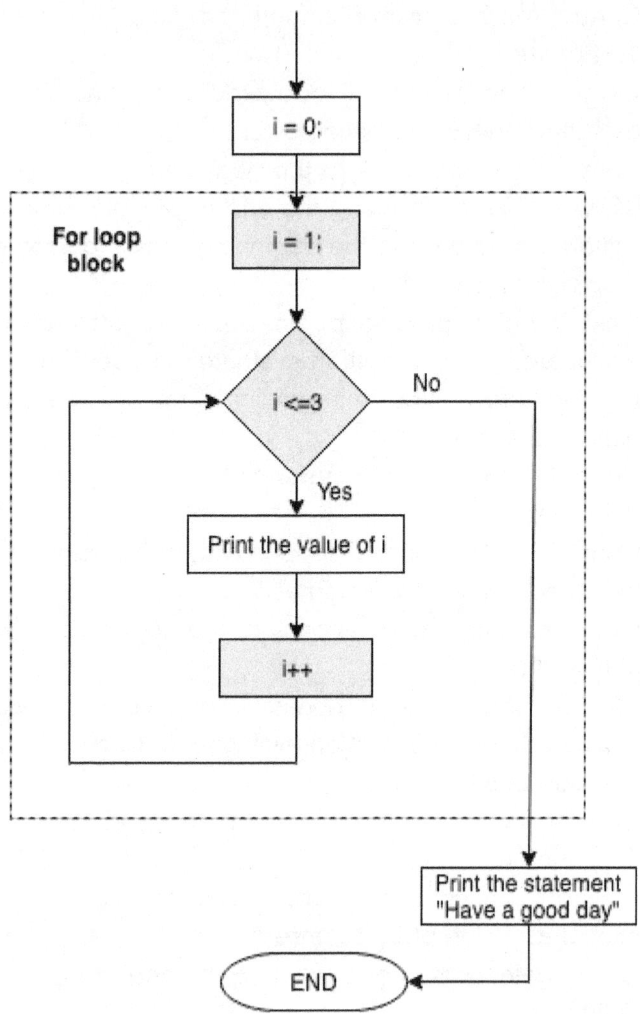

Practice Questions : -

1. Which of the following statements are true.

    a. for loop control statement is executed at end of every iteration.

    b. for loop control statement is executed at beginning of every iteration.

    c. Given a for loop, `for(i=0; 1; i++)`, control will skip loop body and jump to end of the loop.

    d. for loop initialization statement is executed at the beginning of every iteration.

    e. for loop tail statement is executed at beginning of every iteration.

 feedback@thebookofc.com

2. Given a `for` loop, `for(i=0; 0; i++)`, what will be the value of `i` at the end of the loop?
3. Write a program that uses for loop to print numbers from 10 to 1, both inclusive.
4. Write a program to print multiplication table of 2.
5. Write a program to print squares of first ten natural numbers

Few additional things to know about `for` loop:
1. Similar to `if-else`, the braces around the `for` loop block are optional. If braces are left out, one and only one statement immediately after the `for` statement is considered to be part of the loop. It is highly recommended to always use braces.
2. You can use multiple statements separated by a comma as part of loop initialization and tail statement. For example,

    ```
    for (a=-10, b=5; a*b != 0; a++, b--) {
    ```

    In the above example, at the time of loop initialization, a is initialized to -10 and b is initialized to 5. At the end of each loop iteration, a is incremented by 1 and b is decremented by 1.
3. You can use multiple statements separated by a comma as part of loop control condition too. For example,

    ```
    for (i = 10, j = -100;  i != 0, j != 0; i--, j++){
        printf("%d %d\n", i, j);
    }
    ```

    Remember our concept of operator associativity? If you will revisit the table defining precedence and associativity, you will observe that there is an entry for 'comma' operator, and the associativity for the same is left to right. Hence the expression in loop control condition will be evaluated left to right. The rightmost condition will be evaluated last. Hence, irrespective of how many statements we have in the comma separated list, it will be the rightmost statement only which will effectively be the loop control condition.

Hence, in above example, the condition i != 0 will play no role. It is equivalent to

```
for (i = 10, j = -100;  j != 0; i--, j++){
    printf("%d %d\n", i, j);
}
```

4. In a for loop, loop initialization as well as loop tail statements are optional. You can leave them blank. However, in such cases you should be careful to make sure that the loop variables are correctly initialized and loop iterations are set correctly. Here is an example with blank loop initialization and loop tail statements:

```
int a=5; /* Equivalent to loop initialization */
for (; a>0;) {
    printf("%d\n", a*a);
    a--;/* Equivalent to loop tail statement */
}
```

As you can see in for loop above, initialization statement is not specified. However, before entering the loop, a - the variable that plays key role in loop control condition statement - is initialized to value 5.

Similarly, the loop tail statement too is not specified in for loop statement. But, before the for loop ends, variable a is decremented, hence making up for the missing loop tail statement.Note that above code can equivalently be written as follows:

```
for (a = 5; a>0; a--) {
    printf("%d\n", a*a);
}
```

Practice Questions : -

6. Which of the following statements are true.
    a. In a for loop, initialization statement is optional.
    b. If there are multiple comma separated statements in loop control expression then only rightmost statement is executed.

          feedback@thebookofc.com

c. If `for` loop has loop initialization statement then it must also have a tail statement.

7. Which of the following loop constructs are valid.

a.

```c
float a=0, pi=3.14;
for (a=0.2 ; a < 7.1; a=a*pi) {
    printf("%f ",a);
}
```

b.

```c
for (a=0,b=1; a<b) {
    printf("%d %d \n",a,b);
    a++;
    b--;
}
```

8. What will be the output of following code snippets.

a.

```c
for (a=2,b=3,c=7; a<b+c; a++) {
    if (c>b) {
        c--;
    }
    if (b>a) {
        a++;
    }
}
printf("%d %d %d\n",a,b,c);
```

b.

```c
int a=3, b=5, c=10;
if(a+b<c) {
    for(;a<c;a++){
        b++;
    }
} else {
    for(;c<a;a--){
        b--;
    }
}
printf("%d %d %d\n",a,b,c);
```

c.

```c
int a=3, b=5, c=10;
for(;a>b;){
    a--;
    b++;
    c--;
}
printf("%d %d %d\n",a,b,c);
```

9. Write a program that reads a positive number (n) as user input
    and then prints sum of first n natural numbers. The user input
    should be in the range 1 to 1000. If input is outside this range,
    program should print an error message.
10. Write a program that uses `for` loop to print first 5 fibonacci
    numbers.
11. What will be the output of following program.

```c
#include <stdio.h>

int main (int argc, char * argv[]) {
    int a=0, b=1, sum=0;
    for (; a*b<=100; a=a+2, b++) {
        sum = sum + (a*b);
    }
    printf("%d\n", sum);
    return 0;
}
```

While Loop

`while` loop is another loop construct available in C language. It offers
same capability as `for` loop – any loop that can be written with `for`
construct can also be written with `while` construct.

Here is an example of `while` statement

```c
while (counter < 5)
```

`while` is a C language keyword. It is followed by parentheses
enclosing loop control condition statement.

When control reaches the `while` statement, it evaluates the condition
enclosed in parentheses after the keyword `while`. If the statement is
true, control enters the `while` loop block, else control jumps to the
first statement outside the `while` block.

When the execution of `while` block is complete, before beginning
the next iteration, the condition for `while` loop is evaluated again.
Next iteration begins only if the condition is true.

This is equivalent to saying

```c
while(condition is true) {
    /* do this */
}
```

Let's examine our earlier example of printing numbers from 1 to 3 rewritten using while construct.

```c
01: #include <stdio.h>

02: int main (int argc, char * argv[]) {
03:     int i=1;
04:     while (i<=3) {
05:         printf("%d\n", i);
06:         i++;
07:     }
08:     printf("Have a good day!\n");
09:     return 0;
10: }
```

Let's trace control flow for our example above.

1. Integer variable i is declared and initialized to 1 at line 03.
2. Control reaches while statement at line 04. Control condition enclosed in parentheses after keyword while is evaluated.
   a. 1<=3 evaluates to true. Control enters the while block.
3. Print statement at line 05 is executed. Value of i, i.e. 1, is printed. Control advances to next statement.
4. At line 06, value of i is incremented, and it now becomes 2.
5. End of iteration is reached at line 07. Control goes back to beginning of loop. Note that similar to for loop, when the end of while block is reached, the control goes back to the beginning of loop to evaluate loop condition.
6. At line 04, loop condition is evaluated once again.
7. 2<=3 evaluates to true. Control enters the while block.
8. Print statement at line 05 is executed. Value of i, i.e. 2, is printed. Control advances to next statement.
9. At line 06, value of i is incremented, and it now becomes 3.
10. End of iteration is reached. Control goes back to beginning of loop to evaluate loop condition.
11. At line 04, loop condition is evaluated.
12. 3<=3 evaluates to true. Control enters the while block.

13. Print statement at line 05 is executed. Value of i, i.e. 3, is printed. Control advances to next statement.

14. At line 06, value of i is incremented, and it now becomes 4.

15. End of iteration is reached. Control goes back to beginning of loop, i.e line 04.

16. Loop condition is evaluated.

17. 4<=3 evaluates to false. Control jumps to first statement outside the `while` block, i.e. line 08.

18. At line 08, message `Have a good day!` is printed

19. Control reaches the end of the program and terminates

This example is represented in the flow chart below. Loop construct boxes have been shaded.

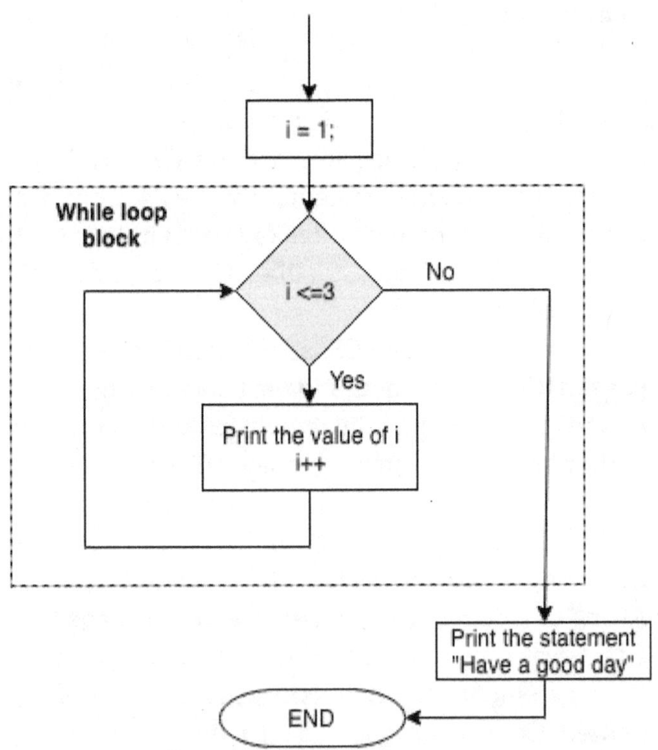

As you would have noticed, unlike `for` loop, `while` loop does not have structurally separate initialization and tail statements. It is up to the programmer to make sure that variables are correctly initialized

     feedback@thebookofc.com

before the loop and loop advancement is taken care of within the `while` block.

Similar to `if-else` and `for` loop constructs, braces around `while` block are optional. If braces are not present, then one and only one statement immediately after the `while` statement is considered to be part of the loop. It is highly recommended to always use braces.

Practice Questions: -

12. Which of the following statements are true.
    a. `while` loop is more powerful than `for` loop.
    b. It is not possible to count down using a `while` loop.
    c. Control expression in `while` loop is optional.
    d. `while(0)` is a valid loop construct.
    e. If control condition of `while` loop is false then control will jump to end of loop.
13. What will be the output of following code snippets.

    a.
```c
int i=1;
while (i<5) {
    printf("%d\n",i+1);
    i++;
}
```
    b.
```c
int a=1, b=3, c=7;
while (a<b && c-b>a) {
    if (a+b>2) {
        printf("%d %d %d",a,b,c);
        b--;
    }
    a++;
    b--;
    c++;
}
```
14. Write a program that reads a positive number (n) as user input and then prints sum of first n natural numbers. The user input should be in the range 1 to 1000. If input is outside this range, program should print an error message. Use `while` loop construct in the program.
15. Write a program using `while` loop that determines the number of digits in an integer. E.g. if input was 25689 then output should be 5.

For Vs While Loop

Capability wise, both `for` and `while` loops are equivalent. Whatever can be written using a `for` loop can also be written using a `while` loop and vice versa. So when should we use `for` and when should we use `while`?

Typically, in the interest of readability, we use `for` loop when number of iterations is known in advance, e.g. printing a multiplication table.

On the other hand, we typically use `while` loop when number of iterations is not known in advance but the condition for loop execution or termination is well understood, e.g. determining the number of digits in an integer. To an extent, it is also a matter of personal preference. As you write more programs, you would develop your own style and preferences.

Break Statement in Loops

Remember the `break` statement that we encountered in `switch case` constructs? `break` is also used inside a loop to force the control to jump outside the loop, irrespective of whether loop termination condition is met or not.

For example, consider the problem of determining whether a number is prime or not. The simplest method is to divide the given number n with all numbers in the range 2 to n/2 in a loop. If division does not leave a remainder of 0 in any iteration, then that number is a prime number.

But, what if one of the iterations has remainder 0? In such case, we know at that point that the given number is not a prime number. Continuing the loop until n/2 is a waste of compute cycles. Here we can use a `break` statement to exit the loop as soon as we discover that the number is not a prime number.

Let's examine source code for this problem.

```c
01: #include <stdio.h>

02: int main (int argc, char * argv[]) {
03:     int num = 0;
04:     int i = 0;

05:     printf("Please enter a number greater than 2: ");
06:     scanf ("%d", &num);
07:     if (num <= 2) {
08:         printf ("Invalid input. Exiting\n");
09:     } else {
10:         for (i=2; i<=num/2; i++) {
11:             if (0 == num%i ) {
12:                 break;
13:             }
14:         }
15:         if (i <= num/2) {
16:             printf ("%d is not a prime number\n",num);
17:         } else {
18:             printf ("%d is a prime number\n",num);
19:         }
20:     }
21:     return 0;
22: }
```

Let's trace the control flow of this program for user input 9.

1. After user input has been read, `if` statement on line 07 is executed.
2. Condition 9 <= 2 is false. Control jumps to `else` block at line 10.
3. At line 10, control reaches `for` loop. `i` is initialized to 2, loop condition 2 <= 4 is true, control enters the loop.
4. Control reaches line 11. `if` statement is evaluated.
    a. Condition 0 == 9%2 is false, control jumps to end of `if` block, line 13.
5. End of loop is reached at line 14, the loop tail statement is executed and `i` is incremented by 1. Its value now becomes 3.
6. Control jumps to line 10. Loop condition is evaluated.
    a. 3 <= 4 is true, control enters the loop.
7. Control reaches line 11. `if` statement is evaluated.

a. Condition `0 == 9%3` is true. Control enters the `if` block.
8. At line 12 `break` statement is encountered. Control jumps outside the loop and goes to line 15.
9. `if` condition is evaluated
   a. `3 < 4` evaluates to true. Control enters the `if` block.
10. At line 16, Message `9 is not a prime number` is printed.
11. End of inner `if-else` block is reached, line 19.
12. End of outer `if-else` block is reached, line 20.
13. End of program is reached and program terminates.

Let's spend some time to understand logic of this program. The purpose of this program is to identify if a given number is prime number or not.

`if` statement at line 11 checks if the number was divisible by another number. If this statement was true for any of the iterations, then our number is not a prime number. In other words, if **break** at line 12 was executed, then input was not a prime number.

However, once the control goes out of `for` loop, there is no direct way to identify if **break** statement caused the loop to terminate or did the loop run through all iterations and exited when control expression became false. To identify that, we use the condition statement of `for` loop (`i<=num/2`). If the loop condition is still true after control has exited the loop, then it implies that the loop did not run all its iterations and was terminated by **break** statement before it could reach the maximum (num/2) + 1 iterations.

We use this knowledge in `if` statement at line 15 to check whether the input number was prime or not.

Practice Questions : -
16. Trace control flow of prime number program for user input 7.
17. Write a program that determines whether a given number is a perfect square or not.
18. What is the output of following code snippet?

          feedback@thebookofc.com

```c
    int a=7, b=11, c=17;
    while (a<c) {
        if (a+c > b+c) {
            c++;
            break;
        }
        a+=2;
        b--;
    }
    printf("%d %d %d\n",a,b,c);
```

Do While Loop

do while loop is a variation of while loop. The basic structure of the
loop is shown below

```c
do {
    /* Loop body goes here */
} while (condition);
```

do, like while, is also a C language keyword.

When control reaches do statement, it simply enters the loop and
executes it. Condition for loop control is evaluated at the end of
iteration as part of while clause. If the condition is true, loop is
executed again else control advances to the first statement outside
the loop.

A flowchart representation of our print from 1 to 3 problem using do
while loop is shown below.

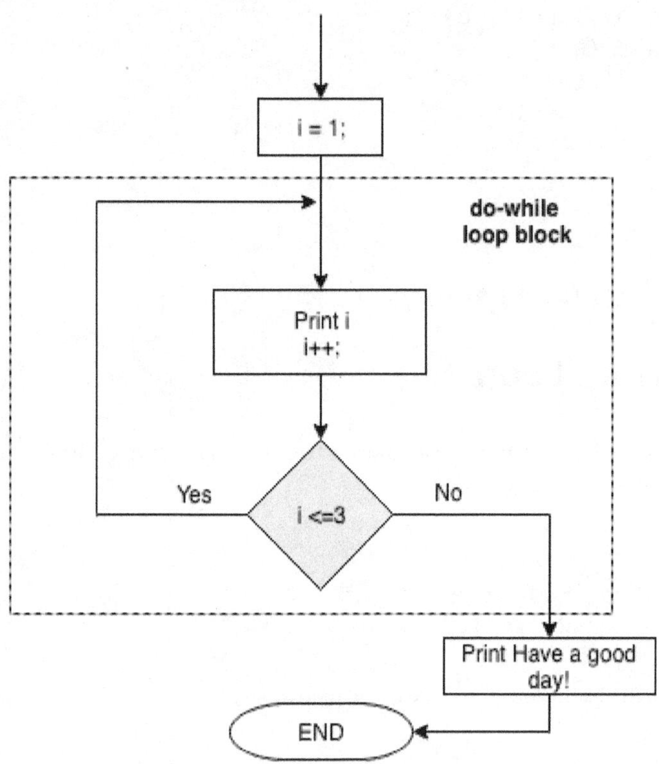

The key difference between **do while** and `while` loop is that since **do while** evaluates the condition at the end of first iteration, the loop body is executed at least once. The same is not true of `while` loop, which may not execute at all if the condition is found to be false in first iteration.

do while construct is useful and intuitive in cases where we have to perform an operation and repeat it a number of times until predefined criterion is hit. For example, consider our prime number example. Suppose we want to update the program to allow user to input the value again in case incorrect value was entered. Additionally we want to allow up to 3 chances to input the value correctly. **do while** loop will be an intuitive fit for this operation. Let's examine the updated snippet for accepting user input.

          feedback@thebookofc.com

```c
01: #include <stdio.h>

02: int main (int argc, char * argv[]) {
03:     int num = 0;
04:     int i = 0, tries = 0;

05:     do {
06:         printf("Please enter a number > 2: ");
07:         scanf ("%d", &num);
08:         tries++;
09:     }while ((tries<3) && (num<=2));

10:     if (num <= 2) {
11:         printf ("Invalid input. Exiting\n");
12:     } else { ...
```

Let's trace control flow for the do while loop.

1. When control reaches line 05, no checks are performed and control simply enters the loop.
2. Control advances to line 06- message is printed to prompt the user to input value >2.
3. Control advances to line 07 – user input is read and placed in variable num. Let's assume user input was -7.
4. Control advances to line 08 - Value of `tries` is incremented and it now becomes 1.
5. Control reaches end of iteration, condition specified with `while` is evaluated
   a. 1<3 is true, -7<=2 is true
   b. Since both conditions evaluate to true, AND of them will also be true.
   c. Since overall condition is true, loop iterates again. Control jumps to line 06.
6. This loop will continue exactly as in steps 2 to 5 above until the `while` condition becomes false. If you examine the `while` condition carefully, it would be false if number of tries becomes >=3 or user input has value >2, i.e. either the user reaches maximum number of retries or user inputs a valid value.

19. Which of the following statements are true.

    a. `for`, `while`, and `do while` loops are equal in capability. Code written using one loop construct can be rewritten using any other loop construct.

    b. `while` loop body is guaranteed to be executed at least once.

    c. `do while` loop body is guaranteed to be executed at least once.

    d. Control condition of `do while` loop is optional.

20. What is the output of following code snippet.

```
int a=1, b=3, c=2;

do {
    if (a+b>c) {
        c+=2;
        a--;
    } else if (!a) {
        break;
    }
}while(a||b||c);

printf("%d %d %d\n",a,b,c);
```

21. Write a program to print multiplication table of 7 using a `do while` loop.

22. Write an addition program that reads values from user and keeps on adding them until user enters 0. On receiving 0 input, program prints the computed sum and terminates.

23. Write a program to print all factors of a number.

24. Write a program to find sum of all digits of an integer. E.g. if user inputs 1590, program should print 15 (1 + 5 + 9 + 0).

Infinite Loops

Infinite loop, as the name indicates, is a loop that never terminates. It is useful when you want your program to continue doing a task forever, e.g. you want your phone or computer to be connected to the network even if you are not browsing.

In other contexts, an infinite loop is typically used in conjunction with a `break` statement to terminate only when a certain criterion is met.

         feedback@thebookofc.com

An infinite loop can be constructed using any of the three loop forms that we have seen.

```c
for(;;) {
    /* Loop body goes here*/
}

while(1) {
    /* Loop body goes here*/
}

do {
    /* Loop body goes here*/
}while(1);
```

As you can see, loop condition is optional in for loop, just like the initialization and tail statement. If no condition is specified as loop condition in a for loop then by default it evaluates to true.

Let's see an example to print multiplication table of 2 using an infinite loop.

```c
#include <stdio.h>

int main (int argc, char * argv[]) {
    int i=1;
    for(;;i++) {
        if (i>10) {
            break;
        }
        printf("2 X %d = %d\n", i, 2*i);
    }
    return 0;
}
```

Practice Questions : -
25. Trace the control flow of infinite loop example above
26. Using an infinite loop write an addition program that reads values from user and keeps on adding them until user enters 0. On receiving 0 input, program prints the computed sum and terminates.

27. Trace the control flow of addition calculator above for following
sequences of user inputs.
   a. -9, -10, 0
   b. -3, -4, 4, 3, 7, -7, 0
   c. 0
   d. 1, 2, 3, 4, 5, 0

Infinite loops are also a possible result of programming error. Few most common causes of this error are,

1. Misplaced semicolon, e.g.

```
while(i<10);
```

Notice the semicolon at the end of while statement. Assuming that i<10 was true, this is an infinite loop that will cause our program to execute forever.

2. Incorrectly programmed loop termination logic, e.g.

```
int i = 1;
while(i<10) {
    printf("%d\n",i);
}
```

Notice that value of i is not being incremented in the loop. This loop will execute forever.

3. Incorrect loop control condition, e.g.

```
for(i = 0; i = 10; i++) {
```

Remember our discussion about using assignment operator (=) instead of relational operator (==) unintentionally? In loop control condition statement here, using an assignment operator will cause the condition to be true always, hence executing the for loop indefinitely.

Another example of incorrect loop control statement causing infinite loop is

                    feedback@thebookofc.com

```
        while(i = 10) {
```

Continue

continue is a C language keyword. It is placed inside a loop block and makes the flow control to jump to the beginning of loop.

```
for(...;...;...) {
    ...
    statement 1;
    continue;
    statement 2;
    ...
}
```

When continue statement in the above block is executed, control will skip statement 2, and up to the end of the block. Tail statement of for will be executed, control will go to for statement again, loop condition will be evaluated and depending on the outcome of loop condition, next action will be performed.

continue comes in handy when you need to carry out further processing only if a certain condition is met. Let's consider an example that takes a number input from the user. It prints all the even digits in that number and skips the odd ones.

```
01: int main(int argc, char * argv[]) {
02:     int number = 0;
03:     int digit = 0;
04:     scanf ("Enter a valid number %d", &number);
05:     while (number != 0) {
06:         digit = number%10;
07:         number = number/10;
08:         if (digit%2 != 0) {
09:             continue;
10:         }
11:         else {
12:             printf("Even digit %d\n", digit);
13:         }
14:     }
15:     return 0;
16: }
```

In above example, observe that if we encounter an odd digit at line 08, we skip the remaining instructions, and go to the beginning of the loop. `continue` comes in handy when we want to perform actions only for a set of iterations and not all iterations.

Note the fundamental difference between `break` and `continue`. `break` statement exits the loop, and moves the control out of the loop. Whereas, a `continue` statement, ends the current iteration, and moves the control to the beginning of the loop to execute the next iteration.

Practice Questions : -

28. Which of the following statements are true.
    a. `continue` is a C language keyword.
    b. `continue` in a `for` loop causes control to jump to beginning of loop and hence loop tail statement is skipped for that iteration.
    c. In following code snippet, `break` statement will never be executed.
        ```
        while(…) {
            …
            if(a>10){
                continue;
                break;
            }
        }
        ```
29. Write a program that reads in 10 integers from the user and prints the sum of all positive numbers in the input.

Nested Loops

Loop constructs can be nested; very similar to the way we nested `if else` statements. Flow chart below presents an overview of logic flow for nested loops.

     feedback@thebookofc.com

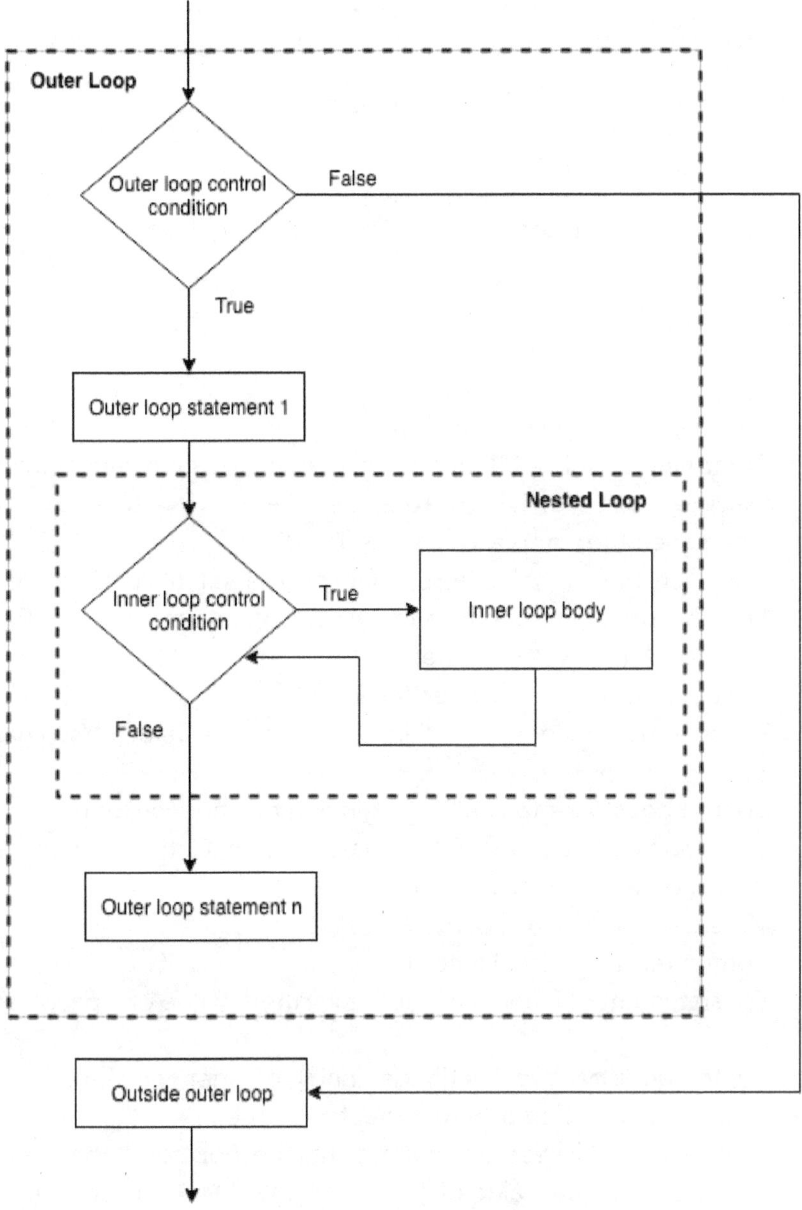

Notice that for every iteration of outer loop we run full iterations of nested loop. If outer loop was to run n times and inner loop was to run m times, then inner loop will run m times for every iteration of outer loop. At the end, inner loop would have n times while nested loop would have run nXm times.

Let's study an example of nested loops to understand them better.

```c
01: #include <stdio.h>

02: int main (int argc, char * argv[]) {
03:     int i = 0, j = 0;
04:     for(i=2; i<5; i++) {
05:         for(j=1; j<=10; j++) {
06:             printf ("%d X %d = %d\n",i,j,i*j);
07:         }
08:     }
09:     return 0;
10: }
```

Let's trace control flow for the above program.

1. Control reaches line 04, outer for loop initialization statement is executed, value of i is set to 2. Condition 2<5 is true, control enters the outer loop and reaches line 05.
2. Inner for loop is initialized, value of j is set to 1. Condition 1<=10 is true, control enters the inner loop and reaches line 06
3. Message 2 X 1 = 2 is printed.
4. Control reaches end of inner for loop.
5. Tail statement of inner for loop is executed. Value of j becomes 2.
6. Control goes back to line 05, beginning of inner for loop.
7. Inner loop condition 2<=10 evaluates to true. Control enters the inner loop and reaches line 06.
8. Message 2 X 2 = 4 is printed.
9. Control reaches end of inner for loop.
10. Tail statement of inner for loop is executed. Value of j becomes 3.
11. Control goes back to line 05, beginning of inner for loop.
12. Inner loop condition 3<=10 evaluates to true.
13. Steps 7 to 11 will keep on iterating until the loop condition j<=10 becomes false, i.e. value of j is incremented to 11 as part of tail statement after 10th iteration. By this time, table of 2 would have been printed.
14. When value of j is 11, inner loop condition becomes false. Hence control jumps out of inner loop.
15. Control reaches line 08, which is end of outer loop iteration.

     feedback@thebookofc.com

16. Outer loop tail statement is executed, value of i is incremented to 3. Outer loop condition 3<5 evaluates to true. Control enters the outer loop and reaches line 05.
17. Inner loop is re-entered. Initialization statement sets value of j to 1. Inner loop condition 1<=10 evaluates to true. Control enters inner loop and reaches line 06.
18. Message 3 X 1 = 3 is printed.
19. Control reaches line 07, end of inner loop.
20. Inner loop tail statement is executed; value of j is incremented to 2. Loop condition 2<=10 evaluates to true. Another iteration of inner loop begins.
21. Message 3 X 2 = 6 is printed.
22. Inner loop will keep on iterating until the loop condition j<=10 becomes false, i.e. value of j is incremented 11 as part of tail statement after 10th iteration. By this time, table of 3 would have been printed.
23. When value of j is incremented to 11, inner loop condition becomes false. Hence, control jumps out of inner loop.
24. Control reaches line 08, which is end of outer loop iteration.
25. Outer loop tail statement is executed, value of i is incremented to 4. Outer loop condition 4<5 evaluates to true. Control enters the outer loop and reaches line 05.
26. Once again as before we will print table of 4. After which j will become 11, inner loop will exit.
27. Control will reach end of outer loop, value of i will be incremented to 5. Outer loop condition 5<5 will evaluate to false. Control will jump to end of outer loop, line 09. It will reach end of program and terminate.

Let's summarise the above example in form of a flowchart. Take a minute to trace the flowchart and build a picture of the flow in your mind for a nested loop.

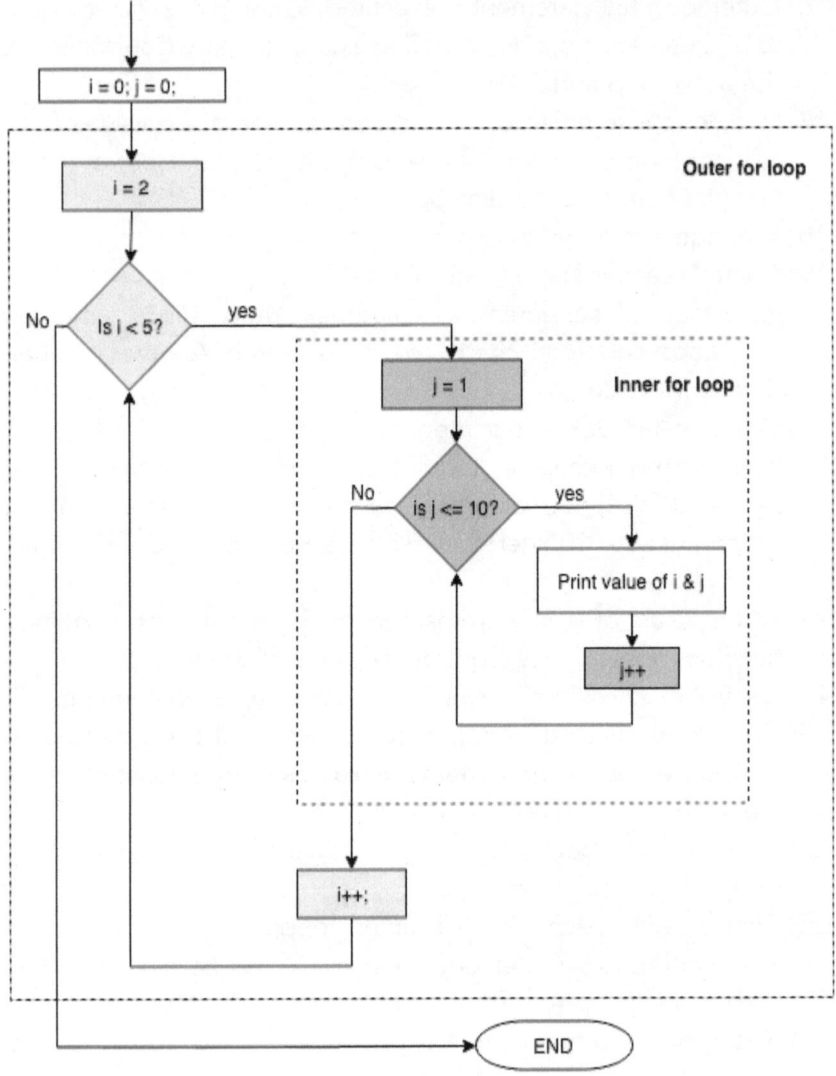

As can be observed from the flowchart, for each iteration of outer loop, inner loop is executed 10 times.

What we just learned was two level nesting of loops. We can nest loops to as many levels as needed to address our needs.

Practice Questions : -

30. Which of the following statements are true.

    a.   for loop can be nested only in another for loop.

    b. Loops can be nested only to maximum 5 levels.

c. A break in nested loop will cause the control to jump to end of outer loop.

d. A continue in nested loop will cause control to jump to next iteration of nested loop.

31. What will be the output of below program?

```c
int main (int argc, char * argv[]) {
    int i = 0, j =0, sum = 0;
    while (i<10) {
        for (j=3; j>0; j--) {
            sum = sum + i + j;
        }
        i++;
    }
    return 0;
}
```

32. Write a program that reads a number n, in the range of 5 to 100, from user and prints nth prime number. E.g. if user input was 5, program should print 5th prime number 11.

Looping with Characters

As we had learned earlier, characters are internally stored as integers and it is possible to use arithmetic operators on them. While using arithmetic operators on characters is discouraged, there are few legitimate uses of applying arithmetic operators on characters. For example, consider the program below for printing all characters from a to z.

```c
#include <stdio.h>

int main (int argc, char * argv[]) {
    char i = 0;
    for (i='a'; i<='z'; i++) {
        printf("%c ",i);
    }
    printf("\n");
    return 0;
}
```

This program applies increment operator to iterate over a range of alphabets.

Character arithmetic can also be used to change alphabet case. Consider the following example.

```c
#include <stdio.h>

int main (int argc, char * argv[]) {
    char i = 0;
    printf("Enter a char: ");
    scanf("%c",&i);
    if (i>='a' && i<='z') {
        i = 'A' + i - 'a';
    }
    printf("Uppercase: %c\n",i);
    return 0;
}
```

The `if` statement checks if the input character is in the range a – z and if so it changes the character to uppercase.

i – 'a' finds the offset of input character from the beginning of alphabet. Adding this offset to 'A' provides the uppercase version of the same alphabet.

The implicit assumption in both these examples is that characters 'a' to 'z' and 'A' to 'Z' have contiguous code which is true of all systems that we have seen even though it is not guaranteed by any standard.

Practice Questions : -
33. Write a program to print all alphabets from 'A' to 'Z'.
34. Modify the above program to print 'A' to 'Z' with alternate characters in lower case, i.e. A b C d E and so on.

          feedback@thebookofc.com

Functions

Functions are segments of code that accomplish a well-defined task.

That definition sounds very similar to definition of a program, and for good reason. You can think of functions being logically coherent but smaller quantities of work that need to be performed in order to complete a larger task – the program.

Let's revisit our Hello World example with a function added to it.

```
01: #include <stdio.h>

02: print_hello(){
03:     printf("Hello World from a function!\n");
04: }

05: int main(int argc, char * argv[]) {
06:     printf("Hello World from main!\n");
07:     print_hello();
08:     printf("Hello again from main!!\n");
09:     return 0;
10: }
```

This program consists of two functions - `main` and `print_hello`.

Every program's execution begins with the `main` function. Hence, each program has one and exactly one `main` function - so that system knows where to begin.

The first statement of `main` function, line 06 is a print statement that prints `Hello World from main!` on the console. Control advances to line 07 which is a call to function `print_hello`. This function call consists of function name followed by a pair of parentheses and semicolon to terminate the statement.

When a function call is encountered, control jumps to the function that was called. In this case control jumps from line 07 to line 02 and execution of `print_hello` function begins.

Control advances to line 03 that prints `Hello World from a function!` on the console. Control reaches end of `print_hello` function and jumps back to where it had come from: `main`, line 07. Function call is complete so control advances to line 08. Print statement is executed and message `Hello again from main!!` is printed on the console. Control advances to end of `main` function and terminates.

The most important thing to note here is the change in control flow.

- o   When a function call is encountered, control jumps from currently executing function to the called function. In our example, `print_hello` was the called function. It was called from `main` on line 07.
- o   When called function has been executed, control returns back to the same point from where the function was called and resumes execution of calling function from that point onwards. In our example `main` was the calling function. It called function `print_hello` on line 07. When `print_hello` execution is completed, control returns to line 07 in `main`.

Let's see one more example to make sure we understand this clearly.

```
01: #include <stdio.h>

02: hello_india(){
03:     printf("Hello from India\n");
04: }

05: hello_china(){
06:     printf("Hello from China\n");
07: }

08: hello_asia(){
09:     printf("Hello from Asia\n");
10:     hello_india();
11:     hello_china();
12: }

13: hello_canada() {
14:     printf("Hello from Canada\n");
15: }

16: hello_usa() {
```

          feedback@thebookofc.com

```
17:        printf("Hello from USA\n");
18: }

19: hello_north_america() {
20:        printf("Hello from North America\n");
21:        hello_canada();
22:        hello_usa();
23: }

24: int main(int argc, char * argv[]) {
25:        printf("Hello World from main!\n");
26:        hello_asia();
27:        printf("Hello again from main!!\n");
28:        hello_north_america();
29:        printf("Hello one more time from main!!\n");
30:        return 0;
31: }
```

Let's trace control flow of this example.

1. Program execution begins with `main` function at line 24.
2. Print statement on line 25 is executed and `Hello World from main!` is printed on the console. Control advances to line 26.
3. This is a function call to `hello_asia`. Control jumps to `hello_asia`, line 08.
4. Print statement on line 09 is executed and `Hello from Asia` is printed on the console. Control advances to line 10.
5. This is a function call to `hello_india`. Control jumps to `hello_india`, line 02.
6. Print statement on line 03 is executed and `Hello from India` is printed on the console.
7. Control advances to end of `hello_india` function and jumps back to where it came from, line 10 in function `hello_asia`.
8. Control advances to line 11. This is a function call to `hello_china`. Control jumps to `hello_china`, line 05.
9. Print statement on line 06 is executed and `Hello from China` is printed on the console.
10. Control advances to end of `hello_china` function and jumps back to where it came from, line 11 in function `hello_asia`.
11. Control advances to end of `hello_asia` function and jumps back to where it came from, line 26 in `main`.
12. Control advances to line 27 and message `Hello again from main!!` is printed on the console.

13. Control advances to line 28. This is call to function `hello_north_america`. Control jumps to function `hello_north_america`, line 19.

14. Print statement on line 20 is executed and `Hello from North America` is printed on the console. Control advances to line 21.

15. This is a function call to `hello_canada`. Control jumps to `hello_canada`, line 13.

16. Print statement on line 14 is executed and `Hello from Canada` is printed on the console.

17. Control advances to end of `hello_canada` function and jumps back to where it came from, line 21 in function `hello_north_america`.

18. Control advances to line 22. This is a function call to `hello_usa`. Control jumps to `hello_usa`, line 16.

19. Print statement on line 17 is executed and `Hello from USA` is printed on the console.

20. Control advances to end of `hello_usa` function and jumps back to where it came from, line 22 in function `hello_north_america`.

21. Control reaches end of function `hello_north_america` and jumps back to where it came from, line 28 in `main`.

22. Control advances to line 29. Print statement is executed and message `Hello one more time from main!!` is printed on the console.

23. Control advances to end of `main` function and terminates.

Above example is designed to help you develop a sense of how control flow works for function calls. It is absolutely critical to understand this well before proceeding further with functions. Revise the above example one more time to make sure you understand every control jump.

Now that we understand how functions work, let's make them do something more useful. Consider the example below that uses a function to add two integers.

   feedback@thebookofc.com

```c
01: #include <stdio.h>

02: int sum (int var1, int var2){
03:     printf("sum of %d and %d is %d\n",var1, var2,
var1+var2);
04:     return 0;
05: }

06: int main(int argc, char * argv[]) {
07:     int num1=2, num2=3;
08:     sum(num1, num2);
09:     sum(7,8);
10:     sum(num1, 5);
11:     return 0;
12: }
```

Let's start with statement on line 02.

```c
int sum (int var1, int var2){
```

This is beginning of a function definition. sum is the name of the function. The comma separated list in the parentheses after function name is called the parameter list. Each entry in parameter list consists of parameter data type and corresponding parameter name. In this example we have two parameters, var1 and var2, both are declared as integers.

Parameters are used to pass data to function. Typically a function would process this data in some fashion to provide us meaningful processed results. In this example, we can pass two integers to the function - one in var1 and other in var2.

Data type int that appears before function name is the return type of the function. We will learn more about return in a bit.

Now let's shift to line 08.

```c
sum(num1, num2);
```

This is the call to function sum. The comma separated list in the parentheses after function name is called the argument list. Each entry in argument list is value that is passed to the function. In this example, we are passing num1 and num2 to function sum. These values are received by sum in its respective parameters using positional matching - num1 is received in var1 and num2 is received in var2.

For the function call on line 08, num1 had value 2 and num2 had value 3. When control jumps from line 08 to line 02, var1 would be given value 2 and var2 would be given value 3.

Now let's trace complete control flow for this program.

1. Execution begins with function main at line 06. Control reaches line 07. Variables num1 and num2 are initialised to 2 and 3 respectively.
2. Control advances to line 08. This is call to function sum with parameters num1 and num2, i.e. 2 and 3 respectively.
3. Control jumps to function sum, line 02. var1 is assigned value 2 and var2 is assigned value 3.
4. Control advances to line 03. Message sum of 2 and 3 is 5 is printed on the console.
5. Control advances to end of function sum and jumps back to calling location, line 08.
6. Control advances to line 09. This is another call to function sum with parameters 7 and 8.
7. Control jumps to function sum, line 02. var1 is assigned value 7 and var2 is assigned value 8.
8. Control advances to line 03. Message sum of 7 and 8 is 15 is printed on the console.
9. Control advances to end of function sum and jumps back to calling location, line 09.
10. Control advances to line 10. This is another call to function sum with parameters num1 and 5. num1 still has value 2.
11. Control jumps to function sum, line 02. var1 is assigned value 2 and var2 is assigned value 5.
12. Control advances to line 03. Message sum of 2 and 5 is 7 is printed on the console.
13. Control advances to end of function sum and jumps back to calling location, line 10.
14. Control advances to end of main and terminates.

       feedback@thebookofc.com

Now let's turn our attention to `int` data type that preceded name of function.

```
int sum (int var1, int var2)
```

This is the data type of return value of the function. Every function can return at most one value back to the calling function. Typically, a function would return either result of data processing or status of processing it was supposed to perform. In our example, function `sum` can return an `int` value.

The value actually returned is specified in the `return` statement. Our last line of each function so far has been

```
return 0;
```

When the function execution completes, this statement returns 0 to the calling function.

Let's put the return value to some good use and return sum of arguments from our `sum` function. Here is a slightly modified example.

```
01: #include <stdio.h>

02: int sum (int var1, int var2){
03:     printf("sum of %d and %d is %d\n",var1, var2,
var1+var2);
04:     return var1+var2;
05: }

06: int main(int argc, char * argv[]) {
07:     int num1=4, num2=8, num3=-2, sum_of_two=0,
sum_of_three=0;
08:     sum_of_two=sum(num1, num2);
09:     sum_of_three=sum(sum_of_two, num3);
10:     printf("sum of %d %d and %d is %d", num1, num2,
num3, sum_of_three);
11:     return 0;
12: }
```

Notice line 04 of above example.

```
return var1+var2;
```

This statement means that our sum function would return sum of these two values back to the calling function, main.

Also note line 08 and 09 of above example. The function call is used as an operand to assignment operator. This statement means that whatever value is returned by our function sum, is assigned to the variable on left side of the assignment operator.

Let's trace the complete control flow for above example.

1. Execution starts with function main, line 06.
2. After variable initialisation, control advances to line 08. This is function call to sum with arguments num1 and num2 which have value 4 and 8 respectively.
3. Control jumps to line 02. var1 is assigned value 4 and var2 is assigned value 8. Control advances to line 03.
4. Print statement is executed and message sum of 4 and 8 is 12 is printed to the console.
5. Control advances to line 04. This is the return statement. Value var1+var2, i.e. 12, is returned back to the calling function - main. Control jumps backs to line 08.
6. Assignment operator on line 08 causes the returned value to be assigned to variable sum_of_two. Now sum_of_two holds value 12.
7. Control advances to line 09. This is another function call to sum with arguments sum_of_two and num3 which have value 12 and -2 respectively.
8. Control jumps to line 02. var1 is assigned value 12 and var2 is assigned value -2. Control advances to line 03.
9. Print statement is executed and message sum of 12 and -2 is 10 is printed to the console.
10. Control advances to line 04. This is the return statement. Value var1+var2, i.e. 10, is returned back to the calling function - main. Control jumps backs to line 09.

          feedback@thebookofc.com

11. Assignment operator on line 09 causes the returned value to be assigned to variable `sum_of_three`. Now `sum_of_three` holds value 10.
12. Control advances to line 10. Message `sum of 4 8 and -2 is 10` is printed on the console.
13. Control advances to line 11. `main` function returns value 0 to the system and program terminates.

Now that we understand how functions work, let's learn a few formal concepts for putting them to use.

The whole body of a function is called function definition. In our example above, function definition of `sum` function was

```
02: int sum (int var1, int var2){
03:     printf("sum of %d and %d is %d\n",var1, var2,
var1+var2);
04:     return var1+var2;
05: }
```

C requires us to declare or define a function before we use (call) it. A function declaration tells the system about a function name, its return type, and data types of its parameters. For example, function declaration of our `sum` function is shown below.

```
int sum (int var1, int var2);
```

Note that a function declaration looks very similar to first line of function definition. Function declarations terminate with a semicolon.

Name of parameters in function declaration are optional. Equivalent declaration of `sum` function is shown below.

```
int sum (int, int);
```

Function name, return type, and list of its parameter types is often also referred to as function signature.

Let's summarise our learning so far.

1. A function declaration contains function name, its return type, and list of data types of its parameters. Parameter names are optional in a function declaration. Function declaration ends with a semicolon.

2. A function definition consists of function name, its return type, and list of types and names of its parameters followed by function implementation enclosed in a pair of braces.

3. Function parameters are names by which values passed to a function are made available to the function implementation.

4. Function arguments are the actual values that are passed to the function during a function call.

5. Before a function call is made in a program, it must either be declared or defined.

6. A function call consists of function name followed by list of arguments. A function call causes control to jump to the called function.

7. Argument values are assigned to function parameters and are available for processing in the function. Positional matching is used to assign argument values to function parameters.

8. Function can return at most one value of the same type as function's return type.

9. Upon completion of function call, control jumps back to the calling function at the same point where function call was made.

10. In the calling function, the function call evaluates to the value returned by the called function.

11. While a function can be called from any other function, a function cannot be defined inside another function.

12. Function call should match function signature. If the number of arguments passed is not equal to the number of parameters defined in function declaration, we will get a compilation error.

Let's turn our attention briefly to `main` function definition that we have been using since the beginning of the book.

```
int main(int argc, char * argv[])
```

          feedback@thebookofc.com

`main` is the name of the function. It's return type is `int`. It has two parameters, an `int` called `argc` and an array of character pointers called `argv`. We will learn more about arrays and pointers in following chapters.

An alternative possible function signature for `main` is

```
int main(void)
```

or equivalently

```
int main()
```

We will learn more about **void** data type later in this chapter. Both variations of `main` function are supported by C11 standard.

Parameter naming follows the same rules as variable naming and parameter names behave exactly like variables inside the function.

Function names also follow the same naming rules as variables. Further, we will use the same naming conventions that we use for variables for naming our functions.

As a good programming practice, we recommend that you use function names that represent the purpose of that function. For example, consider following function declarations

```
float a (int maths, int science);
float average_marks (int maths, int science);
```

The only difference between these two declarations is the name of the function. That minor change makes a huge difference to the readability of the program Function name a does not tell you anything about what the function does - is it average, or is it median or a random number generator. On the other hand, function name **average_marks** clearly communicates the intent of creating that function.

1. Break down the following function declarations to highlight return type, function name, and number of parameters along with their names and data types.

   a. `int largest_factor (int num);`
   b. `float celsius_to_fahrenheit(float celsius);`
   c. `float average (int maths, int science, int english);`

2. Which of the following statements are true.

   a. When a function is called, control jumps from the calling function to the beginning of called function.
   b. A function can return any number of values.
   c. A function can have any number of parameters.
   d. A function must have at least one parameter.
   e. When a called function has been fully executed, control returns to calling function to the same point from where function was called.
   f. `return` statement indicates function processing is complete and causes control to jump back to calling function.

3. Write a function to compute average of three numbers.
4. Write a function to convert temperature from Celsius to Fahrenheit.
5. Write a function to find maximum of two integers. Use this function to determine maximum of three integers.

More Examples

Let's study few more examples in order to understand functions better. Consider the below code for printing all tables from 2 to n where n is input by the user.

```
01: #include <stdio.h>

02: int print_table(int n);

03: int main (int argc, char * argv[]) {
04:     int num=0, i=0;
05:     printf("Enter a number >2: ");
06:     scanf("%d",&num);
```

     feedback@thebookofc.com

```c
07:       if (num<=2) {
08:            printf("Invalid input\n");
09:       } else {
10:            for(i=2; i<=num; i++) {
11:                print_table(i);
12:            }
13:       }
14:       return 0;
15: }
     /* Print table of n */
16: int print_table(int n) {
17:       int i=0;

18:       for(i=1; i<=10; i++) {
19:            printf("%d X %d = %d\n", n,i,n*i);
20:       }
21:       return 1;
22: }
```

Let's examine some key elements in this program.

Line 02 declares a function called `print_table`. The declaration simply tells the compiler that the function returns an integer and accepts one parameter of integer type.

Line 11 is a call to (or invocation of) the function `print_table`.

When control flow reaches a function call, in this case line 11, execution of calling function (`main`) will pause and control will jump to beginning of called function (`print_table`).

The value of argument in the function call will be placed in the parameter of the function and its value will be accessible inside the function by using the corresponding parameter name.

Once the `print_table` function completes its execution, control returns back to `main` and resumes from the point where it was paused.

`print_table` had return type `int`. Line 21 returns an integer 1 back to calling function – `main`. This value will get duly returned back to `main`. However, statement with function call in `main` does not store or process the return value. Hence it will be discarded by `main` and will have no impact in the program.

Let's put it all together and trace control flow for user input value 3.

1. After user inputs value 3, `if` statement on line 07 evaluates to false and control jumps to `else` block, line 09.
2. Control advances to `for` loop, line 10.
   a. Variable `i` is initialized to 2.
   b. Loop condition 2<=3 evaluates to true, control enters the loop block, line 11.
3. Function `print_table` is called with argument 2 (value of variable `i`).
4. Control jumps to function `print_table`, line 16.
5. Value of parameter n is set to 2 (argument with which it was called from `main`).
6. Control advances to line 17, integer variable `i` is declared and initialized to 0.
7. Control advances to line 18, `for` loop. This loop prints multiplication table of n (value 2).
8. When loop condition evaluates to false, control jumps to first statement outside the loop, line 21.
9. `return` statement is encountered. Value 1 is returned to calling function `main`.
10. Control jumps back to same point in `main` from where `print_table` was called, line 11. Function call evaluates to returned value 1. Since we do not capture or use the return value in `main`, it has no effect. It is discarded.
11. Control advances to end of loop, and tail statement is executed. Value of `i` is incremented to 3. Note that variable `i` in main is different from variable `i` in `print_table`. Variable `i` in `print_table` function had value 11 when we returned while variable `i` in `main` had value 2 at that time. We will learn more about this concept later in this chapter.
12. Loop condition 3<=3 evaluates to true. Control enters the loop block, line 11.
13. Function `print_table` is called with argument 3 (value of variable `i`).

                 feedback@thebookofc.com

14. Control jumps to function `print_table`, line 16.

15. Value of parameter n is set to 3 (argument with which it was called from `main`).

16. Control advances to line 17, integer variable `i` is declared and initialized to 0.

17. Control advances to line 18, for loop. This loop prints multiplication table of n (value 3).

18. When loop condition evaluates to false, control jumps to first statement outside the loop, line 21.

19. `return` statement is encountered. Value 1 is returned to calling function `main`.

20. Control jumps back to same point in `main` from where `print_table` was called, line 11. Function call is replaced with returned value 1. Since we do not capture or use the return value in `main`, it has no effect. It is discarded.

21. Control advances to end of loop, and tail statement is executed. Value of `i` is incremented to 4.

22. Loop condition 4<=3 evaluates to false. Control jumps outside the loop, line 13.

23. Control advances to end of **else**. Line 14, we return value 0 from `main` and program terminates.

Note that there was no relation between different calls to `print_table`. All calls are independent of each other and none of variables, values, context was carried over from one call to the next.

Let's look at another example to help solidify our understanding.

Let's write a program to calculate average of three integers.

```
01: #include <stdio.h>
02: float compute_average(int n1, int n2, int n3);
03: int main (int argc, char * argv[]) {
04:     int num1=0, num2=0, num3=0;
05:     float average = 0.0;
06:     printf("Enter first number: ");
07:     scanf ("%d", &num1);
08:     printf("Enter second number: ");
09:     scanf ("%d", &num2);
10:     printf("Enter third number: ");
11:     scanf ("%d", &num3);
```

```
12:      average = compute_average(num1, num2, num3);
13:      printf("Average of these numbers is %f\n",
average);
14:      return 0;
15: }

16: float compute_average(int n1, int n2, int n3) {
17:      float avg = 0.0;
18:      avg = (n1+n2+n3)/3.0;
19:      return avg;
20: }
```

Line 02 declares the function compute_average that returns a float
and has three int parameters.

Let's trace control flow for user input 2, 5, 10.

1. Program execution begins with function main, line 03.
2. After user input has been entered, control reaches line 12. At
    this point variables num1, num2, and num3 have values 2, 5,
    and 10 respectively.
3. On line 12, we encounter a call to function compute_average
    with argument values (2, 5, 10). Control jumps to
    compute_average function, line 16.
4. Positional matching is used and n1 is given value 2, n2 is
    given value 5, n3 is given value 10.
5. Control advances to line 17. Float variable avg is defined and
    initialized to 0.0.
6. Control advances to line 18. (2+5+10)/3.0 evaluates to
    5.66666, which is assigned to variable avg. Note that we
    divided by 3.0 and not 3 in order to avoid an integer division.
7. Control advances to line 19. return statement is
    encountered. Control returns to calling function (main) with
    value 5.66666.
8. Control jumps to line 12. The call to compute_average
    function evaluates to the returned value, 5.66666. This value
    is now assigned to variable average.
9. Control advances to line 13. Message Average of these
    numbers is 5.66666 is printed.
10. Control advances to line 14. main function returns value 0 and
    program terminates.

          feedback@thebookofc.com

Call By Value

If you noticed carefully, when `main` called `compute_average`, the called function received a copy of the values passed as arguments. What that means is, if `compute_average` modified any of these values, it would really be changing only its own copy – the change will not impact the values of variables that were passed as arguments in `main`.

In fact variables defined in the calling function are not visible inside the called function and vice versa. We will learn about this in more detail in a little bit.

> Calling a function using variable names or values as arguments leads to copying of values over to the formal parameters of the called function. This is called *call by value*.

Let's consider another example.

```c
01: #include <stdio.h>
02: int triple_it(int num);

03: int main (int argc, char * argv[]) {
04:     int input = 3, output = 0;
05:     output = triple_it(input);
06:     printf("Value of input after function call = %d\n",input);
07:     printf("Value of output after function call = %d\n",output);
08:     return 0;
09: }

10: int triple_it(int num) {
11:     num = num * 3;
12:     printf("Value of num in function = %d\n",num);
13:     return num;
14: }
```

This example illustrates a function that simply triples the value that is passed to it. We print the tripled value in the function as well as return it from the function. Let's trace control flow for this example.

1. Execution begins with `main` function, line 03.
2. At line 04, variable `input` is initialized to 3 and variable `output` is initialized to 0.
3. At line 05, is a call to function `triple_it` with variable `input` as parameter. Control jumps to line 10.
4. Parameter num receives value of variable input, i.e. 3.
5. At line 11, we assign triple of value of num back to num. Hence, num now has value 9.
6. At line 12 we print the value of num. Message `Value of num in function = 9` appears on the console.
7. At line 13, we return num, i.e. 9, back to the calling function.
8. Control returns to line 05. Variable `output` is assigned the returned value 9.
9. Line 06, we print the value of variable input. Message `Value of input after function call = 3` appears on the console. Note that even though `triple_it` function had modified the value of its parameter, the variable that was passed as argument in `main` remained unchanged. This is because `triple_it` was modifying its own copy of the value. The original variable in `main` remained untouched.
10. Line 07, we print value of variable `output` which is the value returned by the function call. Message `Value of output after function call = 9` appears on the console.
11. At line 08, `main` returns 0 and program terminates.

Above example clearly illustrates that pass by value function call passes a copy of the variables to the called function. Any modification to parameters in called function does not impact the variables that were passed as arguments in calling function.

There is another way to pass data to a function - call by address - that we will learn about when we learn pointers later in the book.

Behind the Scenes of a Function Call

Now that we understand functions and the control flows during a function call, let's examine what happens behind the scenes. Consider the call to function `compute_average` in our example above.

 feedback@thebookofc.com

When control reaches line 12, variables num1, num2, and num3 have already been defined, initialized and assigned some values provided by the user (Let's assume values are again 2, 5, and 10 respectively). Variable average has been defined and initialized. Let's assume that these variables are stored in symbol table and memory as shown below.

num1	24
num2	28
num3	32
average	36

00	04	08	12	16	20	24
						2

28	32	36	40	44	48	52
5	10	0.0				

56	60	64	68	72	76	80

When control reaches line 12, system encounters a function call. Consequently, execution of main function is paused, all these variables and information about current statement being executed is stored in a special area called function stack and control is transferred to the called function, compute_average, line 16.

When a new function is invoked, it is assigned separate independent memory layout for its variables. All arguments are copied over for the called function to use. This what symbol table and memory for compute_average might internally look like.

n1	16
n2	32
n3	36
avg	08

00	04	08	12	16	20	24
		0.0		2		

28	32	36	40	44	48	52
	5	10				

56	60	64	68	72	76	80

When line 18 is executed, result of computation is stored in avg. This is what updated memory of function compute_average would look like.

00	04	08	12	16	20	24
		5.666		2		

28	32	36	40	44	48	52
	5	10				

56	60	64	68	72	76	80

When control advances to line 19, a `return` statement is encountered. Value of `avg` is returned back to `main` and current function – `compute_average` – exits. Control jumps back to `main` function; the entire execution information about `main` is retrieved from the function stack and execution of `main` resumes.

Further execution of line 12 assigns the returned value to variable `average`. This is what updated memory for function `main` would look like.

num1	24
num2	28
num3	32
average	36

00	04	08	12	16	20	24
						2

28	32	36	40	44	48	52
5	10	5.666				

56	60	64	68	72	76	80

Implicit Typecasting

What happens if there is a type mismatch between an argument in calling function and called function parameter. In such case implicit typecasting kicks in. The value of argument in calling function is automatically typecast to data type of parameter of called function. If such typecasting is not feasible we get a compile time error.

For example, consider our `triple_it` example above. It takes an `int` parameter and returns three times its value. If we were to call `triple_it` with a `float` as argument, implicit typecasting will

          feedback@thebookofc.com

truncate the `float` and `triple_it` will get called with typecasted `int` value.

Same principle applies to return values. If there is a mismatch in type of value returned and type of variable to which return value is assigned in calling function, then implicit typecasting applies to the assignment.

Scope of Variable

Recall the average example we discussed above. What would happen if we tried to print value of `num1` in function `compute_average` or if we tried to print value of variable `avg` in `main`?

Modify the print statement in `main` to

```
printf("Average of these numbers is %f\n", avg);
```

and compile the program. You should see compilation errors flagging out use of an undeclared variable. What happened?

As you must have noticed in the behind the scenes discussion above, variables names and values are stored separately for each function in the function stack. One function cannot see variables and values of another function.

Also recall that called function only gets a copy of the arguments in its parameters. Called function cannot access the actual variables in the calling function. That happens because all variables defined inside a function are by default "local" variables – their scope is limited to the function that they are defined in; other functions cannot see them.

Scope of a variable refers to the segment of program within which a variable name is visible.

A ***local variable*** is a variable whose scope is limited to the code block in which it is defined.

A local variable comes into existence when control enters its scope, this is called variable being in-scope. Its existence ends as soon as control exits its scope, this state is called variable being out of scope.

That implies, as soon as control returns from the called function, all local variables of called function cease to exist. Another call to the same function would create new set of local variables.

Note that there is a difference between control exiting the scope and control jumping out for a function call. Control exits when processing is complete and return statement is encountered or end of processing of scope occurs. On the other hand, when a function is called, processing is paused only to be resumed upon return. All local variables of the calling function are in existence through the execution of function call.

Let's apply these principles to our earlier example of average function to make sure we understand these well.
Here is the source code again for ready reference.

```
01: #include <stdio.h>

02: float compute_average(int n1, int n2, int n3);
03: int main (int argc, char * argv[]) {
04:     int num1=0, num2=0, num3=0;
05:     float average = 0.0;
06:     printf("Enter first number: ");
07:     scanf ("%d", &num1);
08:     printf("Enter second number: ");
09:     scanf ("%d", &num2);
10:     printf("Enter third number: ");
11:     scanf ("%d", &num3);
12:     average = compute_average(num1, num2, num3);
13:     printf("Average of these numbers is %f\n",
average);
14:     return 0;
15: }

16: float compute_average(int n1, int n2, int n3) {
17:     float avg = 0.0;
18:     avg = (n1+n2+n3)/3.0;
19:     return avg;
20: }
```

                    feedback@thebookofc.com

argc, argv, num1, num2, num3, and average are local to function main. They are in existence once control reaches line 06. Note that argc and argv are parameters and not variables defined inside main function. Parameters behave like variables and have scope local to the function.

All of these variables continue to exist when control jumps to compute_average function on line 12. However, since they are local to main, they are not visible inside compute_average function. When control returns back to line 12 after completing the function call, they are again visible inside scope of main. They cease to exist when control exits main function - the return statement on line 14.

Likewise, n1, n2, n3, and avg are variables local to function compute_average. They come into existence when control reaches compute_average function and their definition is processed. They cease to exist when control exits compute_average function - the return statement on line 19.

Practice Questions : -

6. Identify all local variables and their scope for table printing example that we saw earlier in this chapter.
7. Which of the following statements are true.
    a. All functions of a program share the same symbol table and have common memory regions.
    b. If we have declared a variable in a function then we cannot use the same variable name in another function.
    c. Every function must have at least one parameter.
    d. 3plus5 is a valid function name.
    e. There is no limit on number of functions that can be defined in a program.
    f. We can define any number of functions inside another function.
8. What will be the return value of triple_it function for following arguments.
    a. float pi = 22.0/7;
    b. char pi = 'p';
    c. double pi = -4.98765;

9. What will be the output of following program.

```c
#include <stdio.h>

float add5(int num);

int main (int argc, char * argv[]) {
    float pi = 3.14;
    float result = 0;

    result = add5(pi);
    printf("Result %f\n",result);
    return 0;
}

float add5(int num) {
    return num + 5.5;
}
```

So far we have been defining all our variables at the beginning of a function. Thus, for all our examples, scope of a local variable spans the entire function.

C also allows you to define variables at the beginning of a code block, for example, following segment of code is valid.

```c
for(int i=1; i<=10; i++) { …
```

Here i is a local variable defined at the beginning of for loop block and it is visible only inside the for loop in which it was defined. In other words, its scope is local to the block in which it was defined - the for loop block.. If you try to print this variable outside the loop, compiler will throw an error.

As all local variables do, this variable i too shall cease to exist once control exits its scope, i.e. the for loop. Completion of the loop or a break statement will terminate its existence.

What happens if there was a variable named i defined at the beginning of the function and it was defined inside the loop as well? While you cannot define two variables with same name in same scope, it is possible to define another variable with same name in nested scope. In such case, when variable name is used, it is

                    feedback@thebookofc.com

interpreted to refer to the innermost scope where that variable name is in scope. Let's understand this with an example.

```c
01: #include <stdio.h>

02: int main (int argc, char * argv[]) {
03:     int i=3;

04:     printf("Value of i at beginning of main =
%d\n",i);
05:     for(int i=10; i>=9; i--){
06:         printf ("Value of i in loop = %d\n",i);
07:     }
08:     printf("Value of i at the end of main = %d\n",i);
09:     return 0;
10: }
```

Let's trace control flow for this program.

1. Execution begins with `main` function, line 02.
2. At line 03, variable `i` is initialised to value 3.
3. At line 04, we print the value of `i` and message `Value of i at beginning of main = 3` is printed on the console.
4. At line 05, `for` loop initialisation again defines a variable named `i` and initialises it to 10. This variable `i` is distinct from variable `i` that was defined on line 03. Hence, now we have two variables named `i` in our program. As we learned, in such cases, innermost in-scope definition takes precedence. Thus, control condition would use variable `i` defined in the `for` loop. 10>=9 evaluates to true. Control enters for loop block.
5. At line 06, we print value of variable `i`. Since innermost scope where variable name `i` is in-scope is the `for` loop, the value that is printed is of the variable `i` defined in the `for` loop. Message `Value of i in loop = 10` appears on the console.
6. This is end of first iteration, tail statement is executed and value of `i` is decremented to 9. Control condition 9>=9 evaluates to true. Control enters for loop block.
7. At line 06, we again print value of variable `i`. Message `Value of i in loop = 9` appears on the console.

8. This is end of second iteration, tail statement is executed and value of i is decremented to 8. Control condition 8>=9 evaluates to false. Control jumps out of for loop.
9. As soon as control jumps outside the for loop, variable i defined inside the for loop goes out of scope. Note that all comparisons, operations, and print statements within the for loop used the variable i that was defined in the innermost scope - for loop.
10. At line 08, we again print value of variable i. The only in scope variable i is the one that was defined in function main at line 03. Hence message Value of i at the end of main = 3 appears on the console. Note that value of this variable i is still 3. The variable i defined in the for loop was a different variable stored at a different memory location. All our operations on variable i inside the loop were on that variable.
11. At line 09 main returns 0 and program terminates.

We highly recommend that you use unique variable names and do not define variables with same name in nested scope. While those are valid constructs, they are error prone and are confusing for readers of your program.

Also note that you can define variables at beginning of any code block, i.e. code segments enclosed in braces { } such as if else block. for loop above was just an example.

Finally, auto is a C language keyword used to explicitly indicate that a variable is local variable. However, since all variables inside any code block are by default local, this keyword is rarely used.

Practice Questions : -

10. Trace control flow of below program for finding nth prime number for user input 6.

```c
#include <stdio.h>
int is_prime (int num);
int main (int argc, char * argv[]) {
    int num = 0, count = 0, i = 0;
    printf("Enter a number between 5 and 100: ");
    scanf("%d",&num);
```

          feedback@thebookofc.com

```c
        if (num < 5 || num > 100) {
            printf("Incorrect input\n");
        } else {
            i=3; count=1;
            while(1) {
                if (is_prime(i)) {
                    count++;
                    if (count == num) {
                        printf("%dth prime number is
%d\n", num, i);
                        break;
                    }
                }
                i++;
            }
        }
    }
}
int is_prime(int num) {
    int i=0;
    for(i=2; i<=num/2; i++) {
        if (num%i== 0) {
            return 0;
        }
    }
    return 1;
}
```

11. What will be the output of following program

```c
#include <stdio.h>
int func1 (int num1, int num2);
int func2 (int param);

int main (int argc, char * argv[]) {
    int a=3, b=7, c=10, d=0;
    d = func1(a, d);
    c = func2(b);
    b = func1(d, c) + func2(a);
    a = func2(a);
    printf("%d %d %d %d\n", a,b,c,d);
}
int func1 (int num1, int num2) {
    num1 = num1 + 3;
    num2 = num2 - num1;
    return ((num1 + num2) * 2);
}
int func2 (int param) {
    return (param * param);
}
```

12. Write a function that determines whether a number is cube of a natural number.
13. Write a function that determines whether a number can be expressed as sum of two prime numbers.

Why Do We Need Functions?

Functions offer several advantages to a programmer. Some of these are:

1. Code reuse: You can write a function once and call it many times to perform the same operation on a different set of inputs. In fact, if you are writing similar code multiple times in your program, it is a sure sign that you should be writing it as a function.
2. Manageability: Since code for a task is written only once, it is easy to manage and update. In case there is some change in logic in future or a bug that needs to be fixed, it would be done in only one place.
3. Readability: Functions make the code very readable, especially when they are used in conjunction with good descriptive names. E.g. it is much more easier to read `is_prime(x)` than having to read a whole loop to understand that this segment of code determines whether a number is prime.
4. Better organization: For any program that is greater than 20 lines, you will find functions invaluable for organizing your code. Write all code in a single function can get messy quickly.

Void Data Type

`void` is a special data type that indicates that there is no data type. It can be used as a return type of a function that does not return anything. For example, the table printing function that we had written did not have to return anything to the calling function. We can specify its return type to be `void`.

```
void print_table(int n);
```

                    feedback@thebookofc.com

A function that has return type specified as **void** cannot return any value. However, it can still use a **return** statement without any value to return control back to the calling function. **void** is a C language keyword.

Here is the print table example again with **void** return data type. Few compiler warnings that you might have been seeing earlier should now have vanished.

```c
#include <stdio.h>

void print_table(int n);

int main (int argc, char * argv[]) {
    int num=0, i=0;

    printf("Enter a number >2: ");
    scanf("%d",&num);

    if (num<=2) {
        printf("Invalid input\n");
    } else {
        for(i=2; i<=num; i++) {
            print_table(i);
        }
    }
    return 0;
}

/* Print table of n */
void print_table(int n) {
    int i=0;

    for(i=1; i<=10; i++) {
        printf("%d X %d = %d\n", n,i,n*i);
    }
    return;
}
```

void is also used as parameter list for functions that do not accept any parameters. We have already seen a variation of **main** function that has void as parameter list. Similarly, the **print_hello** function we saw at the beginning of this chapter can be more aptly defined using signature below.

```
void print_hello (void);
```


Practice Questions : -

14. Which of the following statements are true.
    a. `void` is a data type.
    b. Local variables of called function are visible to calling function.
    c. A function that has return type `void` cannot have any parameters.
    d. `return;` is a valid C statement.
    e. A function with non `void` parameters cannot have `void` return type.
    f. `int func(int a, void b, float c);`
        is a valid function declaration.

15. Modify the hello example that included `hello_asia`, `hello_india` and similar functions such that it should compile without any warnings.

16. What will be the output of following program.

```c
#include<stdio.h>

int silly_function (int num1, int num2) {
    num1 += num2;
    num2 -= 3;
    return (num1+num2);
}
int main (int argc, char * argv[])  {
    int num1 = 5, num2 = 9;
    num2 = silly_function(num1, num2);
    printf("%d %d\n", num1,num2);
}
```

Default Return Type

C99 standard said that if you do not specify a return type of a function, C assumes it to be `int` by default. The declaration

```
print_table(int n);
```

     feedback@thebookofc.com

would have been treated by C as

```c
int print_table(int n);
```

However, C11 standard does not assume a default return type and expects the programmer to always specify the return type explicitly.

As a good programming practice, you should always specify return type of your functions.

Default Return Value

Try compiling a program where you specify a return type but do not actually return a value. While this would lead to a compiler warning, it is not an error and your program will compile and (sometimes) execute successfully.

When we did not specify a return value, what was being returned?

There is no default return value. C standard specifies that if the called function did not return a value and calling function tries to use the returned value then behaviour is undefined.

There is a fine distinction in the text above – behaviour is not undefined if calling function does not try to use the returned value. Behaviour is undefined only if no value is returned AND calling function tries to use returned value.

Expressions As Arguments

So far we have used variables and literals as arguments to functions. We can equally well use expressions as arguments. For example, we could have called our `triple_it` function above using any of the following function calls.

```c
triple_it(3+2);
triple_it(var1+2);
triple_it(var1++);
triple_it(++var1);
```

17. Try out above calls to `triple_it` and explain the results that you observe.

Now let's consider a variation of call to function `sum` that used to add two numbers for us.

`sum(num++, ++num)`

The result in this case depends on two factors:
1. Order of evaluation of arguments, left to right or right to left.
2. Sequencing of operations, if `num` of first argument is incremented before or after evaluation of second argument.

C does not impose a specific ordering of evaluation of arguments. It allows implementations to choose left to right or right to left. We should aim to write code that does not assume any specific order of evaluation of arguments.

Note that this is an example of unspecified behaviour, i.e. there are more than one acceptable behaviours as per the standard. Implementations can choose any one of the supported behaviours.

C also enforces a sequence point between evaluation of arguments and actual function call. In other words, C guarantees that evaluation of all arguments would be complete before called function's execution begins. However, it does not place any sequencing guarantee on order of evaluation of arguments themselves. For example, in our **sum** example above, C guarantees that both arguments would have been fully evaluated before control jumps to function **sum**. However, it does not guarantee whether first argument would be fully evaluated before second argument evaluation begins.

Hence, in the call `sum(num++, ++num)`, we are making two unsequenced modifications to value of num. Therefore, the result of this operation is undefined behaviour.

          feedback@thebookofc.com

Global Variables

C allows us to define variables outside any code block. These are called global variables. As the name indicates, they are visible globally, i.e. from any function in the program. Let's see an example.

```
01: #include <stdio.h>

02: int test_global = 5;

03: int main (int argc, char * argv[]) {
04:     printf("Accessing global variable from main,
value = %d\n",test_global);
05:     return 0;
06: }
```

Note that declaration of `test_global` on line 02 is outside any function. This gives global scope to `test_global`. Hence, when we access it on line 04 to print its value, we are able to access and use it.

Note that the `test_global` variable used in `main` was the actual variable, not a copy local to `main`. This implies that if a function were to modify value of global variable, other functions would be able to see the modified value.

Let's see an example.

```
01: #include <stdio.h>

02: int test_global = 5;

03: void triple_it(void){
04:     test_global *= 3;
05: }
06: int main (int argc, char * argv[]) {
07:     printf("Global variable's value =
%d\n",test_global);
08:     triple_it();
09:     printf("Global variable's value =
%d\n",test_global);
10:     return 0;
11: }
```

This is our earlier `triple_it` example but this time on a global variable. Let's trace control flow of this program.

1. Execution begins with main function, line 06.
2. At line 07, print statement is executed. This statement prints value of global variable `test_global`. Message `Global variable's value = 5` appears on the console.
3. Line 08 is call to `triple_it` function. Control jumps to line 03.
4. Line 04 assigns three times its own value back to `test_global`. As we learned, function accessing a global variable is accessing actual variable. Hence this modification of value would be visible in other functions.
5. Control exits `triple_it` function and jumps back to `main`.
6. Line 09, print statement is executed. This statement prints value of global variable `test_global`. Message `Global variable's value = 15` appears on the console. Note that change in value performed in `triple_it` function is visible inside `main`.
7. Control advances to line 10, `main` returns 0 and program terminates.

Conventionally, all global variables are placed near top of the program, right after the `#include` directives.

We can also define variables with same name as global variables inside a function. As we had learned before, in such scenarios, innermost definition that is in scope is used by the system. Let's see an example.

```c
01: #include <stdio.h>

02: int test = 5;

03: void triple_it(void){
04:     test *= 3;
05:     printf("Value of test in triple_it = %d\n",test);
06: }

07: int main (int argc, char * argv[]) {
08:     int test = 10;
```

          feedback@thebookofc.com

```
09:        triple_it();
10:        printf("Value of test in main = %d\n",test);
11:        for (int test=100; test<=100; test++) {
12:            printf("Value of test in a loop in main =
%d\n",test);
12:        }
13:        printf("Value of test outside a loop in main =
%d\n",test);
14:        return 0;
15: }
```

Notice that we have three definitions of variable test in this program
- at line 02 as a global variable, at line 08 as local to function `main`,
and at line 11 as local to the `for` loop.

Let's trace control flow of this program.
1. Execution begins with function `main`, line 07.
2. On line 08, variable `test` is defined as a local to `main` and
   assigned value 10.
3. Line 09, call to function `triple_it`. Control jumps to line 03.
4. At line 04, value of variable `test` is multiplied by 3 and
   assigned back to it. Note that there is no locally defined
   variable `test` in function `triple_it` and global variable `test`
   is in scope. Hence this statement is acting on the global
   variable `test`.
5. At line 05, value of variable `test` is printed. Note that this is
   still the global variable. Message `Value of test in
   triple_it = 15` appears on console.
6. Control jumps back to `main`, line 09.
7. At line 10, we print the value of variable `test`. Note that there
   is a locally defined variable `test` in function `main` that is in
   scope. It will take precedence over global variable. Hence
   when we print value of `test`, value of local variable `test` will
   get printed. Message `Value of test in main = 10` appears
   on console.
8. At line 10, we define another variable called `test` that is local
   to the `for` loop. `test` is assigned value 100. `for` loop
   condition 100<=100 evaluates to true. Control enters the
   loop block.
9. At line 11 we print value of variable `test`. Since nested scope
   takes higher precedence, variable `test` defined in `for` loop

will take precedence over variable `test` that is local to `main` as well as over global variable `test`. Message `Value of test in a loop in main = 100` appears on screen.

10. First iteration ends. Tail statement is executed and value of `test` is incremented to 101. Control condition 101<=100 evaluates to false. Control jumps to line 14.

11. Note that variable `test` defined in the `for` loop went out of scope as soon as control jumped outside `for` loop. At this point only function local variable `test` and global variable `test` are in scope. When we print the value, local variable `test` gets printed and message `Value of test outside a loop in main = 10` appears on the screen.

12. Control advances to line 15, `main` returns 0 and program terminates.

As good programming practice, we should minimise the use of global variables and use unique names for all our variables. Using same variable name in overlapping scope can lead to confusion and error.

Like we have global variables, we also have global constants. Adding `const` keyword to a global definition would make it a global constant visible across all functions in the program.

C standard requires all global variables to be initialized before program execution begins. If we do not initialize our global variables, system will do it for us. Typically all systems initialize global variables to 0.

Practice Questions : -
18. Which of the following statements are true.
    a. A global variable and a local variable cannot have same name.
    b. A local variable can be declared anywhere within a function.
    c. It is illegal to declare a variable more than once in same scope.

     feedback@thebookofc.com

19. What will be the output of following program.
```c
#include<stdio.h>

int num = 19;

int silly_function (int num1, int num2) {
    num1 += num2;
    num2 -= 3;
    num =- (num1+num2);
    return (num1+num2);
}
int main (int argc, char * argv[])  {
    int num1 = 5, num2 = 9;
    num2 = silly_function(num1, num);
    printf("%d %d %d\n", num,num1,num2);
}
```

Memory Organization of a C Program

Recall our behind the scenes discussion of a function call - all our local variables were stored in a function stack that was saved separately and was invisible to a different function. Where are global variables stored? How are they visible to all functions?

It's time to get deeper into memory organisation of a C program.

Every C program has four distinct memory segments.
1. Text/Code
2. Stack
3. Heap
4. Data

Text segment, also called code segment, stores the binary executable code for the program.

Stack segment, as we have learned, stores context specific to a function including its parameters, local variables, information about current position of control flow etc.

Heap segment stores dynamically allocated memory. We will learn more about dynamic memory allocation and its use later in this book.

Data segment stores global and static data. We will learn more about static data later in the book.

Note that all function invocation specific context goes into the stack segment.

Also note that global variables and constants are stored in the data segment. Since data segment is visible to all functions, global variables are seen by all parts of our program.

Practice Questions : -
20. Which of the following statements are true.
    a. Local variables are stored in the stack segment.
    b. Function specific copy of global data is stored in the stack segment.

          feedback@thebookofc.com

Preprocessing and Macros

Compilation Phases

Typically, a compiler for any language processes the code multiple times before producing the final executable output. That is, the source code that we write, is processed multiple times before final binary is created. We can break this whole process of compilation into logical phases. The output of one phase serves as input to the next phase. Most C compilers broadly consist of following phases.

Phase 1: Preprocessing
We will learn about preprocessing in detail in this chapter. Briefly, in this phase compiler executes all our preprocessing directives and generates final code for conversion into binary executable.

Phase 2: Compilation
Compiler takes the output of first phase, i.e. preprocessing, and generates assembly instructions. Assembly instructions are human readable representation of machine instructions.

Phase 3: Assembly
An assembler converts the set of assembly instructions into object code. Object code is machine readable binary code. Typically, each C file is converted into an individual object code file unless we specify otherwise. Some compilers may have an assembler integrated with the compiler. In that case, no intermediate assembly code may be generated.

Phase 4: Linking
Any practical industry application contains at least a few thousand lines of code split across multiple C files. Typically these multiple source files translate into a several object files. Functions in one object file invoke functions in a different object file. To make these calls work, multiple object files have to be linked together to create final executable binary.

C also provides us with several useful library functions to perform commonly needed actions. For example, `printf` that we have been using extensively in this book is a library function provided by C to write formatted output to console. We know that for any function, we must have a declaration and a definition for the function. For `printf` where is that function declaration and function body?

For declaration, answer lies in `#include<stdio.h>`. We will discuss it in detail in a while. For definition, precompiled object code is available as C libraries. Hence for this library function to execute, a linker links the library code with our binary executable.

This is also the typical code organization – we put all declarations in respective .h files and definition in corresponding .c file.

C Preprocessor

Preprocessor, as the name suggests, does some amount of processing before the actual compilation begins. In C, a line that begins with '#' character is called a preprocessing directive. It is an indicator to the compiler that this preprocessing directive needs to be processed before compilation phase begins.

In all programs that we have written in this book so far, we have already been using a preprocessing directive - `#include <stdio.h>`. The purpose of this directive is to include the header file `stdio.h` in our code – the file that contains declaration of `printf`, `scanf`, and several other standard input output (I/O) functions.

A preprocessing directive begins with '#' symbol. It must be the first character of the line of code. Only whitespace can precede this first element on a new line.

'#' symbol is followed by the type of preprocessing directive. We shall be discussing three most widely used types of directives in this chapter. The complete set of preprocessing directives can be referred at http://thebookofc.com/preprocessing/all-preprocessing-directives-in-c/.

 feedback@thebookofc.com

Finally, a new line character marks end of preprocessing directive.

Following table lists preprocessing directives that we shall be discussing in further detail.

Preprocessing directives	Purpose
#include	Include other files, typically header files
#define #undef	inline text substitution, code and literals Defining and undefining names/symbols
#ifdef #if #elif #endif #if #else #endif	Conditional compilation

#include

In #include <stdio.h>, the first character at the beginning of the line is '#', indicating to the compiler that this line is a preprocessing directive, and hence has to be processed during preprocessing phase of compilation.

#include preprocessing directive tells the preprocessor to include contents of the specified file, as is, within the current source file, at the location of the #include directive.

When we write #include <stdio.h> in our program, it leads to inline inclusion of all contents of stdio.h file in our source code.

There are two variants of #include directive:

```
#include "filename.h"
#include <filename.h>
```

When we include a file by specifying its name in angle brackets, preprocessor starts by looking for the file in the directories configured in the PATH environment variable in the specified order.

If you are not familiar with PATH environment variable then you can find a quick primer at http://thebookofc.com/environment/path-environment-variable/. Simply put, PATH can be viewed as a list of directory paths. The header file in question is looked up in this list of directory paths.

Typically this method is used to include standard library header files. For example, `stdio.h` is a standard library file and we use angular brackets to include it.

When you include a file by specifying its name in double quotes, preprocessor starts by looking for the file in the current directory. If the file is not found in the current directory, it would proceed to search for the file in the directories configured in its PATH variable in the order in which such directories are configured. Typically this method is used to include user-defined header files.

In either case, as soon as a file by the specified name is found, further search is stopped and `#include` directive is replaced with the contents of the file.

Note that subdirectories are not searched. It is required to include the complete path of directory containing the header file in PATH variable.

In case included file is not found in current directory as well as in directories configured in PATH variable, preprocessor will throw an error and compilation would fail.

There is one more way to specify include file paths – as a compiler switch or flag. We encourage you to check your compiler documentation to learn more about compiler switches specific to your system.

Practice Questions : -
1. Which of the following statements are true.
    a. Preprocessing generates object files.
    b. `#include` directive includes a whole file as is at the location of the directive.

                      feedback@thebookofc.com

c. In case included file was not found, system will skip its preprocessing and advance to the next stage.
d. Linker links function calls across object files.

#define

`#define` directive is commonly known as macro. There are broadly two uses of macros:
- o   to define a symbolic name for a literal
- o   to define a symbolic name for a source code snippet

Let us see an example.

```
#define BUFFERSIZE 128
```

As we have learned, '#' symbol at the beginning of the line indicates a preprocessing directive. `#define` is the directive and it defines a symbolic name `BUFFERSIZE` for literal 128.

Once preprocessor encounters this directive, it will replace all following instances of `BUFFERSIZE` with 128.

For example, if our code was

```
...
#define BUFFERSIZE 128
...

...
int my_function(int a, int b) {
    int buffer[BUFFERSIZE] = { 0 };
...
}
```

then preprocessor will replace `BUFFERSIZE` in `my_function` with 128. Consequently, preprocessed code will appear as

```
int my_function(int a, int b) {
    int buffer[128] = { 0 };
...
```

Compiler picks up this preprocessed code as input for compilation in next phase.

Note that preprocessor replaces all uses of the macro after directive is encountered. Hence macro definition has to precede macro use.

Now let us redefine the macro in above code snippet to

```
#define BUFFERSIZE "128"
```

Remember that preprocessor does an as is replacement. Hence the preprocessed code will have double quotes too. It will appear as

```
int my_function(int a, int b) {
    int buffer["128"] = { 0 };
...
```

Subsequently, we will get a compilation error similar to one shown below.

```
main.c:13:9: error: size of array 'buffer' has non-integer type
     int buffer[BUFFERSIZE] = {0};
```

Let us consider another example. Consider following piece of code:

```
01: #include <stdio.h>
02: #define INFINITE_LOOP while (1)

03: int main(int argc, char *argv[]) {
04:     int counter = 0;
05:     INFINITE_LOOP {
06:         counter++;
07:         if (counter != 10) {
08:             printf ("counter = %d\n", counter);
09:         }
10:         else {
11:             break;
12:         }
13:     }
14: }
```

In above example, after preprocessing line 05 will appear as below

    feedback@thebookofc.com

```c
while (1){
```

Remember the thumb rule for macros - a simple textual replacement - find macro name and replace it with macro body, irrespective of contents of macro body.

Following statements are all valid definitions of a macro.

```c
#define PI 3.14
#define NINETY 50+35+5
#define VARIABLE xyz
#define COMPARISON var1 >= var2
#define JUNK_MACRO asd;%$awe
```

Let us dwell upon JUNK_MACRO defined above. Macro body is meaningless invalid code and should give compilation error. However, if this macro is not used at all in the code, there will be no compilation error. Why? In preprocessing stage, if JUNK_MACRO is not found at all in code, no replacement is done at all. Hence this junk piece of code doesn't go to compilation, and the code compiles successfully. We encourage you to write a program to verify the same.

What if we redefine a macro? Let's rewrite one of our previous examples with multiple definitions of a macro.

```c
...
#define BUFFERSIZE 128
#define BUFFERSIZE 256
...

...
int my_function(int a, int b) {
    int buffer[BUFFERSIZE] = { 0 };
...
}
```

We redefined BUFFERSIZE to another value on consecutive lines. Note that macro name is not a variable, and unlike variables, can be redefined. When a macro is redefined, the latest definition takes effect. In above example, all instances of BUFFERSIZE will be replaced by 256, and not 128.

Note that by convention all macro names are in uppercase. This helps to differentiate them from regular variables while reading the code. We will follow this convention throughout this book.

Practice Questions : -
2. Which of the following statements are true.
    a. `#define` macro will replace only first occurrence of macro name with macro body.
    b. #define macro can be used only for replacing literals.
    c. #define macro cannot be placed in a .h file.
    d. Just like a variable, we cannot define a macro more than once in same scope.

Macros With Arguments

So far, we have seen macros with no parameters. Like functions, macros can also be defined with parameters. Let's see an example

```
#define MAX(A,B)   (A>B)?A:B
```

This statement defines a macro called `MAX` that takes two argument `A` and `B`. So how does the replacement take place here? The rules are simple.
    o   Macro `MAX` is replaced by its definition.
    o   Parameters `A` and `B` are replaced by arguments of the macro at the time is use.

Hence macro `MAX(3,5)` will get replaced by `(3>5)?3:5`.

Note that, as stated earlier, preprocessing will perform no validation checks. It will blindly do a text replace.

Practice Questions : -
3. Which of the following statements are true.
    a. In a macro, arguments are passed by value.
    b. Macro arguments data types are matched and validated during preprocessing phase.
    c. Macro arguments are textually substituted, as is, just like macro body.

              feedback@thebookofc.com

4. Point out the error in below program.

```c
#include <stdio.h>
#define MAX(A,B)  (A>B)?A:B
int main(int argc, char *argv[]) {
    int num1 = 5, num2 = 7;
    int max_of_two = 0;
    max_of_two = MAX(num1, B);
    printf ("Max of two numbers is %d\n", max_of_two);
}
```

5. Write a macro that takes 3 arguments and computes their sum.

Predefined Macros

C comes with some predefined macros ready for us to use. Three of the most commonly used predefined macros are `__FILE__`, `__FUNCTION__`, `__LINE__` which expand to the current file name, function name, and line number respectively. Here is an example using these macros.

```c
#define PRINT_LOCATION printf("Control is at %s %s %d",
__FILE__, __FUNCTION__, __LINE__);
```

Now wherever we place `PRINT_LOCATION` in our code, it will print the file name, function name, and line number of that location.

In real world, the code is split into numerous C code files. Hence, when we print log messages in our program, it will be useful if log messages contained exact location from where the log was printed. Let us put our macro knowledge to use and define a useful macro to achieve the same.

```c
#define PRINT_LOG(MSG)  printf("%s: %s: %d: %s", __FILE__,
__FUNCTION__, __LINE__, MSG);
```

`PRINT_LOG` macro will take one argument – the log message to be printed – and print it with file name, function name, and line number. For example,

```c
if (total_marks < 0) {
    PRINT_LOG("Marks < 0. Error condition\n")
}
```

will expand to

```
if (total_marks < 0) {
    printf("%s: %s: %d: %s", __FILE__, __FUNCTION__,
__LINE__, "Marks < 0. Error condition\n");
}
```

Note that in above example, we didn't end the macro use with a
semicolon (;). Why? The answer lies in the expanded code. Since
semicolon was already part of macro definition, expanded code has
the necessary semicolon. It will be equally good if we remove the
trailing semicolon in macro definition, and place it after macro use.
We encourage you to write a program and verify it.

Multiline Macros

Consider the following macro

```
#define IS_ODD(A) if (A%2 != 0) printf ("The number %d is
odd\n", A)
```

Remember our rules for defining a preprocessing directive that we
learned at the beginning of the chapter? A new line character marks
the end of a directive. Hence, if we have to write multiple instructions
in a macro definition, all statements should be written on one single
line. This makes the code unreadable. In order to write a multiline
macro, we can use an '\' at the end of each line. Backslash escapes
the newline character and compiler treats following line to be part of
the current line. Above macro can be rewritten as,

```
#define IS_ODD(A) \
if (A%2 != 0) \
    printf ("The number %d is odd\n", A)
```

Consider the following example.

```
#include <stdio.h>
#define SUBTRACT_AND_RETURN(value1, value2)\
    value1 = value1 - value2;\
    return value1;
```

          feedback@thebookofc.com

```c
int diff(int num1, int num2) {
    if (num1 > num2)
            SUBTRACT_AND_RETURN (num1, num2)
    else
            SUBTRACT_AND_RETURN (num2, num1)
}
```

The above code defines a function to subtract the smaller number from bigger number, and return the difference. If we expand the macros inside function max, it will expand to

```c
int diff(int num1, int num2) {
    if (num1 > num2)
            num1 = num1 - num2;
      return num1;
    else
                num2 = num2 - num1;
      return num2;
}
```

This is clearly not what we wanted. We wanted the multiline macro to execute as a single block. Since we didn't enclose the two statements in macro definition in braces, the `return` statement goes out of `if` block leading to a compilation error. It is good practice to enclose multiline macros in braces to ensure they are part of same block of statements. Modified version of SUBTRACT_AND_RETURN is shown below.

```c
#define SUBTRACT_AND_RETURN(value1, value2) {\
    value1 = value1 - value2;\
    return value1;\
}
```


6. Write a macro that takes three `int` arguments and prints the highest value.

#if #else #elif

#if and #else macros work very similar to `if-else` conditional statements – instead of impacting execution of statement block, they control the compilation of statement block into the executable. Here is an example.

```
#if DEBUG_LEVEL > 3
    printf ("%s %s starting iteration %d\n", __FILE__,
__FUNCTION__, i);
#endif
```

`printf` statement in above example will get compiled into the executable only if `DEBUG_LEVEL` has been defined with value greater than 3. Note that since macros are processed by preprocessor, it is not possible to use variables in condition. We can use defined macro symbols and literals.

Note that we haven't enclosed the comparison expression in parentheses. For preprocessing directive, it is not mandatory to use parentheses. Both `DEBUG_LEVEL > 3` and `(DEBUG_LEVEL > 3)` are valid comparison statements for this directive.

`#if` block ends with an `#endif`.

Similar to `if-else`, `#if` has an optional `#else` clause. If `#if` condition is true, `#if` block is compiled in, otherwise `#else` block is compiled in. Here is an example.

```
#if DEBUG_LEVEL == 3
    PRINT_LOG("Call failed. Counter dump:\n");
    for(int i=0; i<10; i++) {
        printf("counter[%d] = %d\n", i, counter[i]);
    }
#else
    PRINT_LOG("Call failed\n");
#endif
```

If above code was compiled with `DEBUG_LEVEL` as 3, then program will print a log message along with dumping values of counter array else it will simply print a log message.

Similar to combining multiple `if-else` statements to cover multiple scenarios, we can combine multiple `#if` directives as shown below.

                    feedback@thebookofc.com

```
#if DEBUG_LEVEL == 3
    PRINT_LOG("Call failed. Counter dump:\n");
    for(int i=0; i<10; i++) {
        printf("counter[%d] = %d\n",i,counter[i]);
    }
#elif DEBUG_LEVEL == 2
    PRINT_LOG("Call failed. Counter summary:\n");
    printf("Total:%d  Average:%f\n",total,average);
#else
    PRINT_LOG("Call failed\n");
#endif
```

`#elif` (short for else if) in the above code snippet is directive equivalent of `else if`. We can concatenate as many `elif` as required.

Note that `#endif` terminates the entire `#if` `#else` construct.

Practice Questions : -
7. Condition of `#if` directive cannot contain a variable. Why?
8. Which of the following statements are true.
    a. `#if` directive is used to decide what code gets included in the binary executable.
    b. Code in `#elif` gets compiled in irrespective of value of `#if` condition.

Macros for Defining Symbols

```
#define MACRO_DEF
```

This is a valid macro definition. But what does it do? If used, it has no literal defined to replace `MACRO_DEF`. These kind of macros are used to define simply the existence of a symbol.

We can check if a macro was defined or not using `#ifdef` and `#ifndef` directives. We will explore them in next section.

Note that if you use these kind of macros as normal replacements macros, they will be replaced by NULL. Depending on the code where you use it, the compilation may succeed or fail.

#ifdef

#ifdef directives decide if the enclosing block of code will go to the next stage of compilation or not based on whether a symbol has been defined.

#ifdef (short for "if defined") allows us to test if a specific macro symbol has been defined earlier in the program. Depending on the outcome of the check, code is preprocessed and passed to next compilation phase.

Simplest #ifdef construct takes following form.

```
#ifdef <MACRO_NAME>
...
#endif
```

Preprocessed output will include the block of code between #ifdef and #endif only if <MACRO_NAME> had been defined earlier in the program. Else this block of code is excluded, and hence doesn't go to the next compilation stage. Here is an example,

```
#ifdef DEBUG_MODE
    printf("Cumulative sum in iteration %d is %d\n, i,
sum);
#endif
```

The message will be printed only if symbol DEBUG_MODE was defined. Otherwise this statement would not be compiled and would not be part of final executable.

As with regular if statement, #ifdef can also have an #else part. #ifdef with #else takes the form shown below.

```
#ifdef <MACRO_NAME>
...
#else
...
#endif
```

          feedback@thebookofc.com

If <MACRO_NAME> has been defined earlier in the program, statement block between #ifdef and #else is part of preprocessed output and block between #else and #endif is skipped. However, if <MACRO_NAME> has not been defined earlier then the block between #else and #endif is part of preprocessed output and the block between #ifdef and #else is skipped.

Let's see an example

```
#ifdef WEIGHT_REQUIRED
    printf("Please enter height and weight: ");
#else
    printf("Please enter height : ");
#endif
```

If WEIGHT_REQUIRED is defined, prompt for height and weight will be compiled and statement in #else block will not be compiled.

If WEIGHT_REQUIRED is not defined, prompt for only height will be compiled and statement in #ifdef block will not be compiled.

#ifndef

#ifndef (if not defined) is the logical opposite of #ifdef. It evaluates to true if the symbol passed to the directive is not already defined and false otherwise. Here is an example.

```
#ifndef BUFFER_LENGTH
#define BUFFER_LENGTH 128
#endif
```

Above code snippet tests if BUFFER_LENGTH is not defined. If it has not been defined, it defines it with literal 128.

One of the most common use of #ifndef is to avoid multiple inclusion of a header file. Let's understand the problem statement first. Consider having three header files - common.h, userfile1.h and userfile2.h. Contents of these files are shown below.

<File: common.h>

int global_var1;
int func (int var1, var2);

<File:userfile1.h>

#include <common.h>

int user1global;
int user1func(char var2);

<File:userfile2.h>

#include <common.h>

int user2global;
int user2func(char var2);

usercode.c

#include <userfile1.h>
#include <userfile2.h>

Let us derive the preprocessed output of file `usercode.c`. It first includes file `userfile1.h`. The directive will be replaced inline, which in turn includes file `common.h`. During preprocessing `common.h` too will be replaced inline. Hence preprocessed output for `#include <userfile.h>` will appear as shown below.

```
int global_var1;
int func (int var1, var2);
int user1global;
int user1func( char var2);
```

After doing similar preprocessing for `#include <userfile2.h>`, following snippet too will get **added** to preprocessed output of `usercode.c`.

```
int global_var1;
int func (int var1, var2);
int user2global;
int user2func( char var2);
```

      feedback@thebookofc.com

Did you observe that global variable `global_var1` and function prototype `func` got declared twice? In other words, the header file `common.h` got included twice. Duplicate declaration will lead to error during compilation phase.

To avoid this multiple inclusion of header files, we use `#ifndef` directive. Let's rewrite the `common.h` header file as

```
01: #ifndef __COMMON_H__
02: #define __COMMON_H__

03: int global_var1;
04: int func (int var1, var2);

05: #endif
```

At line 01, the `ifndef` directive checks if `__COMMON_H__` is already defined. If defined, the code till line 05 is excluded from preprocessed output.

If `__COMMON_H__` is not defined, then at line 02, it is explicitly defined. Further contents of file get included as part of preprocessing.

Now let's understand the preprocessing of `usercode.c` with this change.

First `userfile1.h` is preprocessed. The preprocessing of `common.h` will check if `__COMMON_H__` is already defined. So far it is not, hence the `#ifndef` directive evaluates to true. Thus the contents of `common.h` will be part of the preprocessed output and will appear as below.

```
int global_var1;
int func (int var1, var2);

int user1global;
int user1func( char var2);
```

However, as part of this preprocessing `__COMMON_H__` is now defined.

Next the file `userfile2.h` is preprocessed. However now, while preprocessing `common.h`, the `#ifndef` directive will evaluate to false. This is because `__COMMON_H__` is already defined during previous step. Hence the entire content of `common.h` is skipped during preprocessing. The remaining contents of `userfile2.h` file get added to the preprocessed output.

```c
int user2global;
int user2func( char var2);
```

The problem of double inclusion of a single header file has been successfully solved.

In real world, code will be distributed across multiple header and C files, and hence running into multiple inclusion of header files is a common problem. It is a good practice to always enclose contents of all header files within `#ifndef` directive to avoid repeated inclusion of the file.

#undef

`#undef` allows us to undefine a previously defined symbol. For example, try out the following code snippet.

```c
#define TEST_SYMBOL
#ifdef TEST_SYMBOL
    printf("TEST_SYMBOL is defined at %s %s %d\n",
__FILE__, __FUNCTION__, __LINE__);
#endif

#undef TEST_SYMBOL
#ifdef TEST_SYMBOL
    printf("TEST_SYMBOL is defined at %s %s %d\n",
__FILE__, __FUNCTION__, __LINE__);
#endif
```

You should see only the first print statement in action. After `#undef` undefined `TEST_SYMBOL` following `#ifdef` check will evaluate to false. As a result, the code within second `#ifdef` would never be compiled into the final executable.

      feedback@thebookofc.com

Once a symbol has been undefined, it may consequently be redefined using #define. The redefinition need not have any resemblance to earlier definition. For example, if earlier definition defined a symbol to have integer value, subsequent redefinition may define it to be a string literal or a macro with arguments.

Practice Questions : -

9. Which of the following statements are true.
    a. We cannot define a symbol again until we have undefined it.
    b. Multiple inclusion of header files can lead to compilation error.
    c. Use of #ifndef to avoid multiple inclusion of header files requires use of a unique symbol for every header file.

Arrays

So far we have seen programming examples that deal with only a few variables related to one entity – score of one student, perimeter of one circle, etc. In real world, our programs have to be capable of handling a lot more entities. For example, consider the problem of calculating the average score for a math test for a class of 50 students. How will we store 50 values? It requires declaring 50 variables and then executing 50 `scanf` statements to read values in those 50 variables.

Note that with 50 different variables, we cannot use a loop to read in the values, because variable names are different, and hence we will have to write 50 `scanf` statements.

Arrays are very helpful in such situations where we have to work with a number of elements of the same type.

What is an Array

An **array** is a collection of elements of same data type.

Consider an egg tray. It has placeholders of same size to keep multiple eggs. Similarly a tray carrying cans of cold drinks has placeholders of same size to keep multiple cans. You can imagine an array as a container that can hold multiple elements of same data type.

Declaring an Array

An array declaration consists of three parts:
- o The data type - defines data type of elements that can be stored in the array.
- o The name - name of the variable for array itself.
- o Size - defines the number of elements that this array can hold.

A sample array declaration is shown below.

```
int age[5];
```
          feedback@thebookofc.com

In this example, **age** is the variable name of the array and it can hold 5 values of type `int`.

Like all other variables that we have discussed, when you declare an array, system allocates enough memory to store all the elements of array. Memory allocated for an array is always contiguous. Above declaration statement would lead to allocation of enough contiguous memory to store 5 integer values. This is illustrated in the figure below.

age				
int	int	int	int	int

Once again, like all other variables, if the array has not been initialized, its contents are not deterministic.

Now that we know how to declare an array, let's learn how to initialize an array.

Initializing an Array

An array can be initialized by providing a comma separated list of values to be stored in that array. This list is enclosed in braces. Following example illustrates the syntax for array initialization.

```
int age[5] = { 5, 8, 7, 2, 15 };
```

Value assignment to array elements is based on position matching. In this case, value 5 is assigned to first element of the array, value 8 is assigned to second element of the array and so on. Result of this initialization will be stored in memory as shown below.

age				
5	8	7	2	15

The number of values in the comma separated list should be the same as the size of the array. Note that the compiler doesn't give an error if size of array and number of elements in initialization list do not match.

If number of elements is less than the size of array, the remaining elements are left uninitialized. If number of elements is more than the size of array, the behaviour is nondeterministic and will be implementation specific. This is another programming error that we should avoid.

If we are initializing individual elements of an array at the time of declaration, then specifying the size of array is optional. In such case system determines size of the array by counting the number of elements in the initialization list.

Hence, initialization statement shown below is equivalent to the above example.

```
int age[] = { 5, 8, 7, 2, 15 };
```

Here, it will be implicitly deduced that the size of array **age** is 5. This way, you can also avoid incorrect array initialization programming error that we talked about above.

If we want to initialize all elements of an array to the same value, we can do so by simply enclosing that single value in braces. The declaration for the same will look like this:

```
int age[5] = { 0 };
```

Above statement will initialize all elements of array **age** to 0. Resulting representation of array **age** is shown below.

age				
0	0	0	0	0

As with other variables, as a good programming practice, you should always initialize your arrays when you declare them.

 feedback@thebookofc.com

1. Which of the following array declarations are valid.

```
a.  int [] arr = { 1, 2, 3, 4 };
b.  int arr[] = { '1', '2', '3', '4' };
c.  float price = { 2.2, 3.4, 5.5 };
d.  double perimeter[7] = { 0 };
e.  char keyword[5] = { 'A' };
```

Accessing an Array Element

So far we have learned how to store multiple elements of same data type in an array. Now let us learn how to retrieve the elements stored in the array and use them in our program.

The position of an element in an array is called index of that element. In C, counting of indices begins at 0. An array element can be accessed by simply writing the name of the array followed by the index of the desired element enclosed in square brackets. For example,

```
int age[5] = { 5, 8, 7, 2, 15 };
```

For the age array shown above,
`age[0]` accesses first element in the array which has value 5.
`age[1]` accesses second element in the array which has value 8.
`age[2]` accesses third element in the array which has value 7.
`age[3]` accesses fourth element in the array which has value 2.
`age[4]` accesses fifth element in the array which has value 15.

Note that valid indices for above example are in the range 0 to 4. Index 5 is not a valid index for this array.

Whatever operations we can perform on an integer variable can also be performed on an integer array element. For example, the way we can read value in an integer variable using `scanf`, we can read value from user in an array element of type integer.

```
scanf("%d",&age[0]);
```

Likewise, we can print value stored in an element, using a similar printf statement.

```
printf("%d",age[0]);
```

We can use array elements as operands in all operations we have learned so far. For example,

```
age[0] = 10; //Assigning literal
age[1] = number + 6; //Assigning result of expression
number = age[4]; //copying value to a variable
age[2] = age[1]++; //increment and assign operators
if (age[4] > age[2]) { //relational operators
        printf("comparison works with array elements\n");
}
```

Array Example

Let's put together our learning so far and write a program that reads marks of a student in five subjects and prints the total marks of that student.

```
01: #include <stdio.h>

02: int main (int argc, char * argv[]) {
03:     int marks[5] = { 0 };
04:     int i=0, total=0;

05:     do {
06:         printf ("Enter marks for subject %d", i+1);
07:         scanf("%d",&marks[i]);
08:         i++;
09:     }while(i<5);

10:     for (i=0; i<5; i++) {
11:         total = total + marks[i];
12:     }

13:     printf("Student's total marks are %d\n",total);
14:     return 0;
15: }
```

Let's trace control flow for this program.

     feedback@thebookofc.com

1. At line 03 an integer array of size 5 - `marks` - is declared and all its elements are initialized to 0.
2. At line 04 integer variables `i` and `total`, are declared and initialized to 0.
3. At line 05, the control enters `do while` loop. Control advances to line 06.
4. A message is printed, prompting the user to enter marks for subject 1. Note that we are printing `i+1` to align prompt to more human friendly count of 1 to 5 instead of 0 to 4 indices of the array.
5. At line 07 user input is read into 0th index of the array `marks`, that is `marks[0]`.
6. At line 08 value of `i` is incremented to 1.
7. At line 09 the loop condition is evaluated. `i<5` evaluates to true and hence control jumps to line 06 for next iteration.
8. Steps 4 to 7 will get repeated till `i < 5`, and hence read in 4 more values from the user and store them at indices 1, 2, 3 and 4 respectively. After reading in 4th value, `i` is incremented to 5. Loop condition on line 09 evaluates to false and control advances to line 10.
9. Control enters the `for` loop. Loop initialization statement sets the value of `i` to 0. Loop execution condition 0<5 evaluates to true. Control advances to line 11.
10. First element of the array (`marks[0]`) is added to `total`.
11. The tail statement of `for` loop is executed. `i` is incremented by 1 to value 2.
12. Loop control goes back to line 10. The condition `i<5` evaluates to true.
13. At line 11, second element of the array (`marks[1]`) is added to the total. Note that `total` is storing the cumulative sum in this example.
14. Likewise, loop continues execution adding array elements one by one to `total` until value of `i` is incremented to 5.
15. When `i` is incremented to 5, loop condition evaluates to false and control advances to line 13.
16. Output message with computed `total` is printed. Control advances to end of program and terminates.

2. Write a program to find highest value in an array of 10 integers.
3. Write a program to compute the average of 10 float numbers in an array.
4. What will be the output of following program.

```c
#include <stdio.h>
int main (int argc, char * argv[]) {
    int arr[] = { 0,1,2,3,4,5,6,7,8,9 };
    int i=0;
    int num_elements = 10;
    for(i=9; i>=0; i--) {
        arr[i] = arr[num_elements - i - 1] + arr[i];
    }
    for(i=0; i<num_elements; i++) {
        printf("arr[%d] = %d\n", i, arr[i]);
    }
    return 0;
}
```

Passing Array as Argument

Like regular variables, array variables can also be passed as arguments to functions. Let's revisit the problem of calculating average score of a class in a math test and use a function to compute the average of scores stored in an array.

Here is the source code for this problem:

```c
01: #include <stdio.h>
02: float compute_average(int marks[], int size);

03: int main (int argc, char * argv[]) {
04:     int marks[50] = { 0 };
05:     int i=0;
06:     float average = 0.0;
07:     do {
08:         printf ("Enter marks for student %d", i+1);
09:         scanf("%d",&marks[i]);
10:         i++;
11:     }while(i<50);
12:     average = compute_average(marks, 50);
13:     printf("Average score is %f\n", average);
14:     return 0;
15: }
```

                    feedback@thebookofc.com

```
16: float compute_average(int marks[], int size) {
17:     int i=0, sum=0;
18:     for(i=0; i<size; i++) {
19:         sum = sum + marks[i];
20:     }
21:     return ((1.0*sum)/size);
22: }
```

At line 02, we have a function declaration with array data type as a parameter.

```
float compute_average(int marks[], int size);
```

The square brackets after the parameter name indicate that this parameter is an array.

When arrays are passed as arguments, the called function also needs to be informed about the size of the array. Hence, we have passed size of the array as an argument to the called function.

Now let's trace control flow for our example.

1. After the variable declaration and initialization, control reaches line 07. Since this is a do while loop, control enters the loop without any checks for the first iteration. Control reaches line 08.
2. Since i was initialized to 0, printf statement prints – Enter marks for student 1. Note that value i+1 is printed instead of i to align prompt to human readable numbers.
3. At line 09, scanf statement reads the user input and saves it at 0th index of the array marks.
4. At line 10, value of i is incremented to 1.
5. At line 11 – while statement 1<50 evaluates to true and control jumps to line 09.
6. Steps 2 to 5 are repeated as the loop continues to iterate for 50 times. User inputs are saved at successive indices in marks array. Loop terminates when value of i becomes 50, i.e. loop has been successful executed for values 0 to 49. Note that

our array of 50 elements has the same range of valid indices – 0 to 49.

7. Once control exits the `do while` loop, it reaches line 12. A call to `compute_average` function is made and `marks` and 50 are passed as arguments. Control jumps to line 16.

8. After initialization of variables `i` and `sum`, control reaches the `for` loop at line 18.

9. `i` is initialized to 0, and the loop condition 0<50 evaluates to true. Control enters the loop.

10. At line 19, value of `sum` is updated to 0 + `marks[0]`, i.e. value at 0th index of marks array is added to current value of `sum`.

11. End of loop is reached. Tail statement increments value of `i`, which now becomes 1.

12. Control goes back to line 18. Loop condition 1<50 evaluates to true. Control enters the loop again.

13. At line 19, value of `sum` is updated to `sum + marks[1]`, i.e. value at 1st index of marks array is added to current value of `sum`.

14. End of loop is reached. Tail statement increments value of `i`, which now becomes 2.

15. Steps 12 to 14 are repeated, as the loop continues until all indices up to 49 have been added to `sum`.

16. When value of `i` is incremented to 50, loop condition `i<50` evaluates to false and control jumps to line 21.

17. Average is calculated as sum/size and returned back to calling function. Note the multiplication with 1.0. Remember our typecasting fundamentals? By multiplying with 1.0, we avoid integer division, and ensure that the precision in the operation isn't lost.

18. Control jumps back to line 12. Returned value is assigned to variable **average**.

19. Control advances to line 13. Value of **average** is printed. Control advances to end of program and terminates.

Practice Questions : -

5. Enhance the above program to add two functions `find_max` and `find_min` to find the highest and lowest scores respectively.

6. Write a program to search a value in an array of integers.

     feedback@thebookofc.com

7. Write a program that inputs two arrays of 10 integers each and
    saves sum of corresponding elements of these arrays in a third
    array and prints them.

sizeof Array

Remember the unary operator `sizeof`? It is a unary operator that tells
us the amount of memory taken, in bytes, by its operand – typically
a variable or a data type. `sizeof` also works on array as an operand.

Let's consider an example:

```c
#include <stdio.h>
int main (int argc, char * argv[]) {
    int a = 5;
    int b[15] = { 0 } ;
    printf ("%lu %lu %lu\n",sizeof(a), sizeof(int),
sizeof(b));
    return 0;
}
```

Since a is an integer hence `sizeof(a)` and `sizeof(int)` will be
identical.

Since b is an array of 15 integers, memory required for storing b will
be 15 times the memory required to store a single integer.

Hence in the output of above program, the first two numbers will be
same and third number will be 15 times as big. As already discussed
in previous chapters, the actual numbers you see may vary on
different systems.

Multidimensional arrays

The arrays that we have discussed so far are called single dimensional
arrays. They are a linear collection of elements that can be accessed
using a single index. C also allows us to declare and use
multidimensional arrays. Let us extend our example of storing marks
in array. If we want to store marks of 5 students in 3 subjects, we can
do so using a 2-dimensional array as shown below.

```
int marks[5][3];
```

The first dimension, that is the first index 5, corresponds to the number of students. And the second index 3, corresponds to the marks of the students in 3 subjects.

We can visualize it as a table shown below.

	Column 1 (subject 1)	Column 2 (subject 2)	Column 3 (subject 3)
Row 1 (student 1)	marks[0][0]	marks[0][1]	marks[0][2]
Row 2 (student 2)	marks[1][0]	marks[1][1]	marks[1][2]
Row 3(student 3)	marks[2][0]	marks[2][1]	marks[2][2]
Row 4 (student 4)	marks[3][0]	marks[3][1]	marks[3][2]
Row 5 (student 5)	marks[4][0]	marks[4][1]	marks[4][2]

If we want to store or retrieve the marks of say, student 4 in subject 2, the array element to look at is `marks[3][1]`.

Let's learn how to initialize a two dimensional array. `marks[5][3]` can be viewed as an array of 5 elements where each element is a single dimensional array of 3 integers. We can initialize this single dimensional array element of 3 integers, for all the 5 elements. A comma separates initialization of rows and this comma-separated list of rows where each row is an array enclosed in another pair of curly brackets. A sample initialization is shown below.

```
int marks[5][3] =  { {80, 92, 77},
                     {69, 84, 73},
                     {68, 52, 81},
                     {49, 89, 82},
                     {97, 91, 88},
                   };
```

        feedback@thebookofc.com

Row major and Column Major order

We talked about how single dimensional arrays are stored in memory earlier in this chapter. How do multidimensional arrays get stored in the memory? When multi-dimensional arrays are to be stored in a linear memory there are two ways to store the same.

Row Major order - The elements are stored row-wise. Refer the table in the above example. First all the elements of row 1 are stored, then row 2 and so on till row 5. The memory storage will appear as shown below.

00	04	08	12	16
marks[0][0]	marks[0][1]	marks[0][2]	marks[1][0]	marks[1][1]
20	24	28	32	36
marks[1][2]	marks[2][0]	marks[2][1]	marks[2][2]	marks[3][0]
40	44	48	52	56
marks[3][1]	marks[3][2]	marks[4][0]	marks[4][1]	marks[4][2]

Column Major order - The elements are stored column-wise. Refer the table in the above example. First all the elements of column 1 are stored, then column 2 and finally column 3. The memory storage will appear as shown below.

00	04	08	12	16
marks[0][0]	marks[1][0]	marks[2][0]	marks[3][0]	marks[4][0]
20	24	28	32	36
marks[0][1]	marks[1][1]	marks[2][1]	marks[3][1]	marks[4][1]
40	44	48	52	56
marks[0][2]	marks[1][2]	marks[2][2]	marks[3][2]	marks[4][2]

C uses row-major order to store multi-dimensional arrays.

Let's put 2D arrays to use in a program. Following program reads marks of 5 students in 3 subjects and prints their total marks.

```c
01: #include<stdio.h>

02: int main (int argc, char * argv[])  {
03:      int marks[5][3] = { 0 };
04:      int student=0, subject=0, sum=0;

05:      for(student=0; student<5; student++) {
06:           for(subject=0; subject<3; subject++) {
07:                printf("Enter marks for student %d
subject %d: ",student,subject);
08:                scanf("%d",&marks[student][subject]);
09:           }
10:      }

11:      for(student=0; student<5; student++) {
12:           sum = 0;
13:           for(subject=0; subject<3; subject++) {
14:                sum = sum + marks[student][subject];
15:           }
16:           printf("Student %d scored total %d\n",
student, sum);
17:      }
18:      return 0;
19: }
```

Processing a 2D array requires nested loops – one loop to go through all the rows and other loop to process all elements of a given row. We see these nested loops on lines 05, 06 and then again on lines 11, 13. Let's understand the program structure in more detail.

1. On line 03, we declare a 2D array, marks, with 5 rows (indices 0 through 4) and 3 columns (indices 0 through 2). All elements of this array are initialized to 0.
2. On line 04, we define 3 integer variables, student, subject, and sum and initialize them to 0.
3. On line 05 we set a loop to iterate through every row of 2D array marks. Visualizing marks as rows corresponding to students and each row containing scores of three subjects for a student, this loop iterates through all students.
4. On line 06 we set a nested loop to iterate through all elements of a row. Visualizing marks as rows corresponding to students and each row containing scores of three subjects for a student, this loop iterates through scores of a student.

          feedback@thebookofc.com

5. On line 08, we read in score of individual subjects for a given student. Once marks for all subjects for all students have been read, control will jump to end of nested loops, line 11.
6. This is beginning of our nested loops for processing the 2D array marks. As before, first loop iterates through every student.
7. Line 12 we set sum to 0. Every time we start processing scores of a student, sum will get reset to 0 allowing us to compute total marks for every individual student.
8. Line 13 we set our nested loop to iterate through subject wise scores of a student.
9. Line 14 we accumulate the sum of scores for a single student.
10. Once we have completed execution of nested loop, we have total score of a student in sum. On line 16 we print this score. When current next iteration of outer loop beings, sum will get reset to 0 (line 12). Hence we have to either print sum before we reset it to 0 or save the value at some other location.

Practice Questions : -
8. Trace control flow of above example.
9. Enhance the above example to print average marks of each student in addition to total marks.
10. Enhance the program further to print class average marks in each subject.

Like a two dimensional array can be imagined as an array of one dimensional arrays, similarly a three dimensional array can be imagined as an array of two dimensional arrays, a four dimensional array can be imagined as an array of three dimensional arrays and so on.

An n-dimensional array can be declared by placing n square brackets with respective dimension size after the array name. For example, declaration of a three-dimensional and a four-dimensional array is illustrated below.

```
int three_dim[5][3][7];
int four_dim[2][5][3][7];
```

Initializing arrays to zero at the time of definition is a good programming practice. We can initialize all elements of a multidimensional array to same value by enclosing that value in a pair of curly braces. For example,

```
/* Initializes all elements to 0 */
int three_dim[5][3][7] = { 0 };

/* Initializes all elements to 3.14 */
float three_dim[5][3][7] = { 3.14 };
```


Pointers

A pointer variable, or simply a pointer, is a variable that stores a memory address.

Consider an integer variable var holding value 9. Then a pointer to var can be visualized as shown below.

Variable Name	Address
ptr	20
var	32

00	04	08	12	16	20	24
					32	

28	32	36	40	44	48	52
	9					

56	60	64	68	72	76	80

As shown in the symbol table, ptr is a variable stored at memory address 20. As we can see from the memory diagram, value stored at memory address 20 is 32 – the address of variable var. Since ptr stores address of var, ptr is a pointer to var.

Declaring a Pointer

A pointer variable is declared by prefixing "*" to the name of the variable. Here is an example,

```
int *ptr;
```

This statement declares a variable called ptr that points to an integer.

Each pointer declaration is for a pointer to a specified data type. For example:

```
char *char_ptr; //Pointer to char
double *dbl_ptr; //Pointer to double
```

You can initialize a pointer using the assignment operator, for example

```c
int *ptr1 = NULL;
```

NULL is a special value, 0. It is illegal to dereference a null pointer. Initializing pointers to NULL makes it easy to test if pointers have proper variable addresses at the time of their use. This is illustrated by skeleton code below.

```c
if(NULL == ptr1) {
    /* Invalid address. Handle error */
} else {
    /* Normal processing goes here */
}
```

One of the hardest programming errors to debug is a dangling pointer, i.e. a pointer that points to some random memory address that may or may not be a valid address. What this means is, in cases when it points to a valid address, program may overwrite data at that location leading to unpredictable consequences; and in case it points to an invalid address, program will crash. In other words, observed program behaviour would be different every time program is run. This makes it hard to isolate and fix the problem.

As a good programming practice, you should always initialize your pointers. If a pointer is no longer required in your program, clear out its address to NULL. If such pointer is mistakenly used after clearing out, program will crash. A consistent NULL pointer crash is much easier to locate and fix as compared to a dangling pointer.

Similar to regular variables, we can declare multiple pointers in the same declaration statement. For example,

```c
int *a = NULL, *b = NULL, *c = NULL;
```

Above statement defines three pointers to int: a, b, and c, and initialises all three to NULL. Note that * is included with each variable name.

          feedback@thebookofc.com

```c
int *a = NULL, b = 10;
```

Above statement declares an `int` pointer a and an `int` b. Note that b is not a pointer variable.

Practice Questions : -
1. Which of the following are valid pointer declarations.
   ```c
   a.  int *Int;
   b.  int *float = NULL;
   c.  char *cptr = NULL;
   ```
2. Which of the following statements are true
   a. A pointer to `float` can store a `float` value.
   b. A pointer is a variable that holds address of another variable.
   c. It is possible to declare an `int` and a pointer to `int` as part of same declaration statement.
   d. It is possible to declare an `float` and a pointer to `double` as part of same declaration statement.

Using Pointers

Remember the "address of" operator (&) that we have been using in `scanf` statements? We can use the same operator to assign "address of" a variable to a pointer. Here is an example.

```c
int var = 9;
int *ptr = &var;
```

Here, we are assigning address of `var` to pointer `ptr`.

If you want to access the value stored in `var` using its pointer ptr, you can use "value at address" operator * which returns the value stored at the address held in the pointer.

```c
printf("ptr points to value %d\n", *ptr);
```

Above statement will print the value stored at address held in ptr. Revisiting our example memory layout, we can see that ptr holds address 32 and at address 32 value 9 is stored. Hence above statement will print, `ptr points to value 9`.

Variable Name	Address
ptr	20
var	32

00	04	08	12	16	20	24
					32	

28	32	36	40	44	48	52
	9					

56	60	64	68	72	76	80

This operation of accessing value at the address stored in a pointer using the * operator is called dereferencing a pointer.

Practice Questions : -
3. What will be printed by code snippet shown below

```c
int var1=7, var2=10;
int *ptr1=&var1, *ptr2=&var2;

printf("var1 = %d var2 = %d\n",*ptr1,*ptr2);
```
4. What will be printed by code snippet shown below.

```c
int var1=7, var2=10;
int *ptr = NULL;

ptr = &var1;
var2 += *ptr;

ptr = &var2;
var1 += *ptr;

printf("var1 = %d var2 = %d\n", var1, var2);
```

Passing Pointers as Arguments

Like regular variables, pointers too can be passed as arguments to functions. Let's consider an example.

           feedback@thebookofc.com

```
01: #include <stdio.h>

02: int add(int *a, int *b);

03: int main (int argc, char * argv[]) {
04:     int var1=7, var2=10, sum=0;
05:     int *ptr1 = &var1, *ptr2 = &var2;

06:     sum = add(ptr1, ptr2);
07:     printf("%d + %d = %d\n", var1, var2, sum);
08:     return 0;
09: }

10: int add(int *a, int *b) {
11:     return(*a + *b);
12: }
```

Line 02 declares function **add** with two integer pointer parameters.

Let's trace control flow of this program.

1. Execution beings with function **main**, line 03. On line 4, we define
    integer variables **var1**, **var2**, and **sum**; and assign them values 7,
    10 and 0 respectively.
2. On line 05, we define two integer pointers, **ptr1** and **ptr2** and
    assign them address of **var1** and **var2** respectively. Below is what
    symbol table and memory may look at this point.

Variable Name	Address
var1	12
var2	16
sum	20
ptr1	24
ptr2	28

00	04	08	12	16	20	24
			7	10	0	12

28	32	36	40	44	48	52
16						

56	60	64	68	72	76	80

Note **ptr1** (address 24) holds value 12 which is address of **var1**
and **ptr2** (address 28) holds value 16 which is address of **var2**.

3. On line 06, is function call to **add**. The call has two arguments,
    ptr1 and **ptr2**. As we had learned earlier, when we call a

function, the called function receives a copy of each argument. Addresses 12 and 16 held in `ptr1` and `ptr2` respectively, get copied over to a and b as control jumps to function add, line 10.

4. Note that variables a and b in add hold address of variables `var1` and `var2` defined in main. While names `var1` and `var2` are not visible inside add, they are still accessible via their address. Recall from our scope discussion earlier that `var1` and `var2` have not gone out of scope, they are simply not visible as variable names in function add. Hence, when we dereference pointers a and b, we get values stored in `var1` and `var2`.

5. On line 11, *a (value at address 12) evaluates to 7 and *b (value at address 16) evaluates to 10. We return their sum, 17. Control jumps back to line 06.

6. Returned value, 17, is assigned to variable sum.

7. Control advances to line 07. Message `7 + 10 = 17` is printed on the console.

8. Control advances to line 08. `main` returns 0 and program terminates.

Practice Questions : -

5. What will be the output of following program.

```c
#include <stdio.h>

int silly_function(int *, int *);

int main (int argc, char* argv[]) {
    int num1=11, num2=13;
    num1 = silly_function(&num1, &num2);
    printf("%d %d\n",num1, num2);
    return 0;
}

int silly_function(int *p1, int *p2){
    int num1=3, num2=5;
    num1 += *p1;
    num2 -= *p2;
    return num1+num2;
}
```

6. Extend the above program to write an integer calculator for operations add, subtract, multiply, and divide. Each operation should be implemented as a separate function. All values should be passed to functions using pointers.

     feedback@thebookofc.com

Call By Address

In our above example of passing pointers as arguments, function `add` we accessed the same variable instances, `var1` and `var2` that were declared in `main`.

Since we passed address of these variables to `add`, the called function was able to access the same memory locations that were referred by variables `var1` and `var2` in `main`.

Passing address as arguments to called function is referred to as "call by address". Contrast this with "call by value", that we had learned earlier, where a copy of variables was passed to the called function and hence called function could not modify the variables in calling function .

A direct consequence of passing address is that called function can modify the value of the original variable. Consider the below variation of our add example.

```c
#include <stdio.h>
int double_and_add(int *a, int *b);

int main (int argc, char * argv[]) {
    int var1=7, var2=10, sum=0;
    int *ptr1 = &var1, *ptr2 = &var2;

    sum = double_and_add(ptr1, ptr2);
    printf("%d + %d = %d\n", var1, var2, sum);
    return 0;
}

int double_and_add(int *a, int *b) {
    /*Following statements double the values contained in
original variables declared in main function */
    *a = *a * 2;
    /* Pointer dereference operator has higher precedence
than multiplication operator. Hence *a * 2 is processed
as ((*a)*2) */
    *b = *b * 2;

    return(*a + *b);
}
```

Since we are passing by address, called function `double_and_add` accesses the variables declared in `main` function using their address and doubles their values.

Notice that the `printf` statement in `main` function will print values of `var1` and `var2` as 14 and 20 respectively after the call to double_and_add.

Some texts also call this method of passing arguments as call by pointer or call by reference. Call by reference has a different meaning in C++. However, in context of C programming, these terms are often used interchangeably.

Practice Questions : -

7. Which of the following statements are true.
    a. A function cannot have some of its parameters passed by value and others passed by reference.
    b. Called function can modify the value of variables defined in calling function if those variables have been passed by value to the called function.
    c. Size of pointer to `double` > size of pointer to `char`.
8. Write a program to print size of pointer to double and pointer to char.
9. Write a function to swap two integers using pointers.
10. Write a function that takes an `int` pointer as parameter and updates the value at that location to next highest perfect square. For example, if parameter was pointer to value 17 then function should update it to 25.

Output Parameters

The ability of called functions to update variables defined in calling function provides us a very powerful way to obtain results from called function – output parameters.

An output parameter is simply a parameter that is updated by the called function with the result of the computations. In many real world applications, the return value is used to indicate status of

          feedback@thebookofc.com

operation (success/failure/failure code) while actual result is passed back using an output parameter. Here is an example.

```c
#include <stdio.h>

int area_and_circumference(float radius, float *area,
float *circumference);

int main (int argc, char * argv[]) {
    float radius = 3.1;
    float area = 0, circumference = 0;
    int status = -1;

    status = area_and_circumference(radius, &area,
&circumference);

    if (status>0) {
        printf ("area=%f circumference=%f\n", area,
circumference);
    } else {
        printf("Error computing area and
circumference\n");
    }

int area_and_circumference(float radius, float *area,
float *circumference) {
    if (radius < 0) {
        return 0;
    }
    *area = 3.14 * radius * radius;
    *circumference = 3.14 * 2 * radius;
    return 1;
}
```

In the above example, values of area and circumference are updated in the respective output parameters and the function returns the status of its execution.

You can also have a parameter that provides an input value to the function as well as gets updated to contain output value. Such a parameter is called "input output parameter".

Practice Questions : -
11. Trace control flow of above example of output parameters.

12. Write a function that takes an `int` n as parameter, returns sum of first n natural numbers, and provides square of n as output parameter.

Scope Revisited

When we learned about scope of variables, we learned that variables are visible within the statement block in which they were defined. In most of our examples we defined variables at the beginning of a function and that meant variables were visible throughout the function.

However, in the examples in preceding section, we were able to access variables outside the functions in which they were defined. Let's review our understanding of scope one more time to make sure we understand why this is valid access.

The scope of a variable begins from its definition statement and ends with the closing brace of the same block in which it was declared. As long as control has not reached end of block, the variable is in scope. What that means is, variable name still refers to a valid memory location that holds the value that was last stored in it.

Consequently, between the definition and end of statement block, any pointer to this variable will be pointing to actual in-scope variable. Such a pointer passed to another function will provide access to in-scope variable from a different function.

We encourage you to re-read the examples in the preceding section to validate this understanding. All pointer access from other functions occurred after the variable was defined and before control exited the statement block that defined the variable.

An attempt to dereference a pointer to an out of scope variable will lead to dangling pointer problem that we mentioned earlier in this chapter. We shall see an example of dangling pointer problem in the next section.

     feedback@thebookofc.com

Returning Pointers

You can return a pointer exactly like you would return a regular variable. The return type of the function should be appropriate pointer type. Here is an example.

```c
int * max(int *a, int *b) {
    if(*a > *b) {
        return a;
    } else if (*b > *a) {
        return b;
    } else {
        return NULL;
    }
}
```

Function `max` takes two integer pointers as argument and returns a pointer to larger integer. In case both integers are equal, `NULL` is returned.

Let's examine one more example, a variant of `add` function.

```c
int * add(int a, int b) {
    int result = a+b;
    return &result;
}
```

Note that `result` is a local variable of function **add**. That means `result` will go out of scope as soon as **add** returns. However, **add** is returning address of `result`.

What would happen if the calling function gets address of variable `result` and `result` is out of scope? This is a dangling pointer access and results are undefined - program might crash or it may provide some random value.

We should never return pointer to a local variable. Local variables go out of scope as soon as function returns. Consequently, when control reaches calling function, the pointer is pointing to an out of scope variable.

13. Which of the following statements are true.
   a. An output parameter is declared in called function.
   b. An output parameter can return address of a variable local to called function.

14. What will be the output of below program.

```c
#include <stdio.h>

int accumulator(int var1, int* var2){
    *var2 += var1;
    return(var1+*var2);
}

int main (int argc, char *argv[]) {
    int var1 = 10, var2 = 20, var3 = 30, result = 0;

    result=accumulator(var1,&var2);
    result=accumulator(var2,&var3);

    printf("%d %d %d %d\n",var1, var2, var3, result);
}
```

Passing Arrays to Functions

We have already learned what an array looks like in memory.

An enhanced illustration of our **age** array with address of each element is shown below.

age					
Value	5	8	7	2	15
Address	20	24	28	32	36

Note that all elements of an array are stored at contiguous memory locations.

Now let's see what happens when we pass an array as an argument to a function.

When we declare a function with an array parameter, system expects to receive ONLY the beginning address (also called base address) of

          feedback@thebookofc.com

the array and it allocates just enough memory for the parameter to hold a memory address. An array parameter of a function is essentially a pointer.

So if we were to pass **age** array to a function, the called function would receive just the address 20. This raises a very important question: how does called function access array elements?

Remember that an array holds elements of the same data type. So if system knows the amount of memory taken by a single element of that data type, system can compute the location of any element in the array by simply adding appropriate offset to the base address of the array.

The formula for computing address of ith index in an array would simply be b + (i * s), where
b is the base address of the array
i is the index to be accessed
s is the size of each element of the given data type

address of arr[i] = b + (i * s)

For accessing the full array, we would need one more piece of information – number of elements in the array. Without this information we have no way of knowing what is the valid range of values for i. Now you know why we had to pass number of elements as argument to the function.

To summarize, when we pass an array as an argument to a function, the called function receives only the base address. Called function accesses various elements in the array by computing the offset of accessed index from the base address.

Passing address to a function has an important implication for programming – since the passed address is of the same variable that was declared in calling function, the called function access the original values – there is no separate copy being used in called function. What this means is that if called function were to update the values held in the array, calling function would see the updated values upon function call return.

It also follows that size of array in the function in which it was defined would be size of memory taken up by whole array. However, if it is passed to a function as parameter then size of receiving parameter in the called function would be size of a pointer.

Let's validate our understanding with an example.

```
01: #include <stdio.h>

02: void double_array (int arr[], int size) {
03:     for (int i=0; i<size; i++) {
04:         arr[i] *= 2;
05:     }
06:     printf("size of array in function = %lu\n",
sizeof(arr));
07: }

08: int main(int argc, char * argv[]) {
09:     int age[5] = { 5, 8, 7, 2, 15 };

10:     for (int i=0; i<5; i++) {
11:         printf ("age[%d] = %d\n", i,age[i]);
12:     }
13:     printf("size of array in main = %lu\n",
sizeof(age));

14:     double_array(age, 5);

15:     for (int i=0; i<5; i++) {
16:         printf ("age[%d] = %d\n", i,age[i]);
17:     }
18:     return 0;
19: }
```

Let's trace control flow of the above example.

1. Execution begin with main, line 08.
2. Line 09, we define an array of 5 integers and initialise it.
3. Lines 10-12 is a **for** loop that prints the array that we just defined. You should see following output on your console.
   ```
   age[0] = 5
   ```

          feedback@thebookofc.com

age[1] = 8
age[2] = 7
age[3] = 2
age[4] = 15

4. Line 13, we print the size of array. Here you should see actual memory taken up by all the elements of array bring printed. Message `size of array in main = 20` gets printed on the console. Note that you may see a different value depending on size of `int` on your system. However, value would be 5 times the size of `int` on your system.

5. Line 14 is call to function `double_array`. Control jumps to line 02. Parameter `arr` is effectively a pointer that is assigned base address of array **age** and parameter **size** is assigned value 5.

6. Lines 03-05 is `for` loop that is simply multiplying every array element by 2 and assigning it back to same array location. Since `arr` had base address of original array, this loop is making modifications to the original array, not a copy. Hence, when we print this array in `main`, we should see doubled values.

7. Line 06 prints the size of parameter `arr` in `double_array`. Since `arr` is simply a pointer, we should see size of pointer printed on the console. Message `size of array in function = 8` is printed on the console. You may see a different value depending on your system implementation. However, value would be same as size of pointer to `int` on your system.

8. Execution of `double_array` is complete. Control returns to calling function - `main`, line 15.

9. Line 15-17 is a `for` loop that prints elements of array **age** in `main`. Since call to `double_array` had doubled the original values, we should see modified values printed on the console.
    age[0] = 10
    age[1] = 16
    age[2] = 14
    age[3] = 4
    age[4] = 30

10. Line 18, `main` returns 0 and program terminates.

Practice Questions : -
15. What is the output of program given below.

```c
#include<stdio.h>

void size_test(int b[]);

int main (int argc, char * argv[]) {
    int a = 5;
    int b[15] = { 0 } ;
    size_test(b);
    printf ("%lu %lu\n",sizeof(a), sizeof(b));
    return 0;
}

void size_test(int b[]) {
    printf("%lu\n",sizeof(b));
}
```

Array Bounds Checking

As we have learned, C processes an array by calculating the right memory location given the base address, index, and element size. C does not check if the accessed index is within the bounds of valid indices for that array, i.e. if you were to access an invalid index in your code, your program will compile fine. However, it may crash at run time due to illegal memory access.

C does not perform any array bounds checking. As a programmer it is your responsibility to make sure that any array access in your program falls within the range of valid locations.

Pointer Arithmetic and Arrays

It is possible to add and subtract integers from pointer variables.

When we add 1 to a pointer, system updates the address to point to the next element of its data type, i.e. new address will be old address + sizeof(data type).

When we subtract 1 from a pointer, system updates the address to point to the previous element of its data type, i.e. new address will be old address - sizeof(data type).

     feedback@thebookofc.com

A typical application of pointer arithmetic is using a pointer to iterate an array.

As we have already learned, arrays are passed by address, i.e. when we pass an array as an argument to a function, what we are really passing as argument is a pointer to the first element of the array.

We can iterate this array in the called function using pointer arithmetic. Here is an example.

```c
01: #include <stdio.h>

02: int add_array(int arr[], int size);

03: int main (int argc, char* argv[]) {
04:     int arr[4] = { 9, 3, 7, 12 };
05:     int sum=0;

06:     sum = add_array(arr, 4);

07:     printf("Sum of array is %d\n",sum);
08: }

09: int add_array(int * arr, int size) {
10:     int result = 0, i = 0;

11:     for(i=0; i<size; i++) {
12:         result = result + *(arr + i);
13:     }
14:     return result;
15: }
```

Notice the statement on line 12.

arr holds address of first element of array that was passed to add_array. Adding i to arr gives us address of ith element of the array. The loop on line 11 iterates through all elements of arr by incrementing i from 0 to size-1.

Key thing to remember is that incrementing a pointer makes it point to next element of the data type that pointer is pointing to.

Adding 1 to an `int` pointer will increment the address by `sizeof(int)`.

Adding 1 to a `long long` pointer will increment the address by `sizeof(long long)`.

Similar result could have also been achieved using increment operator directly on pointer variable. Here is same example rewritten using increment operator

```c
#include <stdio.h>

int add_array(int arr[], int size);

int main (int argc, char* argv[]) {
    int arr[4] = { 9, 3, 7, 12 };
    int sum=0;

    sum = add_array(arr, 4);

    printf("Sum of array is %d\n",sum);
}

int add_array(int * arr, int size) {
    int result = 0, i = 0;

    for(i=0; i<size; arr++,i++) {
        result += *arr;
    }
    return result;
}
```

Pointer subtraction and decrement work in similar fashion. Decrementing a pointer makes it point to previous element of same data type. Subtracting a number n from a pointer makes it point to nth previous element of same data type.

Multiplication and division of memory addresses does not make sense and hence are not supported.

Practice Questions : -
16. Trace control flow of above example.
17. Which of the following statements are true.

            feedback@thebookofc.com

a. Passing an array to a function is equivalent to passing address of first element of the array.

b. Incrementing a pointer pointing to an array element makes the pointer point to next array element.

c. Increment a pointer increases the address stored in pointer by 1.

18. Modify add_array function above to use a countdown loop.

19. Assume `sizeof(double)` is 8, `sizeof(* double)` is 4, `dptr` is a pointer to `double` with address 80 stored in it. What will be the address in `dptr` after `dptr++` is executed.

20. Assume `sizeof(double)` is 8, `sizeof(* double)` is 4, `darr` is a array of `double` with 100 elements. If `darr` is passed to a function in which `sizeof(darr)` is printed, what will be the printed value?

21. Write a function that takes temperature readings of last n days as parameter and provides back average temperature of last seven days and last n days. If n<7 then average of last seven days should be given as zero.

Typecasting Pointers

Like regular data types, pointers too can be typecast; a pointer to `int` can be typecast to pointer to `char` or `double` or any other type. Since all pointers are addresses, there are no compatibility issues – all pointers can hold any address.

The impact of typecasting a pointer is visible when that pointer is dereferenced. Let's assume size of `int` is 4 bytes and size of `double` is 8 bytes. If a pointer to `int` and a pointer to `double` have same address then, dereferencing the `int` pointer will lead to reading 4 bytes at that address and interpreting those bytes as an integer value while dereferencing the `double` pointer will lead to reading 8 bytes at the same address and interpreting those bytes as a `double` value.

Let's see an example.

```
01: #include <stdio.h>

02: int main (int argc, char* argv[]) {
03:     double pi = 22/7.0;
04:     double *dptr = &pi;
05:     int *iptr = NULL;

06:     iptr = (int *)dptr;
07:     printf("%d %f\n",*iptr, *dptr);
08:     return 0;
09: }
```

Line 06 typecasts a **double** pointer to an **int** pointer. Syntax for typecasting pointer remains the same, target type enclosed in parentheses preceding the value, variable, or expression to be typecast.

Above example will print two values, first one is integer interpretation of **double** value **pi** and second one is **double** value of **pi**.

Continuing our assumption of 8 byte **double** and 4 byte **int**, let's analyse impact of typecasting an **int** pointer to a **double** pointer.

```
int count=10;
dptr = (double *) &count;
*dptr = 15;
```

When we declared variable **count**, system allocated 4 bytes for it. If we use **dptr** to access **count**, we access 8 bytes while we were supposed to access only 4. Assignment by dereferencing **dptr** above will write 8 bytes to memory.

In other words, we would be writing data to memory locations that we should not be accessing. We will end up either violating memory access or writing to memory locations that will unintentionally change behaviour of other parts of the program.

There are relatively few scenarios that require pointer typecasting. We should avoid using it to the extent possible. Wherever needed, always document the purpose of using pointer typecasting in comments. This would help you as well as anyone else reading the code to understand the intent behind using pointer typecasting.

Practice Questions : -

22. Which of the following statements are true.
   a. We can typecast pointers of any type to any other type.
   b. Given `iptr` as pointer to `int` and `dptr` as pointer to `double` and typecast
      ```
      dptr = (double *)iptr;
      ```
      Assuming 4 byte `int` and 8 byte `double`, incrementing `dptr` will increase the address in `dptr` by 8.

Pointer to Pointer

A pointer can hold any address, including that of another pointer. Such a variable would be a pointer to pointer. Consider following code snippet.

```
int count = 10;
int *ptr = &count;
int **pptr = &ptr;
```

Here `pptr` is a pointer to pointer to `int`. It holds address of `ptr` which is a pointer to `int`.

Let's examine how these may be stored in memory.

00	04	08	12	16	20	24
					44	

28	32	36	40	44	48	52
	20			10		

56	60	64	68	72	76	80

Variable	Address
count	44
ptr	20
pptr	32

As seen from the symbol table, variable **count** is stored at address 44. We can see value 10 stored at memory address 44.

ptr is stored at memory address 20. It holds address of count. We can see 44 stored at memory address 20.

pptr is stored at memory address 32. It holds address of ptr. We can see 20 stored at memory address 32.

Let's see an example of accessing a value using pointer to pointer.

```c
#include <stdio.h>

int main (int argc, char* argv[]) {
    int count = 10;
    int *ptr = &count;
    int ** pptr = &ptr;

    printf("Integer Value %d %d %d\n",count,*ptr,**pptr);
}
```

Dereferencing pptr would give us value stored at pointed location, i.e. address stored in ptr. Dereferencing it again would give us the value at the address stored at the pointed location.

C does not limit you to a pointer to pointer. You can define a pointer to pointer to pointer to pointer to any number of levels as you may need.

A pointer is sometimes also referred to as indirection and a pointer to pointer is referred to as double indirection. Higher levels of indirection are often called multiple indirection.

Practice Questions : -
23. Which of the following statements are true.
    a. An int ** can only hold address of an int*.
    b. An int ** can only hold address of any integer type.
    c. A pointer to pointer cannot be incremented or decremented.
24. If a pointer to pointer is incremented then what would location would it point to?
25. What will be the output of below program.

         feedback@thebookofc.com

```c
#include <stdio.h>

void mixer(int **pptr){
    int ** temp = pptr;
    for(int i=0; i<2; i++) {
        **temp += **(temp+1);
        temp++;
    }
}

int main (int argc, char *argv[]) {
    int *ptrarr[3] = {0};
    int a=10,b=20,c=30;

    ptrarr[0]=&a;
    ptrarr[1]=&b;
    ptrarr[2]=&c;

    mixer(ptrarr);
    for(int i=0; i<3; i++) {
        printf("%d\n",*ptrarr[i]);
    }
}
```

Strings

A ***string*** is a sequence of `char` terminated by the special character '\0' stored in contiguous memory locations.

In other words, string is an array of `char` terminated by character '\0'. '\0' is also called null byte.

You can declare a string as shown below

```
char first_name[30];
```

In this example, string `first_name` can have maximum length of 29 characters – we need one character space for storing terminating character '\0'.

System reads a string from memory by starting at the base address of the array and reading consecutive memory locations until it encounters '\0'. If '\0' is missing, system will keep on reading memory locations beyond the array limits until it either finds a '\0' or system forcibly terminates the program for invalid memory access. This is called array overrun and often results in a program crash.

Since C does not perform any array bounds checks, as programmer, you are responsible for making sure that your program does not access any out of bound memory location.

Initializing Strings

To initialize a string, you can use either one of the array initialization forms that we had learned earlier. These are also illustrated in the examples below.

```
char first_name[30] = {'p','r','a','g','a','t','i','\0'};

char first_name[30] = {'\0'};

char first_name[] = {'p','r','a','g','a','t','i','\0'};
```

          feedback@thebookofc.com

The first initialization statement initializes `first_name` to string "pragati". Note that you do not need all 30 characters to initialize the array since string processing would terminate at '\0'.

Second initialization statement sets all characters in `first_name` to '\0'.

In the third initialization statement, system automatically determines the array size to be 8 characters and creates an array of 8 char elements for variable `first_name`. Also `first_name` is initialized to string "pragati".

Reading Strings from User

We can use `scanf` with `%s` format specifier to read an input string from user. Following example illustrates this method.

```c
#include <stdio.h>

int main (int argc, char * argv[]) {
    char first_name[32] = { '\0' };

    printf("What is your first name? : ");
    scanf("%s",first_name);

    printf("Hello %s, nice to meet you\n",first_name);
}
```

Note that `%s` format specifier is also used for printing a string using `printf`.

Two important things to note about using `scanf` for reading strings:
1. `scanf` will read input until the first whitespace (a space, a tab, or a newline character). Hence, in its current form if we were to enter "abc def" as input, only abc would be read into `first_name`. String terminating '\0' is automatically appended to the input string.
2. Since there is no check on number of characters read, a user can enter a very long input string - much larger than our array - thereby crashing our program. In this case, `scanf` will keep

on reading and storing input until it hits first whitespace character. When `scanf` writes beyond array boundary, it can lead to undesirable changes to memory content of our program or cause the system to terminate the program for unauthorised memory access.

Below is a version of the same program using with these issues handled using `scanf` format string.

```c
#include <stdio.h>

int main (int argc, char * argv[]) {
    char first_name[32] = { '\0' };

    printf("What is your first name? : ");
    scanf("%31[^\n]s",first_name);

    printf("Hello %s, nice to meet you\n",first_name);
}
```

Notice the format string `%31[^\n]s` used in the above program. There are two elements introduced between `%` and `s`. The number 31 tells the system to read at most 31 characters as part of this input operation. The `[^\n]` bit tells the system to read input until a newline character (`\n`) is encountered. Both of these together instruct the system to read input until `\n` is encountered up to maximum of 31 characters. Reading terminates as soon as either one of those conditions is met.

`scanf` automatically places a '\0' at the end of input string.

If user input is more than 31 characters, it will read only the first 31 characters and leave the remaining in the input queue. If you have subsequent `scanf` statements, those `scanf` statements will consume the remaining input characters – an unintended side effect of using `scanf`.

Practice Questions : -
1. Write a program that reads a string of maximum 30 characters from the user and prints it in uppercase. Note that non-alphabet characters should be printed as is.

              feedback@thebookofc.com

String Literals

A string literal is defined by simply enclosing it in double quotes. For example,

```
char * message = "I am on my way to master strings";
```

Note that `char` pointer `message` is a variable. It can be overwritten with address of another string. However, the string literal itself is read-only. In other words,

```
message  = a_different_address; //Is perfectly legal
message[0] = 'U'; //Won't work
```

Depending on implementation, all literals are stored in text or data segment. All literals are read-only.

String Library Functions

C library provides large number of string manipulation functions that you can invoke directly in your program. These function declarations can be found in header file `string.h`. Let's learn the behaviour of few of these strings related library functions and implement our own versions of those functions.

strlen

`strlen` library function returns the size of a string excluding the terminating null byte. Signature of `strlen` function is shown below.

```
size_t strlen(const char *s);
```

`size_t` is the true standard defined data type of `sizeof` operator result. It is defined in header file `stddef.h`. C requires data type `size_t` to be an unsigned integer type. Implementation is free to choose any unsigned integer type such as `unsigned int` or `unsigned long`.

Note the parameter data type - `const char *s`. This is pointer to a `const` string, i.e. a string whose contents cannot be modified, such as string literal we saw above. If we were to pass a `char *` argument, system would automatically typecast it to a `const char *` when it is passed to `strlen`.

Let's see an example of how we can use `strlen`.

```c
#include <stdio.h>
#include <string.h>

int main (int argc, char * argv[]) {
    char message[256] = { 0 };

    printf("Enter message of the day: ");
    scanf("%255[^\n]s",message);

    printf("Your message is %lu characters long\n",
strlen(message));
    return 0;
}
```

Note the call to `strlen` from `printf` statement. This would lead to a call to `strlen` before call to `printf`. Value returned by `strlen` shall be passed to `printf` function for printing.

Practice Questions : -
2. What shall be the output of above program for input "It's a great time to become a good programmer".

Let's see how we can implement our own version of `strlen` function from what we have learned so far. A `strlen` implementation can be boiled down to iterating through the whole string, i.e. a loop, and counting the number of characters. We have learned that a string terminates with '\0' - our loop termination condition. This can be represented as a flowchart shown below.

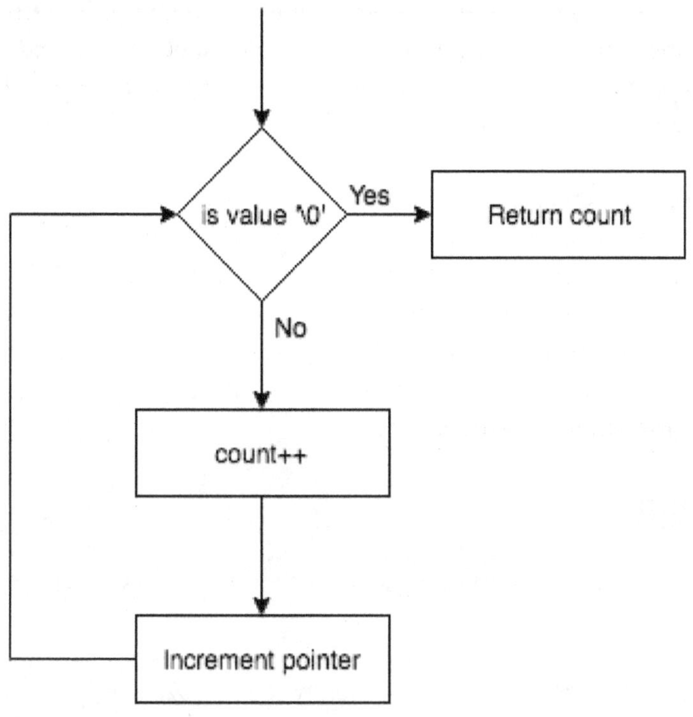

Let's see the source code.

```
01: unsigned long my_strlen (const char * ptr) {
02:     int length = 0;

03:     if (NULL == ptr) {
04:         return length;
05:     }

06:     for (;*ptr!='\0';ptr++) {
07:         length++;
08:     }
09:     return length;
10: }
```

On line 03, we check if pointer that was passed to the function was NULL. It is a good programming practice that helps us ensure that we do not crash in case someone called our function with NULL input value.

Line 06 is a `for` loop that traverses the whole string. Note that `ptr` contains a copy of the address of the original string. Hence we can increment `ptr` and not worry about maintaining starting address of the string.

Practice Questions : -

3. Write a program that reads a string of maximum 30 characters from the user and prints the number of small case alphabets in the string entered by the user.
4. Write a program that reads a string of maximum 30 characters from the user and prints the number of non-alphabet characters in the string entered by the user.

strcmp

`strcmp` library function compares two strings. Its signature is shown below.

```
int strcmp(const char *s1, const char *s2);
```

If string `s1` and `s2` are equal, `strcmp` returns 0.
If string `s1` is greater than string `s2`, `strcmp` returns a value greater than 0.
If string `s1` is lesser than string `s2`, `strcmp` returns a value lesser than 0.

What do we mean by a string being greater than another string? This is character by character comparison where the string with first higher value character encoding would be considered to be greater.

Let's see the source code of a sample implementation.

```
01: int my_strcmp (const char * s1, const char * s2) {
02:     while ( (*s1 != '\0') && (*s1 == *s2) ) {
03:         s1++;
04:         s2++;
05:     }
06:     return (*s1-*s2);
07: }
```

                feedback@thebookofc.com

5.   Draw a flowchart for implementation of strcmp function.

Let's examine the loop condition closely.

We want the comparison to start with first character of both strings and continue until either at least one string ends or we encounter first unequal character.

`*s1 == *s2` checks for equality. It would evaluate to false when we encounter first unequal character while comparing the strings.

`*s1 != '\0'` would evaluate to false if we reach end of string s1 before we find any unequal characters. This could happen in two cases:

1.   s1 was shorter in length as compared to s2, or
2.   s1 and s2 were equal and we reached end of both strings together.

But what if string s2 was shorter and we reach end of s2 before we reach end of s1? In that case our previous equality condition would evaluate to false and we would exit the loop.

The `return` statement on line 06 returns the magnitude of difference between the first unequal characters. If both strings were equal, we would have reached end of string on both and would return 0. Else we would return the difference between first unequal character. This meets the return specification of the `strcmp` function which required us to return any value greater than 0 if s1 was greater than s2 and any value less than 0 if s1 was lesser than s2.

Practice Questions : -
6.   Add NULL error checks to above implementation.
7.   Trace control flow of above function for arguments
     a.   "C" and "Champion"
     b.   "Top programmer" and "Top programmer"

strncmp

strncmp behaves exactly like strcmp except that it compares at most first n characters of both strings. Its signature is shown below.

```
int strncmp(const char *s1, const char *s2, size_t n);
```

If first n characters of string s1 and s2 are equal, strncmp returns 0.
If first n characters of string s1 are greater than first n characters of string s2, strncmp returns a value greater than 0.
If first n characters of string s1 are lesser than first n characters of string s2, strncmp returns a value lesser than 0.

In case s1 or s2 or both have less than n characters then comparison would stop at end of shorter string.

Practice Questions : -
8. Draw a flowchart for function strncmp.
9. Implement function strncmp.

strcpy

strcpy library function copies the contents of one string into another. Its signature is shown below.

```
char *strcpy(char *dest, const char *src);
```

strcpy copies contents of src over to dest, including the terminating null byte. strcpy assumes that dest has enough memory to copy over contents from src. It does not perform any memory validations.

strcpy returns pointer to destination string, i.e. dest.

Let's see a sample implementation.

```c
char * my_strcpy (char *dest, const char *src) {
    int i = 0;
    /*Loop terminates when end of src string is reached*/
    for (i=0; *src != '\0'; i++) {
        dest[i] = src[i];
    }
    dest[i] = '\0'; /*Terminate dest with null byte*/
    return dest;
}
```

Code is a simple `for` loop iterating through `src` that copies every char from `src` to `dest`. Code is self-explanatory.

Practice Questions : -
10. Implement strcpy using while loop.

strncpy

`strncpy` library function behaves similar to `strcpy`. It copies at most first n characters from `src` to `dest`. Its signature is shown below.

```c
char *strncpy(char *dest, const char *src, size_t n);
```

Similar to `strcpy`, it also returns `dest`.

Note that:
1. If terminating null byte is not a part of first n characters then `dest` will not be null terminated.
2. If `src` string was shorter than n bytes, then null bytes are appended to `dest` until all n characters have been written.

Practice Questions : -
11. Draw a flowchart for function `strncpy`.
12. Implement function `strncpy`.

C library offers many more string related functions. It is beyond the scope of this book to discuss all library functions. Our objective of discussion in this chapter was to help demonstrate the utility of pointers and how we can leverage them to solve various problems. It also helps to get a peek into powerful C library and start using some of these functions at this stage.

We encourage you to explore additional library functions as you progress towards solving more complex programming problems. We shall explore few more string library function when we discuss dynamic memory allocation.

const char * Vs char const * Vs char * const

We have encountered `const char *` as data type while discussing string functions above. Let's learn how to read data types like these correctly so that we do not confuse a pointer to a constant with a constant pointer.

`const` keyword applies to the element on its left. If there is nothing on its left, then it applies to the element on its right.

Let's apply this rule to the three variants.

1. `const char *` - there is nothing to the left of `const`, hence it applies to element on its right - `char`. Hence this data type is a pointer to `const char`, i.e. address held in the pointer is that of a constant char while address held in pointer itself is modifiable.
2. `char const *` - `char` is on the left of `const`. Hence `const` will apply to `char`. Hence this data type is also a pointer to `const char`. It is identical to the first variant.
3. `char * const` - `*` is on the left of `const`. This is a constant pointer to a `char`, i.e. value held in this pointer cannot be modified while the `char` that it is pointing to may be modifiable.

Let's validate our learning with a simple program.

  feedback@thebookofc.com

```c
01: #include <stdio.h>

02: int main (int argc, char * argv[]) {
03:     char message[] = "I am getting smarter at C'ing
things";
04:     char alternate_message[] = "may be";

05:     const char *var1 = message + 24;
06:     char const *var2 = message + 30;
07:     char * const var3 = message;

08:     printf("%s\n%s\n%s\n",var1, var2, var3);

09:     //var1[1] = ',';
10:     //var2[1] = ',';
11:     //var3[1] = ',';

12:     printf("%s\n%s\n%s\n",var1, var2, var3);

13:     //var1 = alternate_message;
14:     //var2 = alternate_message;
15:     //var3 = alternate_message;

16:     printf("%s\n%s\n%s\n",var1, var2, var3);
17:     return 0;
18: }
```

Run the above program. You should see following output.

```
C'ing things
things
I am getting smarter at C'ing things
C'ing things
things
I am getting smarter at C'ing things
C'ing things
things
I am getting smarter at C'ing things
```

Start by uncommenting line 09. As we had learned, var1 is a pointer to a const char. If we try to modify a const via it's pointer, we should get an error. Indeed, compiler flags out the error and compilation fails.

Revert back to original program and uncomment line 10. Since `var1` and `var2` declarations are same, we should see same error as before.

Revert back to original program and uncomment line 11. Since `var3` is a constant pointer to a `char`, we should be able to update contents of memory being pointed to by `var3`. Indeed, program compiles and runs successfully. You should see following output.

```
C'ing things
things
I am getting smarter at C'ing things
C'ing things
things
I,am getting smarter at C'ing things
C'ing things
things
I,am getting smarter at C'ing things
```

Notice the comma after I in print statements after line 11.

Revert back to original program and uncomment line 13. Since `var1` is not a constant pointer, we should be able to update address stored in it. Program should compile and run successfully. You should see following output.

```
C'ing things
things
I am getting smarter at C'ing things
C'ing things
things
I am getting smarter at C'ing things
may be
things
I am getting smarter at C'ing things
```

Notice that `var1` printed may be at line 16.

Revert back to original program and uncomment line 14. As before, we should be able to update address stored in `var2` and following output should be printed.

 feedback@thebookofc.com

```
C'ing things
things
I am getting smarter at C'ing things
C'ing things
things
I am getting smarter at C'ing things
C'ing things
may be
I am getting smarter at C'ing things
```

Revert back to original program and uncomment line 15. Since var3 is a constant pointer, system should prevent us from updating a constant. As expected, compiling the program leads to a compilation error.

Revisiting main function

Let's revisit signature of main function and make sure we understand it well.

```
int main (int argc, char * argv[]);
```

We already understand that its return type is int first parameter argc is of data type int. What is the data type of second parameter argv?

argv is an array of char pointers, i.e. an array of strings.

When we launch a program we can pass parameters to main. For example, for a program for finding max of three integers, we can pass three integers as parameters to main. From a command line, this might appear as

```
compute_max 10 20 30
```

Where compute_max is the name of the executable to be launched.

argv is a NULL terminated array of strings where first element is name of the executable and remaining elements are the parameters in the order in which they were supplied on the command line. argc is the highest valid index in array argv. argv[argc] is always NULL.

In above example, value of **argc** would be 4 and **argv** would contain 5 elements. At index 0 will be pointer to executable name "compute_max". At index 1 will be pointer to string "10". At index 2 will be pointer to string "20". At index 3 will be pointer to string "30". At index 4 would be value NULL.

If you launch your program without any arguments, **argc** would be 1 and the index 0 element in **argv** would be the name of executable that was launched.

Below program prints the information stored in **argc** and **argv**. Try launching it with different arguments. You can learn how to launch a program from command line at the URL below.
http://thebookofc.com/environment/launching-from-command-line/

```c
#include <stdio.h>

int main (int argc, char * argv[]) {
    printf ("%d\n",argc);

    for (int i=0; i<argc; i++){
        printf("%s\n", argv[i]);
    }
}
```

We have already learned that passing an array is equivalent to passing base address of an array. Hence, following signature of main is equivalent to the signature we have been using thus far.

```c
int main (int argc, char ** argv)
```

     feedback@thebookofc.com

Dynamic Memory Allocation

So far we have used variables and arrays whose size was known to us upfront - at the time of writing the program. What about instances where we do not know how much memory we would need. For example, if we wanted to write a program to compute average score of a course but we do not know how many students would take the course at the time of writing our program.

Dynamic memory allocation refers to our ability to allocate required amount of memory at run time instead of compile time. In other words, we determine size of memory required and allocate it on the fly, when our program is being executed, and not at the time of writing our program.

malloc & free

`malloc` is a C library function that helps us request and get required amount of memory at run time. Signature of `malloc` function is shown below.

```
void * malloc(size_t size);
```

`malloc` takes one argument, the number of bytes that are to be allocated. Notice the argument data type - `size_t`. We have already learned that `size_t` is an unsigned integer type.

`malloc` returns a pointer to `void`, or simply a void pointer. A void pointer can be typecast to pointer of any data type. We will discuss void pointer in detail later in this chapter.

If call to `malloc` succeeds, then return value is the address of the first byte of a contiguous chunk of `size` bytes. If call fails and `malloc` is unable to allocate requested amount of memory, it would return `NULL`.

We should always check for success of our call to `malloc` before we attempt to use the allocated memory. For example,

```c
memptr = malloc (bytes_required);
if (memptr != NULL) {
      /* Allocation successful. */
} else {
      /* Memory allocation failed. */
}
```

Contiguously allocated memory chunk is in effect an array – only difference being that with arrays their size is determined at compile time while with dynamically allocated memory we determine the size at execution time.

After we are done using memory assigned using `malloc`, we have to call another library function `free` to release this memory. Signature of `free` function is shown below.

```c
void free(void *ptr);
```

Parameter to `free` is the same address that was returned by call to `malloc`. `free` does not return anything and hence its return type is `void`.

Let's see an example of computing average score for a class whose number of students is not known upfront.

```c
01: #include <stdio.h>
02: #include <stdlib.h>
03: int compute_average(int *);
04: void read_score(int *);
05: int main (int argc, char * argv[]) {
06:     int *score = NULL, num_students = 0;
07:     double average = 0;
08:     printf ("Please enter number of students: ");
09:     scanf("%d",&num_students);
10:     if (num_students <= 0) {
11:         printf ("Invalid input. Terminating\n");
12:         return 1;
13:     }
14:     score = malloc (sizeof(int) * num_students);
15:     if (NULL == score) {
16:         printf ("Failed to allocate memory.
Terminating\n");
17:         return 1;
18:     }
```

                feedback@thebookofc.com

```
19:        read_score(score);
20:        average = compute_average(score);
21:        printf("Average score of the class is %f\n",
average);
22:        free(score);
23:        return 0;
24: }
```

Things to note:

1. `malloc` and `free` are declared in `stdlib.h` header file. We have to include it in our program – line 02.

2. Input error checking on line 10. It helps us make sure that we pass a valid positive value to `malloc` call on line 14. Such error checking helps make our code more robust.

3. Argument to `malloc` on line 14 is size of memory chunk required to store one integer for each student. This chunk can be accessed as an `int` array with indices from 0 to `num_students` - 1. The benefit of using `sizeof` operator in size computation is that now our program will compute the right amount of memory irrespective of whether it is running on a system with 2 byte `int` or 4 byte `int` or any size `int`.

4. On line 15, we check if our call to `malloc` was successful. If `malloc` returned `NULL`, then we cannot proceed with reading and processing input as we do not have any memory to store data.

5. Note that return value from `main` function in error conditions is 1. Now we are getting to a point where return value from `main` indicates success (zero) or failure (non-zero) of the program. You can learn about how to examine this return value at http://thebookofc.com/environment/checking-return-value-of-a-program/. Further, you can return different values for different error conditions to make return value even more meaningful.

6. On line 22, after we have finished our computations, we call `free` and give up the memory we had requested.

Practice Questions : -

1. Which of the following statements are true.

    a. Every call to `malloc` may not be successful.

b. Memory allocated by `malloc` is automatically initialised to all zeros.
c. If we do not check return value of `malloc`, our program could crash.
d. We should not call `malloc` again until we have called **free** for already allocated memory.
e. Dynamically allocated memory can be accessed like an array.

2. Implement functions `compute_average` and `read_score` in the above example.

Life of Dynamically Allocated Memory

Dynamically allocated memory comes into existence as soon as it is successfully allocated and remains in existence until **free** is called. If we were to allocate memory inside a function and return from that function without calling **free**, then that memory would still remain accessible as long as we have the address to access it.

Below is an example where we read two input strings and find their longest common prefix. Since we do not know in advance how long the common prefix is, we allocate memory for storing the prefix after we have determined its length. Let's examine the source code.

```
01: #include <stdio.h>
02: #include <stdlib.h>

/* This function returns longest common prefix of strings
ptr1 and ptr2 */

03: char * longest_prefix (char *ptr1, char *ptr2) {

04:     char *itr1 = NULL, *itr2 = NULL, *prefix = NULL;
05:     int count = 0;
06:     itr1 = ptr1;
07:     itr2 = ptr2;
```

        feedback@thebookofc.com

```c
08:      while (*itr1 != '\0' && *itr2 != '\0') {
         /*Loop terminates as soon as end of any one
string is reached*/
09:          if (*itr1 != *itr2) {
         /* strings do not match beyond this point */
10:             break;
         }
11:          count++; /* char matched, increment count*/
12:          itr1++;  /* point itr1 to next char in ptr1*/
13:          itr2++;  /* point itr2 to next char in ptr2*/
14:      }
15:      prefix = malloc (count + 1); /* count holds
number of matched characters in prefix. Allocate 1 extra
byte for terminating '\0' */

16:      if (NULL == prefix) {
17:          printf ("Error allocating memory");
18:          return NULL;
19:      }
         /* Prepare result to return */
20:      for (int i=0; i<count; i++){
21:          prefix[i] = ptr1[i];
22:      }
23:      prefix[count] = '\0';
24:      return prefix;
25: }

26: int main (int argc, char * argv[]) {
27:      char str1[32] = { 0 }, str2[32] = { 0 };
28:      char *result = NULL;

29:      printf("Enter string 1, under 31 characters: ");
30:      scanf("%31s", str1);
31:      printf("Enter string 2:, under 31 characters ");
32:      scanf("%31s", str2);

33:      result = longest_prefix (str1, str2);
34:      if (result) {
35:          printf("longest common prefix is \"%s\"\n",
result);
36:          free (result);
37:      } else {
38:          printf("Error in finding common prefix\n");
39:          return 1;
40:      }
41:      return 0;
42: }
```

3. Trace control flow of above example for user input "Pragati" and "Priyanka".

We strongly recommend that you complete the above exercise before continuing with discussion below.

Let's quickly review some salient points of this example.

1. Memory is allocated in function `longest_prefix` on line 16. However, it is freed in function `main`, line 37, after all required processing is done.
2. Allocated memory is accessible between allocation and freeing. As long as a function has pointer to the chunk of memory between these two statements, it can be legally accessed.
3. Note the difference between accessibility of memory and scope of pointer to that memory. Variable `prefix` in function `longest_prefix` is a local pointer variable. Its scope is limited to `longest_prefix` function. We cannot access variable `prefix` from `main`. However, the memory chunk that it is pointing to is accessible until corresponding call to `free`. We access this memory in `main` using the pointer value returned by `longest_prefix` function.
4. In keeping with our good programming practice, we check return value of `malloc` to make sure it has succeeded, line 17. This helps us avoid an invalid memory access and a crash.
5. We also protect against buffer overrun by limiting `scanf` statement to the capacity of the input array, at line 31 and line 33.
6. Double quote is delimiter for `printf` format string. If we have to print double quote character itself, then we can do so by prepending it (escaping it) with a backslash - line 36.

Recall our discussion on various memory segments of a C program. Dynamically allocated memory is stored in the heap segment.

What happens if we lose the address of allocated memory without freeing it? In such case, this memory would be inaccessible to us

                    feedback@thebookofc.com

(since we do not have its address anymore) and it would not be claimed by the system as we have not called **free**. This scenario is called a memory leak.

A memory leak can be very troublesome over a period of time. With time, it would start showing up as increased memory consumption by our program. Eventually it could exhaust the entire memory available to our program and cause out of memory errors. We should always ensure that we free up all dynamically allocated memory after we have finished using it.

Practice Questions : -
4. Which of the following statements are true.
    a. When address returned by `malloc` is assigned to a pointer, that pointer remains in scope until **free** is called.
    b. Memory leak is a condition in which system's memory has been exhausted.
    c. As a good programming practice, **free** should be called towards end of the program just before `return`.
5. In case of memory leak which segment of memory can be exhausted?
6. Assuming 4 byte `int` and 4 byte pointer, what will be printed by below code snippet?
    ```c
    int *ptr = malloc(10*sizeof(int));
    printf("%lu\n",sizeof(ptr));
    ```

Void Pointer

A **void** pointer is a special pointer that does not have any associated data type. A void pointer can hold address to any data, i.e. a **void** pointer can be assigned value of any other pointer. Also, a **void** pointer can be typecast to any other data type pointer.

Since there is no associated data type, system cannot dereference a **void** pointer. If we wish to access the value stored at **void** pointer, we first have to typecast it to appropriate data type.

As with all other in-built data types, **void** is a C language keyword.

Recall that incrementing or decrementing a pointer makes it point to next or previous element of the same data type. Since there is no data type associated with a **void** pointer, system cannot determine address of next or previous element. Hence, C standard disallows pointer arithmetic on a **void** pointer.

That been said, some compilers do allow pointer arithmetic on **void** pointers. However, given the obvious portability issues and readability issues that stem from such usage, we strongly recommend avoiding such operations.

Practice Questions : -
7.   Which of the following statements are true.
     a.   Return type of `malloc` is **void** *.
     b.   Pointer of any data type can be cast to a **void** *.
     c.   A **void** * can be cast to pointer of any data type.

Initializing Dynamically Allocated Memory

When `malloc` returns pointer to memory, that memory is uninitialized and is likely to have garbage values. There are three ways to initialize dynamically allocated memory.
     1.   Loop through all elements and set them to desired value.
     2.   Use `memset` library function to set all bytes to same value.
     3.   Use `calloc` instead of `malloc`.

memset

`memset` sets entire specified memory to a constant byte. Signature of `memset` function is shown below.

```
void *memset(void *s, int c, size_t n);
```

s is the pointer to beginning of memory to be set to specified value, n is the number of bytes to be initialized and c is the value to which all bytes have to be initialized. `memset` returns pointer to memory that was set – same value as s.

`memset` is declared in `string.h` file.

                    feedback@thebookofc.com

Typical invocation of memset is shown below.

```
arr = malloc(100*sizeof(int));
if (arr) {
    memset(arr, 0, 100*sizeof(int));
}
```

calloc

Signature of calloc library function is shown below.

```
void *calloc(size_t n_memb, size_t s);
```

calloc allocates memory for n_memb elements of size s and sets all allocated bytes to 0. If memory allocation succeeds, then like malloc, it returns pointer to allocated memory, else it returns NULL. calloc is declared in stdlib.h file.

An example invocation of calloc is shown below.

```
arr = calloc(100, sizeof(int));
```

This statement is equivalent to memset example we saw above. They both assign memory for storing 100 int and set them to 0.

What if we need to resize the memory that we have allocated, for example for average score in a course, we have a midsession admission at a later date. To learn how to handle resizing of dynamically allocated memory, visit this link. http://thebookofc.com/pointers/resizing-memory-using-realloc/

User Defined Data Types

C allows a programmer to define new data types, called User Defined Data Types, that are tailor made to their requirement. In simple words, using one or more built-in datatypes and other user defined datatypes, a programmer can define a new data type suitable for their use case. We will learn more about user defined datatypes in this chapter. There are three kinds of user defined data types in C – structure, union and enumeration.

Structure

Consider a problem statement, where we want to print a student's report card. The information required to be printed is name, class, subject wise marks and percentage. If we were to write this program using the built-in data types, a new variable will be declared for each attribute of the student – name, class, marks in each subject, percentage etc. With this approach, the number of variables will increase as the number of attributes increase.

What if we want to write a program to print the report card of entire class? One way to achieve that will be to declare arrays for each attribute we want to print. E.g. an array of strings to store names, an array of `int` for each subject to store marks and so on. Additionally, we will have to maintain relation between these arrays of attributes. For example, for the name stored at index i in array of names, the percentage is stored at same index in another array, marks in a third array and so on. This makes the code complex to read and maintain.

It would be convenient if we had a single data type that could store all the attributes of a student. This is what structure datatype does. In simple words, a structure is a collection of variables of any datatype, bundled in a single datatype. A `struct` (short for structure) for the above use case is shown below.

     feedback@thebookofc.com

```
struct student_info_datatype {
    char* name;
    char* class;
    int english_marks;
    int maths_marks;
    int science_marks;
    float percentage;
};
```

Let's pay attention to the syntax of above declaration. The keyword struct at the beginning of declaration identifies that what follows is a structure datatype. Next, we associate a name with this datatype. In this example the name is student_info_datatype. This name is used to distinguish one struct datatype from another.

Next, within braces we specify the members of struct along with their datatypes. We can use any datatype, including arrays or another struct as a member in a struct datatype. The syntax of declaring a member in a struct is same as declaring a variable of that datatype – datatype followed by member name and ending with a semicolon.

Now that we have defined a new data type, how do we use it in our code?

First, we need to declare a variable of this newly defined datatype. This is similar to the variable declarations we have learned so far - datatype followed by the variable name. For struct, the struct keyword along with the name of the struct is the datatype. For example,

```
struct student_info_type student_info;
```

In above example struct student_info_type is the datatype, and student_info is the name of variable of that datatype.

A variable of type struct can also be initialized during declaration. We can rewrite the above declaration with initialization as shown below.

```c
struct student_info_type alex = {"Alex", "VIII", 80, 85,
84, 83.0};
```

The initialization values for all members are enclosed in a pair of braces and are separated by a comma. Note that the initialization of members is done in the order in which they are defined in **struct** datatype. In above example, member `name` is initialized to "Alex", `class` to "VIII" and so on. Also, each member has to be initialized in accordance with its individual datatype. For example, the first member, `name`, is a pointer to `char`, hence it should be initialized with a string and so on.

Another method to initialize a **struct** during declaration is

```c
struct student_info_type student_info = {0};
```

This declaration initializes all members of the **struct** to value 0 or NULL. Similar to other variables, it is recommended to initialize variables of datatype **struct** at the time of declaration.

Now that we have declared a variable of type **struct**, we need a way to access it's members in order to read or assign values to them. To access the members, syntax is

```c
<variable name of type struct>.<member name>
```

Here, the dot (.), also known as access operator, is used to access individual members of a **struct** (or **union**, as we will see later). For example, members of above **struct** can be accessed using following syntax.

```c
student_info.name = "Student Name";
student_info.class = "VII";
student_info.english_marks = 80;
```

Every member of a **struct** can be used as a variable of their corresponding datatype. E.g. `student_info.english_marks` can be used as any other integer in a C program. Following are perfectly valid statements using the members of above **struct**.

                    feedback@thebookofc.com

```
student_info.percentage = (student_info.english_marks +
                student_info.maths_marks +
                student_info.science_marks)/3.0;
```

```
printf ("%s marks in science are %d\n", student_info.name,
student_info.science_marks);
```

```
if (strcmp(student_info.class, "VII") == 0)
```

Let us put together our learning about **struct** and write a complete program. The following program takes radius of a circle as input, and calculates and prints the area and parameter of the circle. It uses a **struct** to represent a circle.

We define a new **struct** datatype named **circle_type**. It consists of one member of type **int** – **radius**, and two members of type **float** – **perimeter** and **area**.

```
01: #include <stdio.h>

02: struct circle_type {
03:     int radius;
04:     float perimeter;
05:     float area;
06: };

07: #define PI 3.14

08: int main (int argc, char* argv[]) {
09:     struct circle_type circle = {0};

10:     printf ("Enter the radius of circle:");
11:     scanf("%d", &circle.radius);
12:     circle.perimeter = 2*PI*circle.radius;
13:     circle.area = PI*circle.radius*circle.radius;
14:     printf ("Area of circle is %f\nPerimeter of circle
is %f\n", circle.area, circle.perimeter);
15:     return 0;
16: }
```

Note following important aspects of above program.

1. At line 11, user input is taken and stored in corresponding member - `circle.radius`. Note that we have used the format specifier for `int` datatype to read the value.

2. At line 12, perimeter of circle is calculated and stored in `circle.perimeter`. The assignment operator is used to assign value to the member `perimeter`. Similar arithmetic operation is done at line 13 to calculate and assign the value to `float` member `circle.area`

3. To print the `float` members at line 14, we have used format specifier for `float` datatype.

Practice Questions : -
1. Which of the following statements are true.
   a. A variable of type `struct` is automatically initialized to 0 by the system.
   b. A `struct` helps us to keep related data elements together in a single entity.
   c. `struct` is a native data type.

Behind the Scenes

Members of a `struct` are stored in contiguous memory locations in the order in which they are defined in `struct` datatype. The symbol table for our example in previous section may appear as shown below.

circle	14

The variable `circle` is stored at memory location 14. The memory location at address 14 may appear as below.

14	18	22
circle.radius	circle.perimeter	circle.area

Unlike built-in datatypes, `struct` is a bundle of members of different datatypes. Each member will have an individual memory location. However since they are represented by a single variable name, symbol table will have only one entry. The size of `struct circle` shall be 12, assuming four bytes each for its three members. In other

     feedback@thebookofc.com

words, size of `struct` in this example is equal to sum of size of its elements.

However this may not be always true. There could be cases where size of `struct` is larger than sum of size of its elements. Let us see one such example.

```c
#include <stdio.h>

struct example_type {
    int one;
    char two;
    int three;
};
int main (int argc, char *argv[]) {
    printf ("size of int :%u\n", sizeof (int));
    printf ("size of structure :%u\n", sizeof (struct example_type));
}
```

Output of this program is shown below. You may see different values depending on size of data types on your system.

```
size of int :4
size of structure :12
```

If size of `int` is 4, then size of `struct` should have been 4+1+4 = 9. But it is 12. Why? The answer lies in data alignment of the system. In simple words, data alignment of a system determines the address at which a variable can be stored.

For example, if system is 4 byte aligned then all variables are stored at an address divisible by 4. Assume that first element of the `struct` - one starts at address location 04. Since it is an integer of size 4, it takes up bytes from 04 to 07. Next available memory address is 08. Since 08 is divisible by 4, it is a valid address to store a variable, and hence element two is stored at address 08. two is a char and occupies only one byte at address 08. Now the next available memory address is 09, but since it is not 4 byte aligned address, system will look for next 4 byte aligned address which is 12. Hence, next element will be stored at address 12. These unused bytes (three bytes from address 09 to 11) are called padding. If we represent memory for above `struct` pictorially, it appears as shown below.

<pre>
04   08 09   12
+----------------------+------+-----------+----------+
| one | two | <padding> | three |
+----------------------+------+-----------+----------+
</pre>

Please note that a system may be 4, 8, 16 byte aligned, hence size of padding, and subsequently size of `struct` may vary. Above values were chosen only for illustration.

To summarise, the size of a `struct` is greater than or equal to the sum of size of its members.

Practice Questions : -

2. If the system is 8 byte aligned and size of `int` is 4, what will be the size of `struct example_type` in above example? Also work out the memory map for same.

Union

Like `struct`, `union` is also a collection of variables of any datatype, bundled in a single datatype. However, unlike `struct` the members of a `union` share same memory space. `union` allows the use of same memory location to store data of different members at different times.

Let us begin with defining a new `union` data type.

```
union union_example {
    int count;
    float average;
    char name[100];
};
```

The syntax of defining a `union` datatype is similar to that of `struct`, the only difference being that the keyword `struct` is replaced by keyword `union`.

Unlike `struct`, `union` allocates just enough memory to store it's largest member. At any given time only one of the members of a union will have its value stored in a variable of type union. Let's understand this concept with an example using the union we just defined.

```c
01: #include<stdio.h>
02: union union_example {
03:     int count;
04:     float average;
05:     char name[100];
06: };
07: int main (int argc, char* argv[]) {
08:     union union_example example = {0};

09:     printf ("Value of count is %d\n",example.count);
10:     printf ("Value of average is %f\n",
example.average);

11:     example.count = 1103993242;
12:     printf ("Value of count after initializing count
is %d\n",example.count);
13:     printf ("Value of average after initializing count
is %f\n",example.average);

14:     example.average = 2.4;
15:     printf ("Value of count after initializing average
is %d\n",example.count);
16:     printf ("Value of average after initializing
average is %f\n",example.average);

17:     return 0;
18: }
```

At line 02, we have defined a new union datatype - union_example. It has three members, an int, a float and an array of char.

Let's trace control flow of the above program.

1. At line 08, we declare a variable of the newly defined datatype – example - and initialize it to 0.
2. At line 09 and 10, we print values of two members – count and average. As expected, values of both are printed as zero. We see following output on console.
   ```
   Value of count is 0
   Value of average is 0.000000
   ```

3. At line 11 we assign value `1103993242` to member `count`.
4. At line 12, we print the value of member `count`, and it is printed correctly. We see following output on console.
   ```
   Value of count after initializing count is
   1103993242
   ```
5. At line 13, we print the value of member `average`. We see following output on console.
   ```
   Value of average after initializing count is
   25.700001
   ```
   Note that though we didn't assign any value to `average`, the value printed is non-zero. Since `average` shares its memory with member `count`, the value that is printed is integer value `1103993242` interpreted as `float`.
6. At line 14, we assign value 2.4 to member `average`. Since all members share same memory space, this assignment overwrites the earlier assignment to member `count`.
7. At line 15, when we print the value of `count`, it prints different value from the value it was assigned at line 11. We see following output on console.
   ```
   Value of count after initializing average is
   1075419546
   ```
   This time it is `float` value 2.4 interpreted as `int`. As pointed out earlier, this is because members share same memory.
8. At line 16 value of `average` is printed correctly. We see following output on console.
   ```
   Value of average after initializing average is
   2.400000
   ```

To summarise, at any given time only one of the members of a `union` will have its value stored in a variable of `union` datatype. Accessing other members would simply interpret the value at that address as data type of member accessed.

A word of caution – if data type of argument and format specifier in `printf` statement do not match then behaviour is undefined. C does not impose any standard way for interpreting an `int` as a `float` or for interpreting any data type as any other type. Depending on your system you are likely to see different values from what we presented as output here.

     feedback@thebookofc.com

union can be initialized during declaration with syntax similar to
struct initialization. However, as we explained above, at any time
only one member of union has a relevant value. Hence initializer list
can have only one value, and first member of union gets initialized
by default. E.g. in above example, we can initialize example as shown
below.

```
union union_example example = {1};
```

This means the variable example is declared with a default value for
first member i.e. count as 1.

Since all members of a union share the same memory space, the
memory required by a union datatype is the size of the largest
member variable of union. For above example the size of union
union_example will be 100 i.e. size of biggest member variable -
name.

Assuming 4 byte int and 4 byte float, memory map for union in
above example can be represented as,

```
04        08                                                  103
+---------------------------------------------------------------+
| count    <unused>                                             |
| average  <unused>                                             |
| name                                                          |
+---------------------------------------------------------------+
```

The size of union is 100 bytes, starting at address 04. Member count
is of size 4 and hence occupies bytes 04 to 07. Bytes 08 to 103 remain
unused when we store count in this union. Same is the case for
member average. Member name is the largest of all, and it uses all
100 bytes when a value is assigned to it.

In short, the key difference between struct and union is that a
struct has separate memory for each of its member variable,
whereas member variables of a union share the same memory.
Hence assigning value to one member variable of struct doesn't
affect the value of another member. Whereas in case of union,
assigning value to one member can affect other members.

3. Which of the following statements are true.
    a. Size of a `struct` is always greater than sum of size of its members.
    b. A `struct` cannot have just one member.
    c. Size of a `union` is equal to size of largest element of the union.
4. Which of the following will have a larger size.

```
struct trains_s {
    int train_numbers[100];
};
union trains_u {
    int train_numbers[100];
};
```

Typedef

C allows programmers to define a new name or alias for any datatype, including native as well as user defined data types. This alias can then be used in C program to represent the corresponding datatype. Syntax to define a new alias is

```
typedef <data_type> <new alias>;
```

The declaration starts with the keyword `typedef`. It is followed by the datatype for which we want to create a new alias. And finally we specify the new alias. This new alias can be any name, that follows the rules of naming a variable. Let us see a few examples.

```
typedef int INT;
typedef char CHAR;
```

In above example, we have defined a new alias for the built-in datatypes. `INT` is a new alias for `int` and `CHAR` for `char`. We can now use both `int` and `INT` in our program. For example, following declarations are equivalent.

```
INT count = 0;
int count = 0;
```

                    feedback@thebookofc.com

Typically, **typedef** is used to define alias for user defined datatypes. For example, `circle struct` used earlier in this chapter can have an alias defined as shown below.

```
struct circle {
    int radius;
    float perimeter;
    float area;
};
typedef struct circle circle_t;
```

A new name `circle_t` is now available for `struct circle` datatype. Hence following two declarations are equivalent.

```
circle_t circle_instance;
struct circle circle_instance;
```

This makes the code more readable than before. As a naming convention, we will suffix aliases defined with typedef with suffix "_t".

Similarly we can define new alias for **union** datatype.

```
union student_score{
    unsigned int marks;
    float percentage;
};
typedef union student_score student_score_t;
```

A new alias `student_score_t` is now available for union student_score. Hence following two declarations are equivalent.

```
union student_score instance1;
student_score_t instance1;
```

Practice Questions : -
5. Identify which of these are valid typedef declarations.
    ```
    a) typedef unsigned short USHORT;
    b) typedef int[100] INTARRAY;
    c) typedef int char;
    ```

Arrays of Struct

Let's revisit the problem statement we described at the beginning of this chapter - printing the report card for a class of students.

We solved one part of the problem by clubbing all the required attributes of a student in one **struct**. Now let's solve to print the report card for all students of a class.

This requires us to define multiple instances of type **struct**. As we learned earlier in this book, arrays are ideal for defining storage of multiple elements of same data type. If we declare an array of a **struct**, we can store report card information of entire class in that array. Let us learn how to declare an array of **struct**.

```c
struct student_info  {
      char name[32];
      char class[16];
      int english_marks;
      int maths_marks;
      int science_marks;
      float percentage;
};
typedef struct student_info student_info_t;

student_info_t students[50];
```

To declare an array of **struct**, the syntax is same as declaring an array of native datatypes – datatype followed by variable name for array, and finally the size of array specified in square brackets. Here variable **students** is an array of **struct student_info_t** of size 50.

Each element of this array is an individual **struct** and can be accessed using its array index. Individual members of **struct** can then be accessed using access operator. Syntax to access the member name of **struct** at index **i** of array would be **students[i].name**

Let us write a program to understand usage of array of **struct**. Below is source code of a program that takes student's name, class and

            feedback@thebookofc.com

marks as input for a class of size 50 and calculates and prints their percentage.

```c
01: #include <stdio.h>

02: struct student_info {
03:     char name[32];
04:     char class[16];
05:     int english_marks;
06:     int maths_marks;
07:     int science_marks;
08:     float percentage;
09: };
10: typedef struct student_info student_info_t;

11: #define NUM_STUDENTS 50

12: int main (int argc, char *argv[]) {
13:     student_info_t students[NUM_STUDENTS] = {0};

14:     for (int i = 0; i < NUM_STUDENTS; i++ ) {
15:         printf("Enter name of student %d: ", i + 1);
16:         scanf ("%s", &students[i].name);

17:         printf("Enter class of student %d: ", i + 1);
18:         scanf ("%s", &students[i].class);

19:         printf("Enter Marks in English for student
%d: ", i + 1);
20:         scanf ("%d", &students[i].english_marks);

21:         printf("Enter Marks in Maths for student %d:
", i + 1);
22:         scanf ("%d", &students[i].maths_marks);

23:         printf("Enter Marks in science for student
%d: ", i + 1);
24:         scanf ("%d", &students[i].science_marks);

25:         students[i].percentage =
(students[i].english_marks + students[i].maths_marks +
students[i].science_marks ) / 3.0;
26:         printf ("Percentage of Student %d : %f \n", i
+ 1, students[i].percentage);
27:     }
28:     return 0;
29: }
```

6. Trace control flow of above program for first two iterations.

Pointers to User Defined Datatypes

Like built in data types, it is possible to have pointers to user defined datatypes too. The syntax to declare pointer variable remains the same – data type followed by variable name prefixed with "*". Let us declare a pointer to the datatype `student_info_t` defined in previous section.

```
student_info_t *student_info_ptr;
```

In this example, `student_info_ptr` is a variable that points to datatype `student_info_t`.

Remember the "address of" operator? We can use it to assign "address of" a **struct** variable to a **struct** pointer variable. For example,

```
student_info_t student_info_var = {0};
student_info_t *student_info_ptr = &student_info_var;
```

Unlike built-in datatypes, user defined datatypes have members that we want to access. To access a member using a **struct** pointer, arrow operator (->) is used instead of access operator(.). The members for pointer variable `student_info_ptr` can be accessed as shown below.

```
student_info_ptr->english_marks = 78;
strcpy(student_info_ptr->name, "Alex");
```

A pointer to **union** datatype can also be declared and used in same fashion. For example, a pointer to **union** datatype `student_score` defined in **typedef** section can be declared as shown below.

```
student_score_t *student_score_ptr;
```

          feedback@thebookofc.com

Similar to struct pointer, the members of a union pointer can be accessed using the arrow (->) operator.

```
student_score_ptr->marks = 86;
```

Similar to in-built datatype arrays, pointers can also be incremented to iterate through arrays of structs and unions.

Struct as Function Argument

Like built-in data types, user defined datatypes can be passed as arguments to functions – passed by value as well as passed by reference. Consider an example to find difference between two clock time values, where time is measured in hour, minute and seconds.

We define a struct to represent clock time.

```
struct _time{
        int hour;
        int minutes;
        int seconds;
};
typedef struct _time time_t;
```

Next, let's define the function to take start time and end time as arguments, and calculate the time elapsed between start time and end time. The function can be defined as following.

```
01: int diff_in_time (time_t start, time_t end, time_t
*diff) {

02:     if (start.seconds > end.seconds) {
03:         end.minutes--;
04:         end.seconds += 60;
05:     }
06:     diff->seconds = end.seconds - start.seconds;

07:     if (start.minutes > end.minutes) {
08:         end.minutes += 60;
09:         end.hour--;
10:     }
11:     diff->minutes = end.minutes - start.minutes;
```

```
12:        if (start.hour > end.hour) {
13:             printf ("ERROR: start time is greater than
end time\n");
14:             return -1;
15:        }
16:     diff->hour = end.hour - start.hour;
17:     return 0;
18: }
```

The function has three arguments. Two of them – start and end - are of type time_t and passed by value to the function. As we have learned earlier, a copy of these variables is passed to the called function. One argument – diff – is of type pointer to time_t and is passed by reference to the function. Hence any change to struct referenced by this variable will reflect in the calling function.

The logic of function is straight forward. Notice that:
1. At line 06, we subtract start.seconds from end.seconds. The difference in seconds of start and end is stored in seconds of diff. Note that since diff is a pointer variable, hence we have used "->" to access members via a pointer.
2. Similarly difference in minutes and hour is calculated and stored in corresponding members of variable diff using arrow (->) operator.

Let us write a program to take user input for start and end time, and use the above function to calculate the difference and print it.

```
01:int main (int argc, char *argv[]) {

02:     int ret = 0;
03:     time_t start_time={0}, end_time={0}, diff={0};

04:     printf("Enter start time in hh:mm:ss: ");
05:     scanf("%d:%d:%d", &start_time.hour,
&start_time.minutes, &start_time.seconds);

06:     printf("Enter end time in hh:mm:ss: ");
07:     scanf("%d:%d:%d", &end_time.hour,
&end_time.minutes, &end_time.seconds);

08:     ret = diff_in_time (start_time, end_time, &diff);
```

                  feedback@thebookofc.com

```
09:     if (0 == ret){
10:         printf("%d:%d:%d\n", diff.hour, diff.minutes,
diff.seconds);
11:     }
12:     return 0;
13: }
```

In above program, after taking user inputs for start and end time, we pass them to function `diff_in_time` by value at line 08. The variable `diff` however is passed by reference. Note that the syntax to pass a variable by reference is same as built-in datatypes – using the "address of" (&) operator

Dynamic Memory Allocation

Remember our example where we printed the percentage marks for a class of 50 students? What if the size of class is not known in advance? As we have learned, dynamic memory allocation is the answer to such situations.

As with in-built data types, we can allocate memory for user defined data types at run time using `malloc` library function. To determine the size of memory to be allocated, we use `sizeof` operator. For example, to allocate memory for class of n students we can use.

```
student_info_ptr = malloc(sizeof(student_info_t)*n);
```

As before, we should always check for return value of `malloc`. If memory was allocated successfully then we can continue processing the allocated chunk as array of n elements of type `student_info_t`.

Enumeration

Enumeration data type is a list of members that have an integer value assigned to each one of them. The definition of enumeration data type starts with the keyword `enum`, followed by name for this enumeration datatype. Within braces, list of members is specified separated by a comma. Consider the following example.

```c
enum shapes_type {
    rectangle,
    square,
    triangle,
    line
};
```

The above examples defines an **enum** datatype, called **shapes_type**, with four members. All the members of **enum** datatype are integer constants. Let us write a program to validate the same.

```c
#include <stdio.h>

enum shapes_type {
        rectangle, square, triangle, line
};
int main(int argc, char** argv) {
    enum shapes_type shape;
    shape = triangle ;
    printf ("Shape is %d\n", shape);
    return 0;
}
```

The output of above program is

```
Shape is 2
```

The above output shows that the value of member **triangle** is integer value 2.

How are these integer values defined? By default, the first member of an **enum** datatype is assigned a value 0, and subsequent members have incremental values - 1, 2, 3 and so on. In above example, following will be the constant values associated with members:

```
Rectangle = 0
Square = 1
Triangle = 2
Line = 3
```

Few additional things to note about **enum** datatype:
1. If we want specific integer values to be associated with member names, we can assign them as shown below.

```c
enum shapes_type {
        rectangle = 1, square, triangle, line
};
```
Uninitialized members will have incremental values as before - `square` will have value 2, `triangle` 3 and so on. Note that only integer values can be used for initializing an `enum` member.

2. Two members can be assigned same values.
```c
enum shapes_type {
        rectangle = 1, square = 1, triangle, line
};
```
As with previous examples, uninitialized members are assigned the value of previous member plus 1 - `triangle` = 2, `line` = 3.

3. The enum list can have multiple initializations. It need not be in increasing order. For example,
```c
enum colors_type {
        red = 10,
        green,
        blue = 1,
        violet = 5,
        indigo,
        yellow
};
```
Again, the uninitialized members are assigned the value of previous member plus 1.

4. enum constants can be used without declaring a variable of enum datatype. For example, we can use the following `printf` with our `enum colors_type`.

```c
printf("red is %d, blue is %d, violet is %d", red, blue, violet);
```

Output of above `printf` statement is

```
red is 10, blue is 1, violet is 5
```

Hence any `enum` is effectively a list of named integer constants. For this reason, all `enum` constants must be unique in their scope. For example following example will fail during compilation.

```
enum base_colors {
        red, blue, green
};
enum derived_colors{
        red, violet, indigo
};
```

5. Like `struct` and `union`, an alias for `enum` datatype can be defined using `typedef`. The syntax remains the same:

```
typedef enum colors_type colors_type_t;
```

Practice Questions : -

7. Which of the following statements are true.
    a. An `enum` value can be used without defining a variable of enum of type.
    b. `typedef` cannot be used with an `enum` to define new type alias.
    c. Be default, first `enum` member is assigned value 1.
    d. An `enum` cannot be used as a function parameter.

Nested User Defined Datatypes

By definition, members of a `struct` or `union` can be of any datatype. So far we have seen examples where members were of built-in datatypes. A `struct` or `union` datatype can also have another user defined datatype as its member.

Let us extend our report card example to add the address of students, having following attributes – House number, Area, city and pin code. We define a `struct` datatype for address, and then proceed to nesting it in our original datatype.

```
struct _address {
      unsigned short house_num;
      char area[64];
      char city[64];
      unsigned short pincode;
};
typedef struct _address address_t;
```

          feedback@thebookofc.com

This new datatype can now be added as a member in another `struct` like any other native datatype.

```
struct _student {
        char name[32];
        char class[16];
        address_t address;
        int english_marks;
        int maths_marks;
        int science_marks;
        float percentage;
};
typedef struct _student student_t;
```

In above example we added `address` as third member of the `struct` `_student`. Now that we have added this new member, we can access it like any other member of `struct`.

```
01: int main(int argc, char *argv[]){
02:     student_t student;
03:     student.address.house_num = 108;
04:     strcpy(student.address.area,"South Delhi");
05:     strcpy(student.address.city, "Delhi");
06:     student.address.pincode = 110077;
...
```

Few things to note:
1) To access the member `address`, syntax is same as accessing other datatypes as we had already explained, using the access operator - `student.address`.
2) Since `address` is also a `struct`, it's members are in turn accessed using the same syntax, by adding one more access operator - `student.address.<member name>`
3) The above examples shows one level of nesting. Datatypes can be nested to any level. The syntax to access the members is the same, using individual access operator for each level of nesting.

Let us consider another example where we have information about 100 cities. However, we have an integer city code for some of them and city name for others. One possible way to store this information is shown below.

```c
struct _city_info {
    enum city_code {CODE, NAME} code;
    union {
        int citycode;
        char cityname[64];
    } cityinfo;
} ;
#define NUM_OF_CITIES 100
typedef struct _city_info city_info_t;
city_info_t cities[NUM_OF_CITIES];
```

struct _city_info has two members:
1. code which is an enum. It can have two values *CODE, NAME*. This defines whether the value we have stored in union cityinfo is city code or city name.
2. union cityinfo, as the names indicate, it either stores the citycode (of type int) or cityname (of type char array).

Depending on the value of member code, member cityinfo will store the relevant information. Hence code will be the guiding field to access cityinfo members.

Finally we define an array, called cities, for storing NUM_OF_CITIES elements of datatype city_info_t to store information about multiple cities.

Let's write sample code to access the information stored in array cities and print the city code or name, whichever is stored.

```c
for (int i = 0; i < NUM_OF_CITIES; i++ ) {
    if (CODE == cities[i].code){
        printf ("Code for city %d is %d\n", i,
cities[i].cityinfo.citycode);
    }
    else if (NAME == cities[i].code) {
        printf ("Name for city %d is %s\n", i,
cities[i].cityinfo.cityname);
    }
    else {
        printf ("Invalid value for city\n");
    }
}
```

          feedback@thebookofc.com

Scope of User Defined Datatypes

In all examples in this chapter, we have defined new datatype in global scope. Hence they are accessible throughout the program. It is also possible to define a datatype inside a code block. In such case, datatype will available only inside that code block. For example,

```c
int func () {

    struct struct_name {
        int member1;
        char member2;
    };
    struct struct_name var1;
    .
    .
    .
}
```

In the above example, datatype struct struct_name is defined inside function func. Hence we can declare a variable of this datatype only inside func. If we try to declare a variable of type struct struct_name outside the function func, system will throw compilation error.

Like variables, we cannot define two datatypes with same name in same scope. However, it is possible to define another datatype with same name in nested scope. In such case when datatype is used, it refers to the innermost scope where that datatype is defined. Let us extend the above example to define struct_name in nested scopes.

```c
#include <stdio.h>
struct struct_name {
        int gmember1;
        char gmember2;
    };

int func () {

    struct struct_name {
        int member1;
        char member2;
    };
    struct struct_name var1;
```

```c
        .
        .
}

int main (int argc, char* argv[]) {
        .
        .
    struct struct_name var2;
        .
        .
}
```

In above example, in function `func`, variable `var1` will be of type `struct struct_name` defined in scope of `func`, as that is the definition in innermost scope. Thus `var1` will have members `member1` and `member2`.

In `main`, variable `var2` will be of type `struct struct_name` defined in global scope, and hence will have members `gmember1` and `gmember2`.

The scope of aliases defined using `typedef` follow same rules. If an alias is defined inside a block, then that alias can be used to declare variables only inside that block. We cannot define two aliases with same name in same scope. However it is possible to define same alias name in nested or different scopes. When an alias is used, the innermost alias is applicable.

A Few Notes

Variables of type `struct`, `union` and `enum` can also be declared along with datatype definitions as shown below.

```c
struct struct_type {
    int member1;
        .
        .
    char member;
} struct_var;
```

In above example, `struct_var` is declared as a variable of type `struct struct_type`.

We can also omit the datatype name - `struct_type` - to declare the variable in above example. Following is an equivalent declaration for variable `struct_var`.

```
struct {
    int member1;

    .
    .

    char member;
} struct_var;
```

As you can see that with this method, if we want to declare another variable of the datatype, we will need to type the entire `struct` definition again. This will make the code difficult to read and also error prone. Consider a case where we want to add a new member to the `struct`. We will have to add the new member to all variable declarations. Hence it is not advisable to declare variables using this syntax.

To define alias using `typdef` for `struct`, `union` or `enum`, following syntax works equally good.

```
typedef union union_name {
    int member1;

    .
    .

    int member2;
} alias_name;
```

In above example, `typedef` defines the new alias `alias_name` for type `union union_name`. Since we are giving a new alias in single declaration, `union_name` can be omitted to write the above `typdef` as following.

```
typedef union {
    int member1;

    .
    .

    int member2;
} alias_name;
```

8. Which of the following statements are true.
    a. A **union** cannot have an **enum** member.
    b. A **struct** can have a **union** member.
9. Write a program to
    a. Define a **struct** point, that represents a point in 2D space with its x and y coordinates.
    b. Define a **struct** square that stores 4 vertices of the square.
    c. Allow the user to print perimeter and area of the square.
10. Evolve above program to
    a. Define **enum** of shapes – circle, rectangle, square.
    b. Define a **union** to store details of appropriate shape: vertices for square and rectangle, centre and radius for circle.
    c. Print the area and perimeter of the shape entered.

                    feedback@thebookofc.com

Bit By Bit

One of the key advantages of C is that it gives you very high degree of control over your data and logic. You can access and modify any bit or byte of any data (except constants) in your program. C gives you complete control to architect your programs for any amount of performance and wizardry as you can imagine.

Part of that wizardry comes from ability to play around with individual bits - our focus for this chapter. Towards the end of the chapter we explore a real life use case where bitwise operations are useful.

Binary Notation

Before we get into manipulating bits, we need some basic understanding of what data looks like in bits. Let's begin with building up understanding of binary notation, how our integer data appears when converted to binary and stored in the memory.

The regular integers that we are used to dealing with are called base 10 or radix 10 numbers. A base 10 system has 10 distinct digits for representing numbers (0 to 9). Recall the place value notation we used in school for representing decimal numbers. E.g.

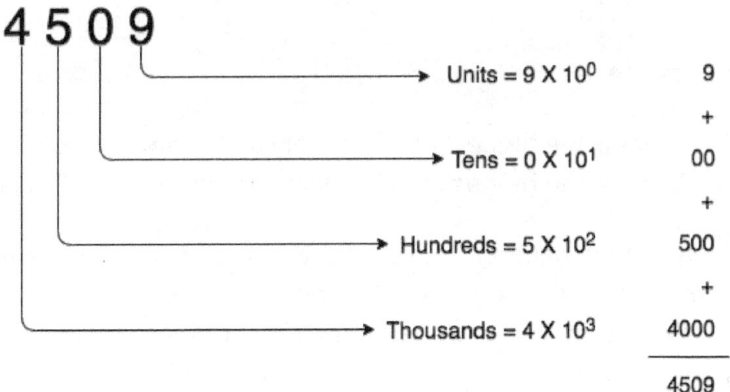

Base 2 or binary numbers behave similarly. Base 2 system has two digits 0 and 1 and each successive place represents an increasing power of 2. For example,

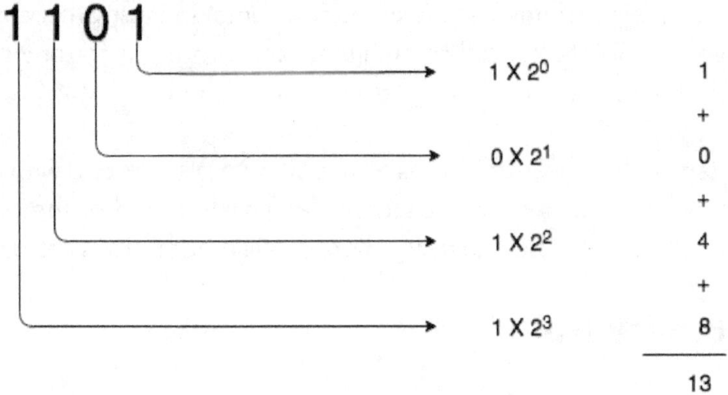

Above example demonstrates how to interpret a binary number and how to convert it to a decimal number.

<u>*Practice Questions : -*</u>
1. Convert following binary numbers into decimal numbers
    1. 1111
    2. 1111 0000
    3. 1010 1011
    4. 1000 1000
    5. 1000
    6. 100
    7. 10
    8. 1
2. What is the highest number that can be stored in 8 bits?
3. What is the highest number that can be stored in 9 bits?

In a binary number, the highest place value bit is called most significant bit or MSB and lowest place value bit is called least significant bit or LSB. Below figure illustrates an example of MSB and LSB.

          feedback@thebookofc.com

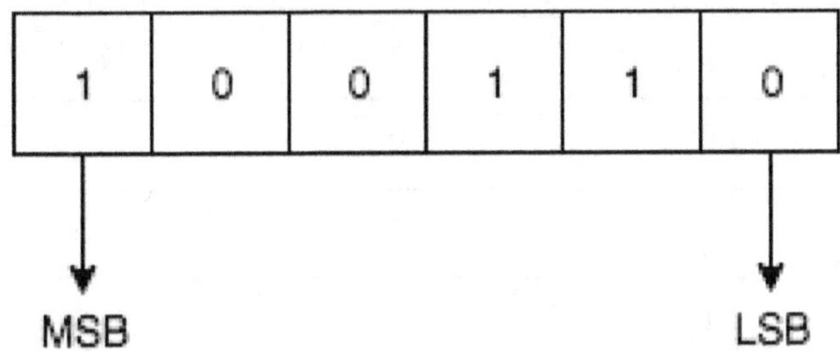

Conventionally we write MSB as the leftmost bit and LSB as the rightmost bit since that is the place value order that we most commonly use.

Hexadecimal Notation

Hexadecimal notation is base 16. It has 16 digits from 0 to 9 followed by A, B, C, D, E, F. Below table provides the interconversion between decimal, hexadecimal, and binary.

Decimal	Hexadecimal	Binary
0	0	0
1	1	1
2	2	10
3	3	11
4	4	100
5	5	101
6	6	110
7	7	111
8	8	1000
9	9	1001

10	A	1010
11	B	1011
12	C	1100
13	D	1101
14	E	1110
15	F	1111

Why are we learning hexadecimal notation?

Because hexadecimal is convenient to use as shorthand for binary. To convert binary to hexadecimal, start from the right and create groups of four bits. Then simply use the above table to convert each group into corresponding hexadecimal digit.

For example, take 1101100. Let's start by creating groups of 4 bits from right end. This gives us two groups: 110 and 1100

Now using the above table, these become 6 and C. Hence, 1101001 in binary is 6C in hexadecimal. It is also expressed as 0x6C. Leading 0x indicates that the following value is represented in hexadecimal.

Practice Questions: -
4.   Convert following binary numbers into hexadecimal
     1.   1101111100
     2.   1000000010000100
     3.   11001100
     4.   1101001

Conversion from hexadecimal to decimal is straightforward. Use place value notation to multiply every hexadecimal digit with appropriate power of 16 to get corresponding decimal value. For example, 0x6C can be written as

$6 \times 16^1 + 12 \times 16^0$
$= 96 + 12$

         feedback@thebookofc.com

= 108

To convert hexadecimal to binary, simply replace every hex digit with corresponding 4 bit binary pattern. E.g. 0xC6 would become 1100 0110 in binary.

Practice Questions : -
5. Convert following hexadecimal numbers into decimal and binary
    1. 0xFF
    2. 0xFF FF
    3. 0x10
    4. 0xF0 00

Decimal to Binary

In order to convert decimal to binary, we can use the divide-by-two method.

We start with the number to convert and keep dividing it by 2 until we get 0 as quotient. The sequence of remainders (from last to first) obtained at each step in the process is the binary representation of that decimal number.

Let's try out an example, 95:

Number	Step	Quotient	Remainder
95	Divide by 2	47	1
47	Divide by 2	23	1
23	Divide by 2	11	1
11	Divide by 2	5	1
5	Divide by 2	2	1
2	Divide by 2	1	0
1	Divide by 2	0	1

Taking the sequence of remainders, from last to first, we get 1011111 as the binary representation for 95.

Practice Questions : -
6. Convert following decimal numbers into binary and hexadecimal
    1. 128
    2. 15
    3. 10
    4. 40
    5. 127

The conversions we have discussed so far are purely mathematical conversions from one base number system to another. This does not imply that a computer has to store the numbers in the same format. In fact most computers do not use these formats. Most computers use two's complement format for storing data. Discussion of two's complement is outside the scope of this book. However, conversion to/from two's complement to mathematical value is fairly straightforward. If you wish to learn more about it, please visit http://thebookofc.com/bit-operations/twos-complement/.

That being said, the mathematical representations that we just learned build a very strong foundation for understanding bit level representation and manipulation.

One final piece of knowledge before we move to bitwise operators - treatment of signed numbers. All signed integer data types (`signed char, short, int, long, long long`) reserve one bit (typically MSB) for storing sign of the value - typically 1 for negative number and 0 for positive number. Remaining bits store the magnitude or value of the number.

An `unsigned char` has 8 bits - all available to store values from 0 to 255. A `signed char` also has 8 bits, 1 sign bit and 7 value bits. 7 bits can store a maximum value of 127; and hence a `signed char` can store values in the range -127 to +127.

         feedback@thebookofc.com

Bit Level Operators

Now that we understand some pieces of bit level data representation, let's get into manipulating data at bit level. C provides us following bit level operators

Operator	Operator Name
&	Bitwise AND
|	Bitwise OR
^	Bitwise XOR
~	Bitwise complement
<<	Bitwise left shift
>>	Bitwise right shift

Bitwise AND

Similar to logical AND operator, bitwise AND operation evaluates to 1 if both its operands are 1 otherwise it evaluates to 0. AND operation can be summarized in following truth table

A	B	A AND B
0	0	0
0	1	0
1	0	0
1	1	1

& is the bitwise AND operator. It takes two integer (`char`, `short`, `int`, `long`, or `long  long`) arguments and performs a bitwise AND of corresponding bits of the operands. In other words, first bit of the result is determined by AND operation of first bit of operand one and first bit of operand two, second bit of the result is determined by AND operation of second bit of operand one and second bit of operand two and so on. For example

Operand 1	1	1	0	0	1	0	1	1
Operand 2	1	0	1	0	1	0	0	0
& Result	1	0	0	0	1	0	0	0

Above table shows the result of operation 1100 1011 & 1010 1000 or to put it more concisely 0xCB & 0xA8 gives us 0x88

Practice Questions : -

7. What is the result of following operations
    1. `0x3B & 0xF0`
    2. `0xFF & 0x01`
    3. `0xFF & 0x00`
    4. `0X87 & 0x78`
8. What would be the output of following program. Note %x prints integer as hexadecimal value.

```c
#include <stdio.h>

int main(int argc, char * argv[]) {
    int operand1 = 0x42;
    int operand2 = 0x32;

    printf("0x%x & 0x%x = 0x%x \n", operand1,
operand2, operand1&operand2);
    return 0;
}
```

What happens when you AND an `int` with a `long`? As we learned earlier, implicit typecasting kicks in - `int` gets upcasted to `long` and result of AND of two `long` operands is a `long` value.

          feedback@thebookofc.com

9.   Explain the output of following program.

```c
#include <stdio.h>
int main(int argc, char * argv[]) {
    int operand1 = 0x42;
    int operand2 = 0x32;
    printf("0x%x & 0x%x = 0x%x \n", operand1, operand2,
operand1&operand2);
    printf("%u %u %u\n",sizeof(operand1),
sizeof(operand2),sizeof(operand1&operand2));
    return 0;
}
```

Bitwise OR

Similar to logical OR operator, bitwise OR operation evaluates to 1 if at least one of its operands is 1 otherwise it evaluates to 0. OR operation can be summarized in following truth table.

A	B	A OR B
0	0	0
0	1	1
1	0	1
1	1	1

| is the bitwise OR operator. Similar to & operator, it takes two integer type operands and performs a bitwise OR of corresponding bits of the operands. For example,

Operand 1	1	1	0	0	1	0	1	1
Operand 2	1	0	1	0	1	0	0	0
| Result	1	1	1	0	1	0	1	1

As can be observed in the above table, 0xCB | 0xA8 gives us 0xEB.

10. What is the result of following operations

```
1.  0x3B | 0xF0
2.  0xFF | 0x01
3.  0xFF | 0x00
4.  0X87 | 0x78
```

11. Explain the output of following program.

```c
#include <stdio.h>

int main(int argc, char * argv[]) {
    long operand1 = 0x100042;
    int operand2 = 0x2;

    printf("0x%lx | 0x%x = 0x%x \n", operand1,
operand2, operand1|operand2);
    printf("%u %u %u\n",sizeof(operand1),
sizeof(operand2),sizeof(operand1|operand2));
    return 0;
}
```

Bitwise XOR

XOR operation evaluates to 1 if exactly one of its operands is 1 otherwise it evaluates to 0. XOR operation can be summarized in following truth table.

A	B	A XOR B
0	0	0
0	1	1
1	0	1
1	1	0

^ is the bitwise XOR operator. Similar to & operator, it takes two integer type operands and performs a bitwise XOR of corresponding bits of the operands. For example,

          feedback@thebookofc.com

Operand 1	1	1	0	0	1	0	1	1
Operand 2	1	0	1	0	1	0	0	0
^ Result	0	1	1	0	0	0	1	1

As can be observed in the above table, 0xCB ^ 0xA8 gives us 0x63.

Practice Questions : -

12. What is the result of following operations

```
1.  0x3B ^ 0xF0
2.  0xFF ^ 0x01
3.  0xFF ^ 0x00
4.  0X87 ^ 0x78
```

Bitwise Complement

Bitwise complement is a unary operator - it takes only one integer type argument and inverses its bits - i.e. 0 bits are converted to 1 and 1 bits are converted to 0.

~ is the bitwise complement operator. It can be summarized in following truth table.

A	~ A
0	1
1	0

Let's see an example.

Operand	1	1	0	0	1	0	1	1
~ Result	0	0	1	1	0	1	0	0

As we can see ~0xCB is 0x34.

<u>***Practice Questions : -***</u>
13. What is the result of following operations
    1. ~0x3B
    2. ~0xFF
    3. ~0x00
    4. ~0X87

Bitwise Left Shift

Bitwise left shift, as the name indicates, shifts the bits in its operand to the left.

<< is the bitwise left shift operator. It takes the form left_operand << right_operand, where left_operand and right_operand are both integer types. Bits in left_operand are shifted left by right_operand places. For example, consider 0x0F << 2.

0x0F	0	0	0	0	1	1	1	1
0x0F<<2	0	0	1	1	1	1	0	0

Note that new bits brought in as a result of shifting are all 0. Also note that one left shift effectively multiplies the number by 2.

If the result of left shift operator is too large to be stored in the data type you used then left shift operation leads to undefined behaviour. Any result you observe in such case is neither reliable nor portable.

<u>***Practice Questions : -***</u>
14. What will be the output of following program
```c
#include <stdio.h>
int main(int argc, char * argv[]) {
    unsigned char result = 0;
    unsigned char operand1 = 1;
    result=operand1<<3;
    printf("%x\n", result);
    return 0;
}
```

          feedback@thebookofc.com

What would happen if we were to left shift a signed integer type? Would a negative value have its sign bit shifted or would just the magnitude of the negative number undergo a bit shift?

If we are using signed data type and the number stored is negative then result of left bit shift is again undefined behaviour. The only case for which left bit shift is defined for signed integer types is if the number stored is non-negative and result can be stored in the data type. We strongly recommend using unsigned integer types if you are expecting to perform bitwise operations on your data.

Practice Questions : -
15. What will be the result of following statements, assume signed char data type is used for storing all operands:
    ```
    1.  0x4 << 1
    2.  0x-1 << 1
    3.  0xA << 1
    ```

Bitwise Right Shift

Bitwise right shift, as the name indicates, shifts the bits in its operand to the right. >> is the bitwise right shift operator. It takes the form left_operand >> right_operand, where left_operand and right_operand are both integer types. Bits in left_operand are shifted right by right_operand places. For example, consider 0x0F >> 2.

0x0F	0	0	0	0	1	1	1	1
0x0F>>2	0	0	0	0	0	0	1	1

Note that new bits brought in as a result of shifting are all 0.

While one left shift effectively multiplied the operand by 2, a right shift divides it by two and yields the integer quotient.

If the value being shifted is a signed negative number then result of the right shift operation is implementation defined, i.e. behaviour is defined by the system you are running on and not by C standard. However, unlike left shift, it is not undefined behaviour.

Practice Questions : -

16. What will be the result of following statements, assume unsigned char data type is used for storing all operands.

```
1.  0x4 >> 2
2.  0x1 >> 1
3.  0xA >> 1
```

17. Write a program to determine behaviour of right shift on negative numbers for your system. Such a program would start with a negative integer and observe the value after successive right shift operations.

What happens if right_operand in bit shift operators is a negative number? As you would expect, such operation has undefined behaviour. Likewise if value of right_operand is greater than or equal to width of left_operand then again behaviour is undefined.

Bitwise Assignment Operators

Similar to += and -= arithmetic assignment operators, we have equivalent bitwise assignment operators.

Assuming a = 4 and b = 2, below table provides a summary result of all bitwise assignment operators.

Operator	Sample Statement	Equivalent to	Result
&=	a &= b	a = a&b	a = 0, b = 2
^=	a ^= b	a = a^b	a = 6, b = 2
|=	a |= b	a = a|b	a = 6, b = 2
<<=	a <<= b	a = a<<b	a = 16, b = 2
>>=	a >>=b	a = a>>b	a = 1, b = 2

          feedback@thebookofc.com

The table is fairly self-explanatory. We have already discussed all operations listed out in the "Equivalent to" column. Note that as with arithmetic assignment operators, precedence of bitwise assignment operators is lower than that of bitwise operators.

Putting It All To Use

One of common uses of bitwise operators is to store status of multiple binary switches or flags indicating their current state. For example, imagine you had 8 different on/off flags such as debug_messages (on/off), log_ip (on/off), require_password(on/off) and so on. You could either use a `char`, which is smallest available data type, for every flag or you could use just one `unsigned` `char` with one bit for each flag.

Using a `char` for each flag would use up 8 bytes while using bit level flags would use up only 1 byte. Such memory saving is critical in embedded systems where your code runs in a resource constrained environment. An increase in memory requirements would imply adding more memory on the chip and consequently increase cost of production per unit.

Let us see some code snippets for storing and setting individual flag bits.

```
/* Initialize all flags to 0 */
unsigned char flags = 0x00;

const int debug_flag = 0; //0th bit is for debug flag
const int ip_flag = 1;   //1st bit is for log IP flag
const int password_flag = 2; //2nd bit is for password flag
```

Note the use of `const` to ensure flag positions do not get mixed up or overwritten anywhere in our program.

```
/* Set IP flag to 1 */
flags = flags | (0x01 << ip_flag);
```

`0x01 << ip_flag` would give us a value that has all bits 0 other than the ip flag bit which would be set to 1. Since OR with 0 gives us the original bit and OR with 1 gives us 1, a bitwise OR with this value would simply ensure that ip flag bit is set to 1 irrespective of its previous value.

Practice Questions : -

18. Write a code snippet to clear out ip flag in the above example. Plug it into a program and validate your code.

Big Endian and Little Endian

Assume we have 4 byte `int`. Let's say it is stored at memory location 100.

```
int var = 0x12345678;
```

There are two possible ways this `int` can be stored in memory. Either system can store most significant byte at lowest address in the 4 byte space.

99	100	101	102	103	104
	12	34	56	78	

Or system can store least significant byte at lowest address in the 4 byte space.

99	100	101	102	103	104
	78	56	34	12	

A system in which most significant byte is stored at lowest address is called a big endian system. A system in which least significant byte is stored at lowest address is called a little endian system.

There are many ways in which we can determine endianness of our system. Let's see an example.

feedback@thebookofc.com

```c
#include <stdio.h>

int main (int argc, char *argv[]) {
    int i = 0x1;
    char * ptr = &i;

    if (*ptr) {
        printf("Little Endian\n");
    } else {
        printf("Big Endian\n");
    }
}
```

Here we have stored value 1 in an integer. As we have learned, this means least significant byte will have value 1 and all other bytes will be 0.

Then we had a `char *` point to this integer. This is the address of first byte of the integer. If this byte has value 1 stored in it, then we know that system is storing least significant byte at lowest address and is a little endian system.

For most applications, endianness of the system remains hidden and is automatically managed by the underlying system. However, if we were to write an application that receives data from another system – such as a network protocol and an `int` is packed with multiple bit level flags, then the order in which int is stored becomes significant.

Discussion on handling such scenarios and serialization is beyond the scope of this book.

Practice Questions : -
19. Determine endianness of your system.
20. Modify the above example for determining endianness by using value 0x12345678 instead of 0x1.

Looping with Bits

Similar to counting loops that we implemented using integer types, we can also implement loops that work through bits of data. Below is a program that loops through bits of an int and prints all individual bits. This in effect, produces int to bit conversion output that we had learned earlier in this chapter.

```c
#include <stdio.h>

int main (int argc, char *argv[]) {
    int value = 8;

    for(;value; value >>= 1) {
        printf("%d ",value&0x1);
    }
}
```

Practice Questions : -

21. Write a program to check if an integer is power of two.
22. Write a program that checks if an integer is negative by checking its MSB.
23. Write a program to count total number of set bits in an integer. A set bit has value 1.

Files

So far in this book we have written programs that take input from user, do the required processing and print output to console. Input or output data has no existence beyond life of the program itself.

Several real life applications require data to be available beyond the programs execution. Let us recollect the use case where we wrote a program that takes input for the marks obtained by students in a class, calculates the percentage obtained by each student, and prints the report card of each student. Recall that we have solved this problem earlier in the book. In our solution, user types in the marks of each student for each subject when prompted. What if the user entered wrong marks for one student by mistake? They will have to rerun the program and enter the input all over again!

Also, we printed the results on console in our program. If user wanted another copy of the output at a later date, they will have to do the entire process again as neither input nor output is stored in persistent memory.

For such applications, it is best if we can provide all input data to program as a file. There will then be no need to re-enter each data element every time. Similarly, if we store output of program so that it is accessible even after program exits, then it can be used to print results later.

This is where files come in handy. Files in digital world are used to organize and store data, similar to the files of real world. C provides the provision to read from as well as write into a file inside a program. Let us get into the details of file operations in C.

File Types

There are two types of files that a C program can work with:
1. Text files – Files that store data in plain text. They can be opened in any text editor, contents are human readable.

2. Binary files – Files that store data in binary format, and hence are not human readable.

Basic File Operations

Let us begin with some basic operations that a user can perform on a file. Basic file operations are:
1. Open file
2. Read from file
3. Write to file
4. Close file

C provides us library functions to perform all file operations mentioned above. Let us explore them in some detail.

fopen

To access the data stored inside a file, we first need to open the file. fopen is one of the commonly used library functions to open a file. Let us begin with signature of fopen.

```
FILE * fopen(const char *filename, const char *mode);
```

First argument to the function is the filename on disk that we want to open. The filename can include the complete path of the file to be opened. If complete path is not specified, the function looks for the file in current directory.

Second argument to the function is mode. When we open a file we need to specify the kind of operation we want to perform on the file. For example, whether we want to read data, write data, read and write both and so on. The parameter mode is used to specify the same. For text files, following can be the values of parameter mode:

r – open the file for read operation only.
r+ – open the file for read and write operations.
w – open the file for write operation only. Create the file if it doesn't exist and truncate the contents of file if it exists.

　　　　feedback@thebookofc.com

w+ – open the file for read and write operations. Create the file if it doesn't exist and truncate the contents of file if it exists.

Note that r/r+ mode doesn't create a file if it doesn't exist. Also note that when we specify w/w+ mode for opening an existing file, it is truncated – i.e. its existing contents are dropped and it effectively becomes an empty file.

For above mentioned modes, the operation (read or write) starts from the beginning of the file. For write mode we may want to append new content to the existing contents of a file. Following modes help us to do the same:

a – open the file in append mode for write operations. Create the file if it doesn't exist.
a+ – open the file for read operations and append mode for write operations. Create the file if it doesn't exist.

For a/a+ modes write operation starts at the end of file. Note that read operation for a+ mode starts at beginning of file though.

The library function returns a pointer to datatype `FILE`. What is `FILE` datatype? `FILE` is an implementation specific structure defined in file `stdio.h`. Library functions use this structure to implement file operations and hence a user need not know the details. From a user's perspective it is a pointer to the file that it is trying to read and is used to read/write contents of a file. If the file can't be opened for any reason, a NULL value is returned.

If we want to open file "abc.txt" in read only mode, following will be the call to `fopen`

```
FILE* fp = fopen ("abc.txt", "r");
```

As a good programming practice, we should always check return value for failure before we start using the returned `FILE *`.

fgetc & fputc

Now that we have opened a file, next step is to read from or write contents to the file. There are several library functions to read/write from a file suitable for different needs. Let's start with simple read/write library functions – `fgetc` to read and `fputc` to write into file. These functions read/write one character at a time. Let us begin with signature of these library functions.

```
int fgetc(FILE *fp);
```

`fgetc` reads the next character from the file pointed to by `fp`. If the read operation was successful, it returns the character it read cast to an `int`. If it hits the end of file, it returns `EOF` (End of File). `EOF` is a macro which is usually defined as -1. As the name suggests, it indicates that end of file was encountered.

```
int fputc(int write_char, FILE *fp);
```

`fputc` writes one character into the file pointed to by `fp`. The `write_char` is the character to be written cast to an `int`. If the write operation is successful, the character that is written is the return value of the function. In case of error, `EOF` is returned.

fclose

Every file that we open, we have to close it. `fclose` is the corresponding library function for closing files opened with an `fopen` call. Signature of `fclose` function is shown below.

```
int fclose(FILE *fp);
```

Parameter `fp` is the same `FILE` pointer that was returned by `fopen`.

`fclose` returns 0 if close operation was successful otherwise it returns EOF.

     feedback@thebookofc.com

Now that we know some basic file operations, let us write a simple copy program – copy contents of a file "read.txt" to another file "write.txt".

```
01:#include <stdio.h>
02:int main(int c , char** argv){
03:     FILE *fp_read = NULL, *fp_write = NULL;
04:     char ch = 0;
05:     fp_read = fopen("read.txt", "r");
06:     if (NULL == fp_read) {
07:         printf("Cannot open file for read operation");
08:         return -1;
09:     }
10:     fp_write = fopen("write.txt", "w");
11:     if (NULL == fp_write) {
12:         printf("Cannot open file for write opn");
13:         fclose(fp_read);
14:         return -1;
15:     }
16:
17:     while(1) {
18:         ch = fgetc(fp_read) ;
19:         fputc(ch, fp_write);
20:         if (EOF == ch) {
21:             break;
22:         }
23:     }
24:     fclose(fp_read);
25:     fclose(fp_write);
26:     return 0;
27:}
```

In the above program we copy contents of one file to another file, one character at a time. Note the following about the above program.

1. At line 04, when the file "read.txt" is opened using fopen, the mode is set to r (read only). Remember the mode "r" doesn't create a file if it doesn't exist.

2. At line 06, we check the value of fp_read. A NULL value indicates fopen failed. fopen can fail for various reasons, such as, file didn't exist. We will learn how to find the error reason in a while.

3. At line 10, when the file "write.txt" is opened, the mode is set to "w". Remember the mode "w" will create this file if it

doesn't exist, and it will truncate the contents of file if it already exists. So if we have a pre-existing file from a previous run of the program, it will automatically get cleared out.

4. At line 21, we break the loop when we encounter an EOF.

5. At line 24 and 25, note that we explicitly closed the file pointers. If `fclose` operation is not performed, then depending on system implementation, the files may be in unusable state. Hence, it is very important to close all the file pointers once we are done using the files.

6. At line 13, if call to open "write.txt" failed, we still closed `fp_read` pointer that we had opened at line 10.

7. We only read from the file pointer which we opened using "r" mode. Similarly, we have written only to the file pointer which we opened using write mode "w". If we try to read from a file pointer which is opened with write mode or vice versa, the library call will give an error.

Practice Questions : -
1. Run the above program when file "read.txt" doesn't exist.
2. Run the above program when file "write.txt" already exists and has some content.
3. Rewrite the above program with mode being passed to `fopen` as "a" at line 08. Execute the above program multiple times and observe the contents of file "write.txt".

fgets & fputs

For a large majority of real world programming applications we will have to read and write whole strings. Let us explore some file operations that can read/write strings with a single function call.

fgets (short for file get string) reads a string from a file. Let us begin with signature of `fgets` library call.

```
char *fgets(char *str, int n, FILE *fp);
```

fgets reads a line from the file represented by `fp`. fgets reads till a new line or EOF is encountered or n-1 number of bytes are read, and

          feedback@thebookofc.com

stores the bytes read in str. String str is terminated by placing a NULL character at nth byte in str.

On success, the library function return the same str pointer that was passed to it as input. On failure, NULL pointer is returned.

Similarly fputs (short for file put string) writes a string to a file.

```c
int fputs(const char *str, FILE *stream);
```

fputs writes a string into the file represented by fp. fputs writes the content of str into the file except for the string terminating null character. It return a non-negative number in case of success, and EOF in case of an error.

Let us rewrite our example of copying a file using fgets and fputs.

```c
01:#include <stdio.h>
02:int main(int c, char** argv) {
03:    FILE *fp_read = NULL, *fp_write = NULL;
04:    char buffer[512] = { 0 };
05:    char *ret = NULL;
06:    fp_read = fopen("read.txt", "r");
07:    if (NULL == fp_read) {
08:        printf("Cannot open file for read operation");
09:        return -1;
10:    }
11:    fp_write = fopen("write.txt", "w");
12:    if (NULL == fp_write) {
13:        printf("Cannot open file for write opn");
14:        fclose(fp_read);
14:        return -1;
15:    }
16:    while(1) {
17:        ret = fgets(buffer, 512, fp_read);
18:        if (NULL == ret) {
19:            break ;
20:        }
21:        fputs(buffer, fp_write);
22:    }
23:    fclose(fp_read);
24:    fclose(fp_write);
25:    return 0;
26:}
```

At line 04 we declared a char array by name buffer of size 512. Since this variable can only hold a string of size 512, when we pass the buffer to fgets at line 17, we specify the size to be read as 512.

In case the line to be read from "read.txt" exceeds 511 characters, the read operation will read up to 511 characters and we will not write beyond our array's capacity.

errno & perror

In all the file operations that we have learned above, if the library function call returns an error, we are unable to determine the reason for the error. There can be multiple reasons for failure of a file operation, and hence to debug, it is very important to know the reason of failure.

The solution to the problem is errno. errno is a global integer variable declared in system header file - errno.h. It is set by library function calls in case an error occurred. The value of errno represents a unique error code, which gives us an insight into what went wrong.

perror is a library function that converts this errno into a human readable error message. Signature of perror is shown below.

```c
void perror(const char *msg);
```

perror prints the const string passed as msg, followed by the system error message corresponding to errno.

```c
int main(int argc ,char *argv[]) {
    FILE* fp_read;
    fp_read= fopen ("read1.txt", "r");
    if (NULL == fp_read) {
        perror("File open error");
        return -1;
    }
    return 0;
}
```

                    feedback@thebookofc.com

If the file "read1.txt" doesn't exist, the output of above program would appear as shown below.

```
File open error: No such file or directory
```

Let's take another example, where we try to read from a file pointer that was opened in write only mode.

```c
int main(int argc , char** argv) {
    FILE* fp_read = NULL,*fp_write = NULL;
    fp_read = fopen ("read.txt", "r");
    if (NULL == fp_read) {
        perror("Read file open error");
        return -1;
    }
    fp_write = fopen ("write.txt", "w");
    if (NULL == fp_write) {
        perror("Write file open error");
        fclose(fp_read);
        return -1;
    }
    ret = fgets(buffer, 512, fp_write);
    if ( NULL == ret ) {
        perror("File read error");
        break ;
    }
    fclose(fp_read);
    fclose(fp_write);
    return 0;
}
```

If read.txt file exists and write.txt file could be opened successfully, the output of the above program will be:

```
File read error: Bad file descriptor
```

As we learned, errno is a global variable. Every time its value gets updated, earlier value is lost. That implies that we should invoke perror immediately after a failure to emit out appropriate error message. If a subsequent call fails, this diagnostic information will no longer be available to us.

stdin, stdout, and stderr

Every program that is launched has three file pointers available to it by default. These are,

1. stdin – Standard input file stream that is automatically linked to our keyboard input. This is the default input stream.
2. stdout – standard output file stream that is automatically linked to our console. This is the default output stream.
3. stderr – standard error file stream that is also automatically linked to our console. This is the default stream for printing any errors that occur in our program. `perror` writes to `stderr` file pointer.

We do not have to open these file pointers. They are automatically made available to us by the system. We will learn how to use these file pointers later in this chapter.

fprintf & fscanf

`fprintf` and `fscanf` sound very similar to the `printf` and `scanf` library functions that we have been using so far in the book – and they indeed are very similar. Only difference is that instead of console they operate on a file.

Here are function signatures of `printf` and `fprintf`.

```c
int printf(const char *format, ...);
int fprintf(FILE *fp, const char *format, ...);
```

`fprintf` prints formatted output to a file just as `printf` prints it on console. It takes one extra input parameter as compared to `printf`. The first parameter to `fprintf` is a file pointer.

So the following statement prints the output on console:

```c
printf("Hello world\n");
```


feedback@thebookofc.com

Whereas the following statement using `fprintf` will print the output into the file pointed by `fp`.

```
fprintf(fp,"Hello world\n");
```

Note the ... in the parameter list. This indicates that a function can take variable number of arguments. Indeed, we are able to print any number of variables using `printf`. Implementation of functions or macros with variable number of arguments is outside the scope of this book.

`fprintf` returns an integer value. In case of success, it is equal to the number of bytes written by the function. In case of failure, it returns EOF.

We can use `stdout` as file pointer to make `fprintf` print to console. Following two statements are equivalent.

```
printf("Hello world\n");
fprintf(stdout,"Hello world\n");
```

We encourage you to write a program and validate it yourself.

Similarly `fscanf` takes formatted input from a file instead of taking it from console. Like `fprintf`, it takes one extra input parameter to indicate the file from where to read the input.

Here are function signatures of `scanf` and `fscanf`.

```
int scanf(const char *format, ...);
int fscanf(FILE *stream, const char *format, ...);
```

Following statement takes input from the console.

```
scanf("%d", &count);
```

Whereas the following statement using `fscanf` will read the input from the file pointed by `fp`.

```
fscanf(fp, "%d", &count);
```

`fscanf` returns an integer value. In case of success, it is equal to the number of items read by the function. In case of failure, it returns EOF.

`fscanf` reading from `stdin` will behave exactly like `scanf`. Following statements are equivalent.

```
scanf("%d", &count);
fscanf(stdin, "%d", &count);
```

A Complete Example

Now that we have learned the basics of file operation, let us use this knowledge to build a program for the students report card problem that we talked about in the beginning of the chapter.

Instead of taking input from console, we take it from a file. Following is how we design the input file.

```
                <file : student_data.txt>
Name: Peter English: 75 Maths: 88 Science: 83
Name: John English: 77 Maths: 83 Science: 63
Name: Alexa English: 75 Maths: 92 Science: 86
```

Now let us modify the program we had written in chapter for User Defined Datatypes to achieve the same result.

```
#include <stdio.h>

struct student_info {
    char name[32];
    char class[16];
    int english_marks;
    int maths_marks;
    int science_marks;
    float percentage;
};
typedef struct student_info student_info_t;

int main (int argc, char** argv) {
```

          feedback@thebookofc.com

```c
    student_info_t student_info = {0};
    FILE* student_fp = NULL, *result_fp = NULL;
    int ret = 0;

    student_fp = fopen("student_data.txt", "r");
    if (NULL == student_fp) {
        perror("Error in opening file for read");
        return -1;
    }
    result_fp = fopen("results.txt", "w");
    if (NULL == result_fp) {
        perror("Error in opening file for write");
        fclose(student_fp);
        return -1;
    }

    while (1) {
        ret = fscanf(student_fp, "Name: %s English: %d Maths: %d Science: %d\n",
                     &student_info.name,
                     &student_info.english_marks,
                     &student_info.maths_marks,
                     &student_info.science_marks);
        if (EOF == ret) {
            break;
        }
        student_info.percentage =
(student_info.english_marks + student_info.maths_marks +
student_info.science_marks ) / 3.0;
        fprintf (result_fp, "Name :%s Percentage %f\n",
student_info.name, student_info.percentage);
    }
    fclose(student_fp);
    fclose(result_fp);

    return 0;
}
```

The output file of above program appears as shown below.

```
                    <file: results.txt>
  Name :Peter Percentage 82.000000
  Name :John Percentage 74.333336
  Name :Alexa Percentage 84.333336
```

Use of files in this program allows us to persist input as well as output data. Also, if any error occurs during data entry then the user can simply fix it in input file, and re-run the program to obtain the results. Since results are also stored in a file, they can be accessed anytime in the future.

Practice Questions : -

4. Which of the following statements are true.
   a. `fgets` with `size` parameter set to 1 is equivalent to `fgetc`.
   b. Every program has three `FILE *` open by default – `stdin`, `stdout`, and `stderr`.
   c. `perror` writes errors to `stdout`.
   d. Value of `errno` should be checked immediately after a library call fails.
   e. Format strings for `printf` and `fprintf` are identical.
5. Write a program that reads int value from a file, one value per line and prints the sum
6. Write a program that asks user to input a word and then finds number of occurrences (case insensitive) of that word in a file.

This chapter has focused on text files. Operations on binary files are similar. You can learn more about binary files I/O at http://thebookofc.com/files/binary-files-i-o-tutorial/.

The Rest Of It

In this chapter we take on few concepts that we must know so that we can wield complete power offered by C. These can be very helpful in future. However, we may not need these frequently at our current learning stage.

Goto

goto is a C language keyword. It forces the control to jump to a specific location. The location is identified by a label. Concept of label is similar to what we saw in switch case – a symbol identifying a location in code. Let's see an example.

```
01: #include <stdio.h>

02: int main (int argc, char *argv[]) {
03:     int value = 0;

04:     printf("Roll a dice. What did you get? :");
05:     scanf("%d",&value);

06:     if (value < 1 || value > 6) {
07:         printf("Couldn't roll a dice?\n");
08:         goto end;
09:     }
10:     if (value%2 == 0) {
11:         printf("Oh too bad. You lose.\n");
12:         goto end;
13:     } else {
14:         printf("I win!\n");
15:         goto end;
16:     }

17:     end:
18:     printf("House Always Wins.\n");
19:     return 0;
20: }
```

Observe the label on line 17. A label can be placed between any two statements. Labels do not have to be declared. All we need is a unique name followed by a colon symbol to place a label.

Note goto statements on line 08, 12, and 15. Syntax of goto statement is fairly straightforward – keyword goto followed by name of the label to which you want control to jump. Whenever a goto statement is executed, control jumps to the label specified by goto.

Let's trace control flow for above example assuming input was 3.

1. After user input, control reaches line 06. if condition evaluates to false. Control skips if block and reaches line 10.
2. if condition evaluates to false. Control skips if block and enters else block, line 13.
3. Message I win! is printed on line 14. Control advances to line 15.
4. goto is encountered. Control jumps to label end, line 17.
5. Message House Always Wins. is printed on line 18. Control advances to line 19 and program terminates.

Scope of a label name is local to the function, i.e. if a label is defined in function A, then you can use it with goto statements in function A only.

Since goto jumps are ad-hoc, it is very difficult to read and maintain code riddled with goto statements. Anything that we can do with goto can also be achieved using other constructs such as if else and loops.

We strongly recommend you to avoid using goto.

Practice Questions : -
1. Which of the following statements are true.
   a. We have to declare a label before using it.
   b. Scope of a label is limited to the function in which it is placed.
   c. A label can be placed in the middle of an expression.
   d. As a good programming practice we should avoid using goto statement.
   e. Use of goto is recommended only for cases where we do not know how control will flow.

      feedback@thebookofc.com

Extern

Consider an application written over multiple files using a global variable `int var1` that is accessed across multiple .c files.

We have learned that
1. We need to declare a variable before we can use it.
2. A variable can be defined only once in a given scope.
3. Each .c file gets compiled into an object file and these files get linked together at linking stage.

Where would we define the global variable such that each file that it using it compiles successfully till linking stage?

If we define the variable in a .c file then other .c files will not find that definition during compilation phase. If we define the variable in a .h file and include it in all .c files then we will have multiple definitions of that variable.

`extern` helps solve exactly that problem. `extern` is a C language keyword that helps declare a variable but does not define it. What is the difference between declaring and defining a variable?

Declaring a variable simply tells the system about the data type and name of the variables but does not allocate memory for it while defining a variable leads to allocation of memory along with informing about data type and variable name.

```
extern int var1;
```

Above statement tells the compiler that there is a variable called `var1` of type `int` that is defined in some other file. Based on this information compiler can successfully compile the .c file which is then linked with the definition of `var1` during linking phase.

Static

`static` is a C language keyword that can be applied to variables as well as functions.

Static With Local Variables

When a local variable is declared as a static variable,
1.   It is initialized only once – ever, and
2.   It retains its value across multiple invocations of the function.

While local variables are allocated space in the stack segment, a static variable is allocated space in the data segment. Hence it retains its value throughout the life of the program. Let's see an example.

```
01: #include <stdio.h>

02: int adder(int val) {
03:     static int sum = 0;
04:     printf("sum = %d\n",sum);
05:     sum += val;
06:     return sum;
07: }

08: int main (int argc, char *argv[]) {
09:     int result = 0;
10:     result = adder(10);
11:     result = adder(20);
12:     result = adder(30);
13:     printf("result = %d\n", result);
14:     return 0;
15: }
```

Notice variable definition on line 03. Variable sum is defined as a static int. We have initialized it to 0. If we had left it uninitialized, system would have initialized it to a default value – typically 0.

Let's trace control flow of the above example.

1.   Execution begins with main, line 08 and proceeds to adder function call on line 10.
2.   Control jumps to line 02. val has value 10.
3.   Control proceeds to line 03. This initialization occurs only once and it has happened before the program execution began.

          feedback@thebookofc.com

4. Control advances to line 04. Since we have not updated the value of `sum`, it prints as 0. Message `sum = 0` appears on console.
5. Line 05, value in `sum` gets updated to 10.
6. Line 06, control returns to `main` with value 10.
7. Line 10, value 10 is assigned to `result`. Control advances to line 11. `adder` is called with argument 20. Control jumps to line 02.
8. As we learned static variable is initialized only once. Control advances to line 04. When adder returned last time, sum had value 10. It still has same value. Message `sum = 10` appears on console.

Further control flow trace is left as an exercise for you.

Static With Global Variables

When `static` is used with a global variable it limits the visibility of that variable to the .c file it was declared in. All functions in the same .c file will be able to access that variable and no functions outside that .c file will be able to see or access that variable.

Static With Functions

By default, all functions in an application are visible across all files. Any function in any .c file can call any other function in any other .c file.

`static` keywords when applied to a function has the same effect it has on global variable – that function's visibility gets limited to its .c file.

Inline Functions

Recall that when we call a function, all its context is stored in a function stack and only then control jumps to the called function. Similarly on return, the function context is restored from the function stack before execution can proceed in calling function. All this context saving and restoring takes some CPU time.

If processing time of our function is very small, such as sum function that simply added two numbers, then the function call overhead may be significant as compared to function execution time. For such cases, we have an option to suggest to the system to make a function call fast.

inline is a C language keyword that tells the system to make the function call as fast as possible. Note that C standard does not tell how to make it fast. That choice is left up to the implementation. Also, inline is merely a suggestion. It is up to the system to choose the extent to which such a suggestion is effective.

Some textbooks erroneously indicate that inline keyword makes the compiler substitute function call with function body in order to avoid a function call completely. It is important to understand that inline is not textual substitution, and is definitely not enforced by C standard. Discussion of ways of speeding up function calls inside an implementation is beyond the scope of this book.

Let's see an example of defining an inline function.

```
01: #include <stdio.h>

02: static inline int triple_it(int num){
03:      return num*3;
04: }

05: int main (int argc, char * argv[]) {
06:      int result = 0;
07:      result = triple_it(10);
08:      printf("Result = %d\n",result);
09:      return 0;
10: }
```

Focus on line 02 that defines an inline function triple_it.

To declare a function to be inline, we simply add keyword inline before the return type of the function. Also note that we have another C keyword in the declaration - static.

          feedback@thebookofc.com

Note that call to inline function on line 07 is identical to a regular function call.

Remember that inline is recommendation. It does not force the system to actually inline the function. What happens if system decides not to inline the function? In such case, for successful compilation, we still would need a compiled version of the function definition for linking.

`static` keyword forces the compiler to produce a file scoped version of function in the object code and ensures that appropriate definition is available to ensure successful compilation.

Practice Questions : -
2. Which of the following statements are true.
    a. Inline functions are textually substituted in the program.
    b. `inline` is a hint to compiler to optimize execution time of a function.
    c. A `static` variable is initialized before program execution begins.
    d. A local static variable can be accessed by any function in the file.
    e. An `extern` variable declaration does not allocate any memory for the variable.

Register

Registers are special storage units located on the processor chip. Access to registers is significantly faster than access to RAM. `register` is a C language keyword that serves as hint to the system to keep a variable in register.

```
register int i = 7;
```

Above declaration tells the system to define an `int` variable called `i` with initial value 7 and possibly keep it in a register.

We use this hint when faster access to a variable is likely to speed up processing time, such as loop counter that is accessed many times.

Most modern systems have plenty of in-built optimisation and we typically do not need to use `register` keyword. However, it may be useful for certain kinds of systems – particularly embedded systems.

Note that `register` is just a hint. It does not force use of a register.

Volatile

`volatile` is a C language keyword that tells the system to not optimise any access to a variable. It indicates that value of a variable may change in way that is not evident from the code – for example, in case of a device driver, a location could be written by the device itself. Hence, if system optimises under assumption that variable value is being changed only within the program then it may generate incorrect results.

Here is an example declaring a volatile variable.

```
volatile int device_status = 0;
```

Detailed treatment of `volatile` scenarios is outside the scope of this book.

Restrict

`restrict` is a C language keyword used with pointers that tells the system that this specific pointer is the only way pointed variable will be accessed. This declaration of intent by the programmer allows compiler to generate more optimized object code. Here is an example.

```
restrict int * ptr = &device_status;
```

`restrict` is applicable for the life of the pointer. If pointed object is accessed in any other way during this time then behavior is undefined.

feedback@thebookofc.com

Short Circuit Evaluation

Short circuit evaluation refers to control expression evaluation that does not require full condition evaluation to determine the outcome and hence only a partial evaluation is performed.

Recall our discussion of AND logical operator (**&&**). AND evaluates to false if any one of its operands is false. For example,

```
if (a && b)
```

In above expression, if a evaluates to false, then system does not have to evaluate b at all to know that the expression will evaluate to false.

Short circuit evaluation becomes important when we change values in control expressions. For example,

```
int a = 7, b = 0;
```

```
if (a>10 && b++)
```

In above expression, system can evaluate a>10 to false and skip evaluating b++ altogether. In other words, b may not get incremented.

Recursion

Recursion is a problem solving method where a larger problem is solved by solving smaller instances of the same problem. For example, consider computing sum of first n natural numbers. This problem can in turn be defined as

Sum(n) = n + Sum(n-1)

Now we just need to find sum of first n-1 natural numbers and we can then compute sum of first n natural numbers using a simple addition. Sum(n-1) can in turn be defined as

Sum(n-1) = n-1 + Sum(n-2)
=> Sum(n) = n + n-1 + Sum(n-2)

and so on.

This line of reasoning requires a base case where result is known so that we can start building back the solution. In this case, base case is Sum(1) which is known to be 1.

Since each instance of problem is expressed as a smaller instance of same problem, solution would involve a function calling itself again and again. Let's see recursive solution source code for problem we just discussed.

```c
01: #include <stdio.h>

02: int sum_n(int val) {
03:       int retval = 0;

    /* This is our base case */
    /* If val was 1 then we know sum_n will be 1 */
04:       if (1 == val) {
05:           return val;
06:       }

07:       retval = val + sum_n(val-1);
08:       return retval;
09: }

10: int main (int argc, char *argv[]) {
11:       int result = 0, n = 0;

12:       printf("Enter value of n: ");
13:       scanf("%d",&n);
14:       if (n<1) {
15:           printf("Invalid input\n");
16:           return 1;
17:       }

18:       result = sum_n(n);
19:       printf("Sum of first %d numbers is %d\n", n,
result);
20:       return 0;
21: }
```

          feedback@thebookofc.com

Let's trace control flow for user input 3. We will skip input validation and jump straight to line 18.

1. Function `sum_n` is called with argument 3. Control jumps to line 02. `val` has value 3.
2. Line 03, `retval` is initialized to 0.
3. Line 04, we evaluate our base case. `val` is not 1, control jumps to line 07.
4. This is where magic happens. We assign `retval` value equal to 3 + recursive call to `sum_n` with value 2.
5. Function `sum_n` is called a second time, this time from within `sum_n`. Control jumps to line 02. `val` has value 2.
6. Line 03, `retval` is initialized to 0. Note that since `retval` is a local variable, this instance of `retval` is different from the instance from previous invocation.
7. Line 04, we evaluate our base case. `val` is not 1, control jumps to line 07.
8. We assign `retval` value equal to 2 + recursive call to `sum_n` with value 1.
9. Function `sum_n` is called a third time. Control jumps to line 02. `val` has value 2.
10. Line 03, `retval` is initialized to 0.
11. Line 04, we evaluate our base case. `val` is 1. Function call returns 1.
12. Control returns to line 07 from second invocation. Call to `sum_n` has evaluated to 1. Hence `retval` is assigned value 2 + 1, i.e. 3.
13. Control advances to line 08. Value 3 is returned to calling function – first invocation of `sum_n`.
14. Call to `sum_n` has evaluated to 3. Hence `retval` is assigned value 3 + 3, i.e. 6.
15. Control advances to line 08. Value 3 is returned to calling function – `main`. Control jumps back to line 18.
16. `result` is assigned value 6.
17. Control advances to line 19. Message `Sum of first 3 numbers is 6` is printed to the console.
18. Control advances to line 20 and program terminates.

Few things to note:
1. Successive calls to sum_n brought us closer and closer to the base case.
2. In our recursive function, we check for base case before we make a recursive call.

Both these conditions are essential otherwise we will keep on making recursive calls infinitely – a condition known as infinite recursion.

Above control flow can be pictured as shown below.

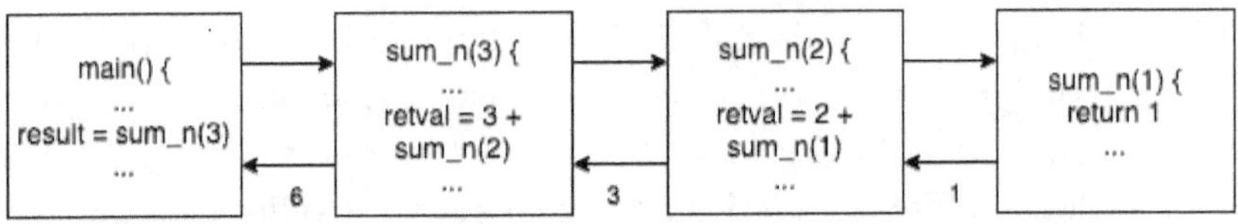

There are several problems that lend themselves naturally to a recursive solution. Most common among them are factorial and Fibonacci Series.

Factorial of a number n is the product of all numbers from 1 to n. Sounds very similar to sum of all numbers from 1 to n problem that we just solved using recursion.
Fibonacci Series is defined as below.

Fib(n) = Fib(n-1) + Fib(n-2)
Fib(0) = 0
Fib(1) = 1

The first statement in the definition is recursive definition of a fibonacci number while second and third form our base case for recursion.

There are two forms of recursion – direct recursion and indirect recursion. Direct recursion is when a function call its itself – the one that we just implemented. Indirect function is when a function calls another function which in turn, directly or indirectly, leads to a call to the calling function.

          feedback@thebookofc.com

For example, if function A called function B which in turn called function A then it is indirect recursion. If function A called function B which called function C which called function A – again indirect recursion.

Practice Questions : -
3. Which of the following statements are true.
    a. In a recursive function, we should check base condition before recursive call.
    b. An infinite recursion will eventually evaluate to zero.
    c. A recursive function cannot be called with pointer arguments.
    d. If a function calls itself, it is called direct recursion.
4. Implement recursive program for computing n factorial.
5. Implement recursive program for computing n^{th} Fibonacci number.

Acknowledgements

Even though title carries our name as authors, this book would not have seen light of the day without support from a lot of kind people who helped us in many different ways to reach our goal. Our heartfelt gratitude to all.

Praful Kumar
Vrinda Dhingra
Harish Verma
Santosh Verma
Madhuri Verma
Dr. Shailesh Tiwari
Narasimha Karumanchi
Satish Bommareddy
All our teachers, mentors, and peers who have taught us everything.